THE LIFE

OF

MICHELANGELO BUONARROTI

VOLUME 2

THE LIFE OF

MICHELANGELO BUONARROTI

BASED ON STUDIES IN THE ARCHIVES OF THE

BUONARROTI FAMILY AT FLORENCE

JOHN ADDINGTON SYMONDS

Introduction by Creighton E. Gilbert

Volume 2

University of Pennsylvania Press

Philadelphia

Originally published by J.C. Nimmo and Charles Scribner's Sons
Third Edition 1911

Introduction copyright © 2002 University of Pennsylvania Press

Published 2002 by
University of Pennsylvania Press
Philadelphia, Pennsylvania 19104-4011

10 9 8 7 6 5 4 3 2 1

Library of Congress Cataloging-in-Publication Data

Symonds, John Addington, 1840–1893.
  The life of Michelangelo Buonarroti : based on studies in the archives of
the Buonarroti family at Florence / by John Addington Symonds ; intro-
duction by Creighton E. Gilbert.—
    p.cm
  Originally published: 3rd ed. New York : J.C. Nimmo and C. Scribner's
Sons, 1911. With new introd.
  Includes bibliographical references and index.
  ISBN 0-8122-3611-4 (cloth : alk. paper)—ISBN 0-8122-1761-6 (pbk. :
alk. paper)
  1. Michelangelo Buonarroti, 1475–1564. 2. Artists—Italy—Biography. I.
Michelangelo Buonarroti, 1475–1564. II. Title.
N6923.B9 S9 2001
709'.2—dc21
[B]   2001043629

CONTENTS

LIFE OF MICHELANGELO.

CHAPTER X.

1. The Church of S. Lorenzo at Florence.—Founded in part by a Medici.—Members of that family buried there.—The Medicean Popes, Leo and Clement, design its completion. The Façade, the new Sacristy, the Library.—History of the Medicean monuments.— 2. Michelangelo's innovations in architecture.—Italian Gothic, the early Italian Renaissance style.—Vitruvian influences leading up to the Barocco manner and Palladian purism.—Michelangelo's importance in this process.—3. Vasari's account of his work at S. Lorenzo.—The introduction of Barocco freedom.—4. In these works Michelangelo always contemplated architecture as a framework for statuary.—5. He also studied picturesque effects.—The structural importance of the building is sacrificed to plastic art and superficial decoration.—Faults inherent in Italian Gothic, partly overcome by fifteenth-century architects, revived by Michelangelo. —In what sense he was an amateur of genius.—Only in the Cupola of S. Peter's did he attack a great problem of the builder's art, and solve it architecturally.—6. The Sacristy.—Its internal arrangement is a scheme for marble panelling to frame sculpture and bronze, with vast fresco decoration for the dome and blank wall-spaces.—Viewed in this way, it remains imperfect, but the part performed is excellent.—Michelangelo left the whole in 1534 incomplete and unsettled.—Difficult points regarding his intentions as to details.—Duke Cosimo's project of finishing the Sacristy in the last year of Michelangelo's life.—7. Vasari's letter explaining the Duke's scheme.—Its failure.—8. Criticism of the Sacristy as it now exists.

I.

THE collegiate church of S. Lorenzo at Florence had long been associated with the Medicean family, who were its most distinguished benefactors. Giovanni d'Averardo dei Medici, together with the heads of six other Florentine houses, caused it to be rebuilt at the beginning of the fifteenth century. He took upon himself the entire costs of the sacristy and one chapel; it was also owing to his suggestion that Filippo Brunelleschi, in the year 1421, designed the church and cloister as they now appear. When he died, Giovanni was buried in its precincts, while his son Cosimo de' Medici, the father of his country, continued these benevolences, and bestowed a capital of 40,000 golden florins on the Chapter. He too was buried in the church, a simple monument in the sacristy being erected to his memory. Lorenzo the Magnificent followed in due course, and found his last resting-place at S. Lorenzo.

We have seen in a previous chapter how and when Leo X. conceived the idea of adding a chapel which should serve as mausoleum for several members of the Medicean family at S. Lorenzo, and how Clement determined to lodge the famous Medicean library in a hall erected over the west side of the cloister. Both of these undertakings, as well as the construction of a façade for the front of the church, were assigned to Michelangelo. The ground-plan of the monumental chapel corresponds to Brunelleschi's sacristy, and is generally known as the Sagrestia Nuova. Internally Buonarroti altered its decorative panellings, and elevated the vaulting of the roof into a more ambitious cupola. This

portion of the edifice was executed in the rough
during his residence at Florence. The façade was
never begun in earnest, and remains unfinished.
The library was constructed according to his designs,
and may be taken, on the whole, as a genuine specimen of his style in architecture.

The books which Clement lodged there were the
priceless manuscripts brought together by Cosimo
de' Medici in the first enthusiasm of the Revival, at
that critical moment when the decay of the Eastern
Empire transferred the wrecks of Greek literature
from Constantinople to Italy. Cosimo built a room
to hold them in the Convent of S. Marco, which
Flavio Biondo styled the first library opened for the
use of scholars. Lorenzo the Magnificent enriched
the collection with treasures acquired during his lifetime, buying autographs wherever it was possible to
find them, and causing copies to be made. In the
year 1508 the friars of S. Marco sold this inestim-
able store of literary documents, in order to discharge
the debts contracted by them during their ill-consi-
dered interference in the state affairs of the Republic.
It was purchased for the sum of 2652 ducats by the
Cardinal Giovanni de' Medici, second son of Lorenzo
the Magnificent, and afterwards Pope Leo X. He
transferred them to his Roman villa, where the
collection was still further enlarged by all the
rarities which a prince passionate for literature
and reckless in expenditure could there assemble.
Leo's cousin and executor, Giulio de' Medici, Pope

Clement VII., fulfilled his last wishes by transferring them to Florence, and providing the stately
receptacle in which they still repose.

The task assigned to Michelangelo, when he
planned the library, was not so simple as that of
the new sacristy. Some correspondence took place
before the west side of the cloister was finally
decided on. What is awkward in the approach to
the great staircase must be ascribed to the difficulty of fitting this building into the old edifice ;
and probably, if Michelangelo had carried out the
whole work, a worthier entrance from the piazza
into the loggia, and from the loggia into the vestibule, might have been devised.

II.

Vasari, in a well-known passage of his Life of
Michelangelo, reports the general opinion of his
age regarding the novelties introduced by Buonarroti into Italian architecture. The art of building
was in a state of transition. Indeed, it cannot be
maintained that the Italians, after they abandoned
the traditions of the Romanesque manner, advanced
with certitude on any line of progress in this art.
Their work, beautiful as it often is, ingenious as
it almost always is, marked invariably by the individuality of the district and the builder, seems to

be tentative, experimental. The principles of the Pointed Gothic style were never seized or understood by Italian architects. Even such cathedrals as those of Orvieto and Siena are splendid monuments of incapacity, when compared with the Romanesque churches of Pisa, S. Miniato, S. Zenone at Verona, the Cathedral of Parma. The return from Teutonic to Roman standards of taste, which marked the advent of humanism, introduced a hybrid manner. This, in its first commencement, was extremely charming. The buildings of Leo Battista Alberti, of Brunelleschi, and of Bramante are distinguished by an exquisite purity and grace combined with picturesqueness. No edifice in any style is more stately, and at the same time more musical in linear proportions, than the Church of S. Andrea at Mantua. The Cappella dei Pazzi and the Church of S. Spirito at Florence are gems of clear-cut and harmonious dignity. The courtyard of the Cancelleria at Rome, the Duomo at Todi, show with what supreme ability the great architect of Casteldurante blended sublimity with suavity, largeness and breadth with naïveté and delicately studied detail. But these first endeavours of the Romantic spirit to assimilate the Classic mannerism —essays no less interesting than those of Boiardo in poetry, of Botticelli in painting, of Donatello and Omodei in sculpture—all of them alike, whether buildings, poems, paintings, or statues, displaying the genius of the Italic race, renascent, recalcitrant

against the Gothic style, while still to some extent
swayed by its influence (at one and the same time
both Christian and chivalrous, Pagan and precociously
cynical; yet charmingly fresh, unspoiled by dogma,
uncontaminated by pedantry)—these first endeavours
of the Romantic spirit to assimilate the Classic
mannerism could not create a new style representative of the national life. They had the fault inherent
in all hybrids, however fanciful and graceful. They
were sterile and unprocreative. The warring elements,
so deftly beautifully blent in them, began at once
to fall asunder. The San Galli attempted to follow
classical precedent with stricter severity. Some
buildings of their school may still be reckoned
among the purest which remain to prove the sincerity of the Revival of Learning. The Sansovini
exaggerated the naïveté of the earlier Renaissance
manner, and pushed its picturesqueness over into
florid luxuriance of decorative detail. Meanwhile,
humanists and scholars worked slowly but steadily
upon the text of Vitruvius, impressing the para-
mount importance of his theoretical writings upon
practical builders. Neither students nor architects
reflected that they could not understand Vitruvius;
that, if they could understand him, it was by no
means certain he was right; and that, if he was
right for his own age, he would not be right for the
sixteenth century after Christ. It was just at this
moment, when Vitruvius began to dominate the
Italian imagination, that Michelangelo was called

upon to build. The genial adaptation of classical elements to modern sympathies and uses, which had been practised by Alberti, Brunelleschi, Bramante, yielded now to painful efforts after the appropriation of pedantic principles. Instead of working upon antique monuments with their senses and emotions, men approached them through the medium of scholastic erudition. Instead of seeing and feeling for themselves, they sought by dissection to confirm the written precepts of a defunct Roman writer. This diversion of a great art from its natural line of development supplies a striking instance of the fascination which authority exercises at certain periods of culture. Rather than trust their feeling for what was beautiful and useful, convenient and attractive, the Italians of the Renaissance surrendered themselves to learning. Led by the spirit of scholarship, they thought it their duty to master the text of Vitruvius, to verify his principles by the analysis of surviving antique edifices, and, having formed their own conception of his theory, to apply this, as well as they were able, to the requirements of contemporary life.

Two exits from the false situation existed: one was the picturesqueness of the Barocco style; the other was the specious vapid purity of the Palladian. Michelangelo, who was essentially the genius of this transition, can neither be ascribed to the Barocco architects, although he called them into being, nor yet can he be said to have arrived at the Palladian solution.   He held both types within himself in embryo, arriving at a moment of profound and complicated difficulty for the practical architect; without technical education, but gifted with supreme genius, bringing the imperious instincts of a sublime creative amateur into every task appointed him.   We need not wonder if a man of his calibre left the powerful impress of his personality upon an art in chaos, luring lesser craftsmen into the Barocco mannerism, while he provoked reaction in the stronger, who felt more scientifically what was needed to secure firm standing-ground.   Bernini and the superb fountain of Trevi derive from Michelangelo on one side; Vignola's cold classic profiles and Palladio's resuscitation of old Rome in the Palazzo della Ragione at Vicenza emerge upon the other.   It remained Buonarroti's greatest glory that, lessoned by experience and inspired for high creation by the vastness of the undertaking, he imagined a world's wonder in the cupola of S. Peter's.

III.

Writing in the mid-stream of this architectural regurgitation, Vasari explains what contemporaries thought about Michelangelo's innovations.   "He wished to build the new sacristy upon the same lines as the older one by Brunelleschi, but at the same

time to clothe the edifice with a different style of
decoration. Accordingly, he invented for the interior
a composite adornment, of the newest and most
varied manner which antique and modern masters
joined together could have used. The novelty of his
style consisted in those lovely cornices, capitals, base-
ments, doors, niches, and sepulchres which trans-
cended all that earlier builders, working by measurements, distribution of parts, and rule, had previously
effected, following Vitruvius and the ancient relics.
Such men were afraid to supplement tradition with
original invention. The license he introduced gave
great courage to those who studied his method, and
emboldened them to follow on his path. Since that
time, new freaks of fancy have been seen, resembling
the style of arabesque and grotesque more than was
consistent with tradition. For this emancipation
of the art, all craftsmen owe him an infinite and
ever-during debt of gratitude, since he at one blow
broke down the bands and chains which barred the
path they trod in common." [1]

If I am right in thus interpreting an unusually
incoherent passage of Vasari's criticism, no words
could express more clearly the advent of Barocco
mannerism. But Vasari proceeds to explain his
meaning with still greater precision. "Afterwards
he made a plainer demonstration of his intention in
the library of S. Lorenzo, by the splendid distribution of the windows, the arrangement of the upper

[1] Vasari, xii. 205.

chamber, and the marvellous entrance-hall into that enclosed building. The grace and charm of art were never seen more perfectly displayed in the whole and in the parts of any edifice than here. I may refer in particular to the corbels, the recesses for statues, and the cornices. The staircase, too, deserves attention for its convenience, with the eccentric breakage of its flights of steps; the whole construction being so altered from the common usage of other architects as to excite astonishment in all who see it."

What emerges with distinctness from Vasari's account of Michelangelo's work at S. Lorenzo is that a practical Italian architect, who had been engaged on buildings of importance since this work was carried out, believed it to have infused freedom and new vigour into architecture. That freedom and new vigour we now know to have implied the Barocco style.

IV.

In estimating Michelangelo's work at S. Lorenzo, we must not forget that at this period of his life he contemplated statuary, bronze bas-relief, and painting, as essential adjuncts to architecture. The scheme is, therefore, not so much constructive as decorative, and a great many of its most offensive qualities may be ascribed to the fact that the purposes for which it was designed have been omitted. We know that the façade of S. Lorenzo was intended to abound in bronze and marble carvings. Beside the Medicean tombs, the sacristy ought to have contained a vast amount of sculpture, and its dome was actually painted in fresco by Giovanni da Udine under Michelangelo's own eyes. It appears that his imagination still obeyed those leading principles which he applied in the rough sketch for the first sepulchre of Julius. The vestibule and staircase of the library cannot therefore be judged fairly now ; for if they had been finished according to their maker's plan, the faults of their construction would have been compensated by multitudes of plastic shapes.

M. Charles Garnier, in *L'Œuvre et la Vie*, speaking with the authority of a practical architect, says : " Michelangelo was not, properly speaking, an architect. He made architecture, which is quite a different thing ; and most often it was the architecture of a painter and a sculptor, which points to colour, breadth, imagination, but also to insufficient studies and incomplete education. The thought may be great and strong, but the execution of it is always feeble and naïve. . . . He had not learned the language of the art. He has all the qualities of imagination, invention, will, which form a great composer ; but he does not know the grammar, and can hardly write. . . . In seeking the great, he has too often found the tumid ; seeking the original, he has fallen upon the strange, and also on bad taste."

There is much that is true in this critique, severe
though it may seem to be. The fact is that Michelangelo aimed at picturesque effect in his buildings;
not, as previous architects had done, by a lavish use
of loosely decorative details, but by the piling up and
massing together of otherwise dry orders, cornices,
pilasters, windows, all of which, in his conception,
were to serve as framework and pedestals for statuary.
He also strove to secure originality and to stimulate
astonishment by bizarre modulations of accepted
classic forms, by breaking the lines of architraves,
combining angularities with curves, adopting a vio-
lently accented rhythm and a tortured multiplicity
of parts, wherever this was possible.

V.

In this new style, so much belauded by Vasari,
the superficial design is often rich and grandiose,
making a strong pictorial appeal to the imagination.
Meanwhile, the organic laws of structure have been
sacrificed; and that chaste beauty which emerges
from a perfectly harmonious distribution of parts,
embellished by surface decoration only when the
limbs and members of the building demand em-
phasis, may be sought for everywhere in vain. The
substratum is a box, a barn, an inverted bottle;
built up of rubble, brick, and concrete; clothed with

learned details, which have been borrowed from the pseudo-science of the humanists.   There is nothing here of divine Greek candour, of dominant Roman vigour, of Gothic vitality, of fanciful invention governed by a sincere sense of truth.   Nothing remains of the shy graces, the melodious simplicities, the pure seeking after musical proportion, which marked the happier Italian effort of the early Renaissance, through Brunelleschi and Alberti, Bramante, Giuliano da Sangallo, and Peruzzi.   Architecture, in the highest sense of that word, has disappeared.   A scenic scheme of panelling for empty walls has superseded the conscientious striving to construct a living and intelligible whole.

The fault inherent in Italian building after the close of the Lombard period, reaches its climax here. That fault was connected with the inability of the Italians to assimilate the true spirit of the Gothic style, while they attempted its imitation in practice. The fabrication of imposing and lovely façades at Orvieto, at Siena, at Cremona, and at Crema, glorious screens which masked the poverty of the edifice, and corresponded in no point to the organism of the structure, taught them to overrate mere surface-beauty.   Their wonderful creativeness in all the arts which can be subordinated to architectural effect seduced them further.   Nothing, for instance, taken by itself alone, can be more satisfactory than the façade of the Certosa at Pavia ; but it is not, like the front of Chartres or Rheims or Amiens, a natural

introduction to the inner sanctuary. At the end
of the Gothic period architecture had thus come to
be conceived as the art of covering shapeless struc-
tures with a wealth of arabesques in marble, fresco,
bronze, mosaic.

The revival of learning and a renewed interest in
the antique withdrew the Italians for a short period
from this false position. With more or less of
merit, successive builders, including those I have
above mentioned, worked in a pure style : pure
because it obeyed the laws of its own music,
because it was intelligible and self-consistent, aim-
ing at construction as the main end, subordinating
decoration of richer luxuriance or of sterner severity to the prime purpose of the total scheme. But
this style was too much the plaything of particular
minds to create a permanent tradition. It varied in
the several provinces of Italy, and mingled personal
caprice with the effort to assume a classic garb.
Meanwhile the study of Vitruvius advanced, and
that pedantry which infected all the learned movements of the Renaissance struck deep and venomous
roots into the art of building.

Michelangelo arrived at the moment I am attempt-
ing to indicate. He protested that architecture was
not his trade. Over and over again he repeated
this to his Medicean patrons ; but they compelled
him to build, and he applied himself with the predilections and prepossessions of a plastic artist to
the task. The result was a retrogression from the

point reached by his immediate predecessors to the vicious system followed by the pseudo-Gothic architects in Italy. That is to say, he treated the structure as an inert mass, to be made as substantial as possible, and then to be covered with details agreeable to the eye. At the beginning of his career he had a defective sense of the harmonic ratios upon which a really musical building may be constructed out of mere bricks and mortar—such, for example, as the Church of S. Giustina at Padua. He was overweighted with ill-assimilated erudition; and all the less desirable licenses of Brunelleschi's school, especially in the abuse of square recesses, he adopted without hesitation. It never seems to have occurred to him that doors which were intended for ingress and egress, windows which were meant to give light, and attics which had a value as the means of illumination from above, could not with any propriety be applied to the covering of blank dead spaces in the interiors of buildings.

The vestibule of the Laurentian Library illustrates his method of procedure. It is a rectangular box of about a cube and two thirds, set length-way up. The outside of the building, left unfinished, exhibits a mere blank space of bricks. The interior might be compared to a temple in the grotesque-classic style turned outside in: colossal orders, meaningless consoles, heavy windows, square recesses, numerous doors—the windows, doors, and attics having no right to be there, since they lead to nothing, lend view to nothing, clamour for bronze and sculpture to explain their existence as niches and receptacles for statuary. It is nevertheless indubitably true that these incongruous and misplaced elements, crowded together, leave a strong impression of picturesque force upon the mind. From certain points and angles, the effect of the whole, considered as a piece of deception and insincerity, is magnificent. It would be even finer than it is, were not the Florentine *pietra serena* of the stonework so repellent in its ashen dulness, the plaster so white, and the false architectural system so painfully defrauded of the plastic forms for which it was intended to subserve as setting.

We have here no masterpiece of sound constructive science, but a freak of inventive fancy using studied details for the production of a pictorial effect. The details employed to compose this curious illusion are painfully dry and sterile ; partly owing to the scholastic enthusiasm for Vitruvius, partly to the decline of mediæval delight in naturalistic decoration, but, what seems to me still more apparent, through Michelangelo's own passionate preoccupation with the human figure. He could not tolerate any type of art which did not concede a predominant position to the form of man. Accordingly, his work in architecture at this period seems waiting for plastic illustration, demanding sculpture and fresco for its illumination and justification.

It is easy, one would think, to make an appeal to

the eye by means of colossal orders, bold cornices, enormous consoles, deeply indented niches. How much more easy to construct a box, and then say, "Come, let us cover its inside with an incongruous and inappropriate but imposing parade of learning," than to lift some light and genial thing of beauty aloft into the air, as did the modest builder of the staircase to the hall at Christ Church, Oxford! The eye of the vulgar is entranced, the eye of the artist bewildered. That the imagination which inspired that decorative scheme was powerful, original, and noble, will not be denied; but this does not save us from the desolating conviction that the scheme itself is a specious and pretentious mask, devised to hide a hideous waste of bricks and mortar.

Michelangelo's imagination, displayed in this distressing piece of work, was indeed so masterful that, as Vasari says, a new delightful style in architecture seemed to be revealed by it. A new way of clothing surfaces, falsifying façades, and dealing picturesquely with the lifeless element of Vitruvian tradition had been demonstrated by the genius of one who was a mighty amateur in building. In other words, the *Barocco* manner had begun; the path was opened to prank, caprice, and license. It required the finer tact and taste of a Palladio to rectify the false line here initiated, and to bring the world back to a sense of seriousness in its effort to deal constructively and rationally with the pseudo-classic mannerism.

The qualities of wilfulness and amateurishness

and seeking after picturesque effect, upon which I
am now insisting, spoiled Michelangelo's work as
architect, until he was forced by circumstance, and
after long practical experience, to confront a problem
of pure mathematical construction.   In the cupola
of S. Peter's he rose to the stern requirements of his
task.   There we find no evasion of the builder's duty
by mere surface-decoration, no subordination of the
edifice to plastic or pictorial uses.   Such side-issues
were excluded by the very nature of the theme.   An
immortal poem resulted, an aërial lyric of melodious
curves and solemn harmonies, a thought combining grace and audacity translated into stone uplifted
to the skies.   After being cabined in the vestibule to
the Laurentian Library, our soul escapes with gladness
to those airy spaces of the dome, that great cloud
on the verge of the Campagna, and feels thankful
that we can take our leave of Michelangelo as
architect elsewhere.

VI.

While seeking to characterise what proved pernicious to contemporaries in Michelangelo's work as
architect, I have been led to concentrate attention
upon the Library at S. Lorenzo.   This was logical;
for, as we have seen, Vasari regarded that building
as the supreme manifestation of his manner.   Vasari

never saw the cupola of S. Peter's in all its glory, and it may be doubted whether he was capable of learning much from it.

The sacristy demands separate consideration. It was an earlier work, produced under more favourable conditions of place and space, and is in every way a purer specimen of the master's style. As Vasari observed, the Laurentian Library indicated a large advance upon the sacristy in the development of Michelanglo's new manner.

At this point it may not unprofitably be remarked, that none of the problems offered for solution at S. Lorenzo were in the strictest sense of that word architectural. The façade presented a problem of pure panelling. The ground-plan of the sacristy was fixed in correspondence with Brunelleschi's; and here again the problem resolved itself chiefly into panelling. A builder of genius, working on the library, might indeed have displayed his science and his taste by some beautiful invention adapted to the awkward locality; as Baldassare Peruzzi, in the Palazzo Massimo at Rome, converted the defects of the site into graces by the exquisite turn he gave to the curved portion of the edifice. Still, when the scheme was settled, even the library became more a matter of panelling and internal fittings than of structural design. Nowhere at S. Lorenzo can we affirm that Michelangelo enjoyed the opportunity of showing what he could achieve in the production of a building independent

in itself and planned throughout with a free hand.
Had he been a born architect, he would probably
have insisted upon constructing the Medicean mausoleum after his own conception instead of repeating
Brunelleschi's ground-plan, and he would almost
certainly have discovered a more genial solution
for the difficulties of the library. But he protested
firmly against being considered an architect by inclination or by education. Therefore he accepted
the most obvious conditions of each task, and devoted himself to schemes of surface decoration.

The interior of the sacristy is planned with a
noble sense of unity. For the purpose of illuminat-
ing a gallery of statues, the lighting may be praised
without reserve; and there is no doubt whatever
that Michelangelo intended every tabernacle to be
filled with figures, and all the whitewashed spaces of
the walls to be encrusted with bas-reliefs in stucco or
painted in fresco. The recesses or niches, taking
the form of windows, are graduated in three degrees
of depth to suit three scales of sculptural importance.
The sepulchres of the Dukes had to emerge into
prominence; the statues subordinate to these main
masses occupied shallower recesses; the shallowest
of all, reserved for minor statuary, are adorned above
with garlands, which suggest the flatness of the
figures to be introduced. Architecturally speaking,
the building is complete; but it sadly wants the
plastic decoration for which it was designed, together
with many finishing touches of importance. It is

clear, for instance, that the square pedestals above the double pilasters flanking each of the two Dukes were meant to carry statuettes or candelabra, which would have connected the marble panelling with the cornices and stucchi and frescoed semicircles of the upper region. Our eyes are everywhere defrauded of the effect calculated by Michelangelo when he planned this chapel. Yet the total impression remains harmonious Proportion has been observed in all the parts, especially in the relation of the larger to the smaller orders, and in the balance of the doors and windows. Merely decorative carvings are used with parsimony, and designed in a pure style, although they exhibit originality of invention. The alternation of white marble surfaces and mouldings with *pietra serena* pilasters, cornices, and arches, defines the structural design, and gives a grave but agreeable sense of variety. Finally, the recess behind the altar adds lightness and space to what would otherwise have been a box. What I have already observed when speaking of the vestibule to the library must be repeated here : the whole scheme is that of an exterior turned outside in, and its justification lies in the fact that it demanded statuary and colour for its completion. Still the bold projecting cornices, the deeper and shallower niches resembling windows, have the merit of securing broken lights and shadows under the strong vertical illumination, all of which are eminently picturesque.

No doubt remains now that tradition is accurate

in identifying the helmeted Duke with Lorenzo de'
Medici, and the more graceful seated hero opposite
with Giuliano.[1] The recumbent figures on the void
sepulchres beneath them are with equal truth desig-
nated as Night and Day, Morning and Evening.
But Michelangelo condescended to no realistic portraiture in the statues of the Dukes, and he also
meant undoubtedly to treat the phases of time which
rule man's daily life upon the planet as symbols for
far-reaching thoughts connected with our destiny.[2]
These monumental figures are not men, not women,
but vague and potent allegories of our mortal fate.
They remain as he left them, except that parts of
Giuliano's statue, especially the hands, seem to have
been worked over by an assistant.   The same is true
of the Madonna, which will ever be regarded, in her
imperfectly finished state, as one of the finest of his
sculptural conceptions.   To Montelupo belongs the
execution of S. Damiano, and to Montorsoli that of
S. Cosimo.   Vasari says that Tribolo was commissioned by Michelangelo to carve statues of Earth
weeping for the loss of Giuliano, and Heaven rejoic-
ing over his spirit.[3]   The death of Pope Clement,

[1] See Heath Wilson, pp. 563–566. He was present at the opening
of these sarcophagi in 1875, and saw the remains of Duke Alessandro
enclosed with those of his supposed father in the sepulchre of Lorenzo,
Duke of Urbino.

[2] This view is confirmed by what Condivi writes about the statues
in question. He says that, taken together, they represent "Time, who
consumes all things," cap. xlv. p. 50.

[3] Michelangelo even prepared clay models for them. See Lettere,
No. cdxix. ; Vasari, x. 250 ; Springer, ii. 384.

however, put a stop to these subordinate works,
which, had they been accomplished, might perhaps
have shown us how Buonarroti intended to fill the
empty niches on each side of the Dukes.

When Michelangelo left Florence for good at the
end of 1534, his statues had not been placed; but
we have reason to think that the Dukes and the
four allegorical figures were erected in his lifetime. There is something singular in the malad-
justment of the recumbent men and women to the
curves of the sarcophagi, and in the contrast between
the roughness of their bases and the smooth polish
of the chests they rest on. These discrepancies do
not, however, offend the eye, and they may even
have been deliberately adopted from a keen sense of
what the Greeks called *asymmetreia* as an adjunct
to effect. It is more difficult to understand what
he proposed to do with the Madonna and her two
attendant saints. Placed as they now are upon a
simple ledge, they strike one as being too near the
eye, and out of harmony with the architectural tone
of the building. It is also noticeable that the saints
are more than a head taller than the Dukes, while
the Madonna overtops the saints by more than
another head. We are here in a region of pure
conjecture; and if I hazard an opinion, it is only
thrown out as a possible solution of a now impene-
trable problem. I think, then, that Michelangelo
may have meant to pose these three figures where
they are, facing the altar; to raise the Madonna

upon a slightly projecting bracket above the level
of SS. Damiano and Cosimo, and to paint the wall
behind them with a fresco of the Crucifixion. That
he had no intention of panelling that empty space
with marble may be taken for granted, considering
the high finish which has been given to every part
of this description of work in the chapel. Treated
as I have suggested, the statue of the Madonna, with
the patron saints of the House of Medici, over-
shadowed by a picture of Christ's sacrifice, would
have confronted the mystery of the Mass during
every celebration at the altar. There are many
designs for the Crucifixion, made by Michelangelo
in later life, so lofty as almost to suggest a group
of figures in the foreground, cutting the middle
distance.

At the close of Michelangelo's life the sacristy
was still unfinished. It contained the objects I have
described—the marble panelling, the altar with its
candelabra, the statues of the Dukes and their attendant figures, the Madonna and two Medicean patron
saints—in fact, all that we find there now, with the
addition of Giovanni da Udine's frescoes in the
cupola, the relics of which have since been buried
under cold Florentine whitewash.[1]

All the views I have advanced in the foregoing

---

[1] I often wonder why people abuse the churchwardens of the last
century in England, while they withhold their censure from the men
of Florence, who have obliterated really great work, and rendered the
task of reconstructing it impossible, by a remorseless application of
mere whitewash to damaged frescoes.

paragraphs as to the point at which Michelangelo
abandoned this chapel, and his probable designs for
its completion, are in the last resort based upon an
important document penned at the instance of the
Duke of Florence by Vasari to Buonarroti, not long
before the old man's death in Rome. This epistle
has so weighty a bearing upon the matter in hand
that I shall here translate it. Careful study of its
fluent periods will convince an unprejudiced mind
that the sacristy, as we now see it, is even less representative of its maker's design than it was when
Vasari wrote. The frescoes of Giovanni da Udine
are gone. It will also show that the original project
involved a wealth of figurative decoration, statuary,
painting, stucco, which never arrived at realisation.

VII.

Vasari, writing in the spring of 1562, informs
Michelangelo concerning the Academy of Design
founded by Duke Cosimo de' Medici, and of the
Duke's earnest desire that he should return to
Florence in order that the sacristy at S. Lorenzo
may be finished.[1] "Your reasons for not coming
are accepted as sufficient. He is therefore considering—forasmuch as the place is being used now for

---

[1] The despatch is printed in Bottari's *Lett. Pitt.*, vol. iii. pp. 78-84.
It exists in manuscript in the Arch. Buon., Cod. xi. No. 765.

religious services by day and night, according to the
intention of Pope Clement—he is considering, I say,
a plan for erecting the statues which are missing
in the niches above the sepulchres and the tabernacles above the doors. The Duke then wishes that
all the eminent sculptors of this academy, in competition man with man, should each of them make
one statue, and that the painters in like manner
should exercise their art upon the chapel. Designs
are to be prepared for the arches according to your
own project, including works of painting and of
stucco; the other ornaments and the pavement are to
be provided; in short, he intends that the new academicians shall complete the whole imperfect scheme,
in order that the world may see that, while so many
men of genius still exist among us, the noblest work
which was ever yet conceived on earth has not been
left unfinished. He has commissioned me to write
to you and unfold his views, begging you at the
same time to favour him by communicating to himself or to me what your intentions were, or those of
the late Pope Clement, with regard to the name and
title of the chapel; moreover, to inform us what
designs you made for the four tabernacles on each
side of the Dukes Lorenzo and Giuliano; also what
you projected for the eight statues above the doors
and in the tabernacles of the corners; and, finally,
what your idea was of the paintings to adorn the
flat walls and the semicircular spaces of the chapel.
He is particularly anxious that you should be assured

of his determination to alter nothing you have already done or planned, but, on the contrary, to carry out the whole work according to your own conception. The academicians too are unanimous in their hearty desire to abide by this decision. I am furthermore instructed to tell you, that if you possess sketches, working cartoons, or drawings made for this purpose, the same would be of the greatest service in the execution of his project; and he promises to be a good and faithful administrator, so that honour may ensue. In case you do not feel inclined to do all this, through the burden of old age or for any other reason, he begs you at least to communicate with some one who shall write upon the subject; seeing that he would be greatly grieved, as indeed would the whole of our academy, to have no ray of light from your own mind, and possibly to add things to your masterpiece which were not according to your designs and wishes. We all of us look forward to being comforted by you, if not with actual work, at least with words. His Excellency founds this hope upon your former willingness to complete the edifice by allotting statues to Tribolo, Montelupo, and the Friar (Giovanni Angelo Montorsoli). The last named of these masters is here, eagerly desirous to have the opportunity of doing you honour. So are Francesco Sangallo, Giovanni Bologna, Benvenuto Cellini, Ammanato, Rossi and Vincenzio Danti of Perugia, not to mention other sculptors of note. The painters, headed by Bronzino, include many talented young men, skilled in design, and colourists, quite capable of establishing an honourable reputation. Of myself I need not speak. You know well that in devotion, attachment, love, and loyalty (and let me say this with prejudice to no one) I surpass the rest of your admirers by far. Therefore, I entreat you, of your goodness, to console his Excellency, and all these men of parts, and our city, as well as to show this particular favour to myself, who have been selected by the Duke to write to you, under the impression that, being your familiar and loving friend, I might obtain from you some assistance of sterling utility for the undertaking. His Excellency is prepared to spend both substance and labour on the task, in order to honour you. Pray then, albeit age is irksome, endeavour to aid him by unfolding your views; for, in doing so, you will confer benefits on countless persons, and will be the cause of raising all these men of parts to higher excellence, each one of whom has learned what he already knows in the sacristy, or rather let me say our school."

This eloquent despatch informs us very clearly that the walls of the sacristy, above the tall Corinthian order which encloses the part devoted to sculpture, were intended to be covered with stucco and fresco paintings, completing the polychromatic decoration begun by Giovanni da Udine in the cupola. Twelve statues had been designed for the niches in the marble panelling; and one word used by Vasari, *facciate*, leaves the impression that the blank walls round and opposite the altar were also to be adorned with pictures. We remain uncertain how Michelangelo originally meant to dispose of the colossal Madonna with SS. Damian and Cosimo.

Unhappily, nothing came of the Duke's project. Michelangelo was either unable or unwilling— probably unable—to furnish the necessary plans and drawings. In the eighth chapter of this book I have discussed the hesitations with regard to the interior of the sacristy which are revealed by some of his extant designs for it. We also know that he was not in the habit of preparing accurate working cartoons for the whole of a large scheme, but that he proceeded from point to point, trusting to slight sketches and personal supervision of the work.[1] Thus, when Vasari wrote to him from Rome about the staircase of the library, he expressed a perfect readiness to help, but could only remember its construction in a kind of dream.[2] We may safely assume, then, that he had not sufficient material to communicate; plans definite enough in general scope and detailed incident to give a true conception of his whole idea were lacking.

---

[1] The cartoon for the Battle of Pisa, the cartoons for the Sistine, and the model for the cupola of S. Peter do not invalidate this statement. In the case of the frescoes above mentioned, the work was actually in hand and had to be got through ; the model was only made at the urgent instance of friends, who were anxious lest he should die and leave no record of his conception.

[2] Lettere, No. cdlxxxv.

VIII.

Passing to æsthetical considerations, I am forced
to resume here what I published many years ago
about the Sacristy of S. Lorenzo, as it now exists.
Repeated visits to that shrine have only renewed
former impressions, which will not bear to be reproduced in other language, and would lose some of
their freshness by the stylistic effort. No other course
remains then but to quote from my own writings,
indorsing them with such weight as my signature
may have acquired since they were first given to
the world.[1]

"The sacristy may be looked on either as the
masterpiece of a sculptor who required fit setting
for his statues, or of an architect who designed
statues to enhance the structure he had planned.
Both arts are used with equal ease, nor has the
genius of Michelangelo dealt more masterfully with
the human frame than with the forms of Roman
architecture in this chapel. He seems to have paid
no heed to classic precedent, and to have taken no
pains to adapt the parts to the structural purpose of
the building. It was enough for him to create a
wholly novel framework for the modern miracle of
sculpture it enshrines, attending to such rules of
composition as determine light and shade, and seek-

---

[1] *Renaissance in Italy,* "Fine Arts," pp. 86, 87, 415-419.

ing by the relief of mouldings and pilasters to enhance the terrible and massive forms that brood
above the Medicean tombs. The result is a product
of picturesque and plastic art as true to the Michelangelesque spirit as the Temple of the Wingless
Victory to that of Pheidias. But where Michelangelo achieved a triumph of boldness, lesser natures
were betrayed into bizarrerie; and this chapel of
the Medici, in spite of its grandiose simplicity,
proved a stumbling-block to subsequent architects
by encouraging them to despise propriety and violate
the laws of structure.

"We may assume then that the colossal statues of
Giuliano and Lorenzo were studied with a view to
their light and shadow as much as to their form;
and this is a fact to be remembered by those who
visit the chapel where Buonarroti laboured both as
architect and sculptor. Of the two Medici, it is not
fanciful to say that the Duke of Urbino is the most
immovable of spectral shapes eternalised in marble;
while the Duke of Nemours, more graceful and
elegant, seems intended to present a contrast to
this terrible thought-burdened form. The allegorical
figures, stretched on segments of ellipses beneath
the pedestals of the two Dukes, indicate phases of
darkness and of light, of death and life. They are
two women and two men; tradition names them
Night and Day, Twilight and Dawning. Thus in
the statues themselves and in their attendant genii
we have a series of abstractions, symbolising the

sleep and waking of existence, action and thought, the gloom of death, the lustre of life, and the intermediate states of sadness and of hope that form the borderland of both. Life is a dream between two slumbers; sleep is death's twin-brother; night is the shadow of death; death is the gate of life:— such is the mysterious mythology wrought by the sculptor of the modern world in marble. All these figures, by the intensity of their expression, the vagueness of their symbolism, force us to think and question. What, for example, occupies Lorenzo's brain? Bending forward, leaning his chin upon his wrist, placing the other hand upon his knee, on what does he for ever ponder?

"The sight, as Rogers said well, 'fascinates and is intolerable.' Michelangelo has shot the beaver of the helmet forward on his forehead, and bowed his head, so as to clothe the face in darkness. But behind the gloom there lurks no fleshless skull, as Rogers fancied. The whole frame of the powerful man is instinct with some imperious thought. Has he outlived his life and fallen upon everlasting contemplation? Is he brooding, injured and indignant, over his own doom and the extinction of his race? Is he condemned to witness in immortal immobility the woes of Italy he helped to cause? Or has the sculptor symbolised in him the burden of that personality we carry with us in this life, and bear for ever when we wake into another world? Beneath this incarnation of oppressive thought there lie, full

length and naked, the figures of Dawn and Twilight,
Morn and Evening. So at least they are commonly
called, and these names are not inappropriate; for
the breaking of the day and the approach of night
are metaphors for many transient conditions of the
soul. It is only as allegories in a large sense, comprehending both the physical and intellectual order,
and capable of various interpretation, that any of
these statues can be understood. Even the Dukes
do not pretend to be portraits, and hence in part
perhaps the uncertainty that has gathered round
them. Very tranquil and noble is Twilight: a giant
in repose, he meditates, leaning upon his elbow,
looking down. But Dawn starts from her couch,
as though some painful summons had reached her,
sunk in dreamless sleep, and called her forth to
suffer. Her waking to consciousness is like that of
one who has been drowned, and who finds the return
to life agony. Before her eyes, seen even through
the mists of slumber, are the ruin and the shame of
Italy. Opposite lies Night, so sorrowful, so utterly
absorbed in darkness and the shade of death, that
to shake off that everlasting lethargy seems impossible. Yet she is not dead. If we raise our voices,
she too will stretch her limbs, and, like her sister,
shudder into sensibility with sighs. Only we must
not wake her; for he who fashioned her has told
us that her sleep of stone is great good fortune.
Both of these women are large and brawny, unlike
the Fates of Pheidias, in their muscular maturity.

The burden of Michelangelo's thought was too tremendous to be borne by virginal and graceful beings. He had to make women no less capable of suffering, no less world-wearied, than his country.

"Standing before these statues, we do not cry, How beautiful! We murmur, How terrible, how grand! Yet, after long gazing, we find them gifted with beauty beyond grace. In each of them there is a palpitating thought, torn from the artist's soul and crystallised in marble. It has been said that architecture is petrified music. In the Sacristy of S. Lorenzo we feel impelled to remember phrases of Beethoven. Each of these statues becomes for us a passion, fit for musical expression, but turned like Niobe to stone. They have the intellectual vagueness, the emotional certainty, that belong to the motives of a symphony. In their allegories, left without a key, sculpture has passed beyond her old domain of placid concrete form. The anguish of intolerable emotion, the quickening of the consciousness to a sense of suffering, the acceptance of the inevitable, the strife of the soul with destiny, the burden and the passion of mankind :—that is what they contain in their cold chisel-tortured marble. It is open to critics of the school of Lessing to object that here is the suicide of sculpture. It is easy to remark that those strained postures and writhen limbs may have perverted the taste of lesser craftsmen. Yet if Michelangelo was called to carve Medicean statues after the sack of Rome and the fall of Florence—if he was obliged in sober sadness to make sculpture a fit language for his sorrow-laden heart—how could he have wrought more truthfully than this? To imitate him without sharing his emotions or comprehending his thoughts, as the soulless artists of the decadence attempted, was without all doubt a grievous error. Surely also we may regret, not without reason, that in the evil days upon which he had fallen, the fair antique *Heiterkeit* and *Allgemeinheit* were beyond his reach."

That this regret is not wholly sentimental may be proved, I think, by an exchange of verses, which we owe to Vasari's literary sagacity.[1] He tells us that when the statue of the Night was opened to the public view, it drew forth the following quatrain from an author unknown to himself by name:[2]—

> The Night thou seest here, posed gracefully
> In act of slumber, was by an Angel wrought
> Out of this stone; sleeping, with life she's fraught:
> Wake her, incredulous wight; she'll speak to thee.

Michelangelo would have none of these academical conceits and compliments. He replied in four verses, which show well enough what thoughts were

[1] Vol. xii. p. 208. Compare what Condivi says about the statues having been executed under an impulse of fear rather than of love, p. 49.

[2] The writer was Giovan Battista Strozzi.

in his brain when he composed the nightmare-
burdened, heavy-sleeping woman : [1]—

> Dear is my sleep, but more to be mere stone,
> So long as ruin and dishonour reign :
> To hear naught, to feel naught, is my great gain ;
> Then wake me not ; speak in an undertone.

---

[1] There are numerous transcripts of the verses. The first word of the quatrain was originally *grato*, but he changed it finally to *caro*. See Guasti, *Rime*, p. 3. In the Codex Vaticanus, as I have seen, the hand of a scribe wrote *grato*, and Michelangelo wrote over the word *caro*.

CHAPTER XI.

I.

AFTER the death of Clement VII., Michelangelo never returned to reside for any length of time at Florence. The rest of his life was spent in Rome, and he fell almost immediately under the kind but somewhat arbitrary patronage of Alessandro Farnese, who succeeded to the Papal chair in October 1534, with the title of Paul III.

One of the last acts of Clement's life had been to superintend the second contract with the heirs of Julius, by which Michelangelo undertook to finish the tomb upon a reduced scale within the space of three years. He was allowed to come to Rome and work there during four months annually. Paul, however, asserted his authority by upsetting these arrangements and virtually cancelling the contract.

"In the meanwhile," writes Condivi,[1] "Pope Clement died, and Paul III. sent for him, and requested him to enter his service. Michelangelo saw at once that he would be interrupted in his work upon the Tomb of Julius. So he told Paul that he was not his own master, being bound to the Duke of Urbino until the monument was finished. The Pope grew angry, and exclaimed : ' It is thirty years that I have cherished this desire, and now that I am Pope, may I not indulge it ? Where is the contract ? I mean to tear it up.' Michelangelo, finding himself reduced to these straits, almost resolved to leave Rome and take refuge in the Genoese, at an abbey held by the Bishop of Aleria, who had been a creature of Julius, and was much attached to him. He hoped that the neighbourhood of the Carrara quarries, and the facility

[1] Condivi, p. 57.

of transporting marbles by sea, would help him to
complete his engagements. He also thought of
settling at Urbino, which he had previously selected
as a tranquil retreat, and where he expected to be
well received for the sake of Pope Julius. Some
months earlier, he even sent a man of his to buy a
house and land there. Still he dreaded the greatness of the Pontiff, as indeed he had good cause to
do, and for this reason he abandoned the idea of
quitting Rome, hoping to pacify his Holiness with
fair words.

"The Pope, however, stuck to his opinion; and
one day he visited Michelangelo at his house, attended by eight or ten Cardinals. He first of all
inspected the cartoon prepared in Clement's reign
for the great work of the Sistine; then the statues
for the tomb, and everything in detail. The most
reverend Cardinal of Mantua, standing before the
statue of Moses, cried out: 'That piece alone is
sufficient to do honour to the monument of Julius.'
Pope Paul, having gone through the whole workshop, renewed his request that Michelangelo should
enter his service; and when the latter still resisted,
he clinched the matter by saying: 'I will provide
that the Duke of Urbino shall be satisfied with three
statues from your hand, and the remaining three
shall be assigned to some other sculptor.' Accordingly, he settled on the terms of a new contract
with the agents of the Duke, which were confirmed
by his Excellency, who did not care to displeasure

the Pope. Michelangelo, albeit he was now relieved from the obligation of paying for the three
statues, preferred to take this cost upon himself, and
deposited 1580 ducats for the purpose. And so
the Tragedy of the Tomb came at last to an end.
This may now be seen at S. Pietro ad Vincula;
and though, truth to tell, it is but a mutilated and
botched-up remnant of Michelangelo's original design,
the monument is still the finest to be found in Rome,
and perhaps elsewhere in the world, if only for the
three statues finished by the hand of the great
master."

II.

In this account, Condivi has condensed the events
of seven years. The third and last contract with
the heirs of Julius was not ratified until the autumn
of 1542, nor was the tomb erected much before the
year 1550. We shall see that the tragedy still cost
its hero many anxious days during this period.

Paul III., having obtained his object, issued a
brief, whereby he appointed Michelangelo chief
architect, sculptor, and painter at the Vatican. The
instrument is dated September 1, 1535, and the
terms with which it describes the master's eminence
in the three arts are highly flattering.[1] Allusion is
directly made to the fresco of the Last Judgment,

[1] Gotti, ii. p. 123.

which may therefore have been begun about this date. Michelangelo was enrolled as member of the Pontifical household, with a permanent pension of 1200 golden crowns, to be raised in part on the revenues accruing from a ferry across the Po at Piacenza. He did not, however, obtain possession of this ferry until 1537, and the benefice proved so unremunerative that it was exchanged for a little post in the Chancery at Rimini.[1]

When Michelangelo began to work again in the Sistine Chapel, the wall above the altar was adorned with three great sacred subjects by the hand of Pietro Perugino. In the central fresco of the Assumption Perugino introduced a portrait of Sixtus IV. kneeling in adoration before the ascending Madonna.[2] The side panels were devoted to the Nativity and the finding of Moses. In what condition Michelangelo found these frescoes before the painting of the Last Judgment we do not know. Vasari says that he caused the wall to be rebuilt with well-baked carefully selected bricks, and sloped inwards so that the top projected half a cubit from the bottom. This was intended to secure the picture from dust.[3] Vasari also relates that Sebastiano del

[1] See Ricordo, January 2, 1537, in Lettere, p. 604, and Lettere, No. cciii., date August 10, 1548. It appears that Michelangelo refused to profit by the benefice at Rimini.

[2] This must have resembled Pinturicchio's fine portrait of Alexander VI. in a similar attitude, reproduced in Yriarte, *Autour des Borgias*, at p. 72.

[3] Vasari, xii. p. 219. The projection is not apparent now ; and if it kept off dust, it would rather have increased the injury from rising smoke.

Piombo, acting on his own responsibility, prepared this wall with a ground for oil-colours, hoping to be employed by Michelangelo, but that the latter had it removed, preferring the orthodox method of fresco-painting.[1] The story, as it stands, is not very probable; yet we may perhaps conjecture that, before deciding on the system to be adopted for his great work, Buonarroti thought fit to make experiments in several surfaces. The painters of that period, as is proved by Sebastiano's practice, by Lionardo da Vinci's unfortunate innovations at Florence, and by the experiments of Raphael's pupils in the hall of Constantine, not unfrequently invented methods for mural decoration which should afford the glow and richness of oil-colouring. Michelangelo may even have proposed at one time to intrust a large portion of his fresco to Sebastiano's executive skill, and afterwards have found the same difficulties in collaboration which reduced him to the necessity of painting the Sistine vault in solitude.

Be that as it may, when the doors of the chapel once closed behind the master, we hear nothing whatsoever about his doings till they opened again on Christmas Day in 1541. The reticence of Michelangelo regarding his own works is one of the most trying things about him. It is true indeed that his correspondence between 1534 and 1541 almost

[1] *Life of Sebastiano del Piombo*, vol. x. p. 135. Vasari refers to this occasion Michelangelo's famous saying that oils were only meant for women and lazy fellows. He also ascribes Michelangelo's rupture with his old friend and gossip to the bad feeling caused by the incident.

JUDGING CHRIST, DETAIL OF LAST JUDGMENT, fresco, Sistine
Chapel, Vatican, 1535–42. Alinari/Art Resource, NY.

entirely fails; still, had it been abundant, we should probably have possessed but dry and laconic references to matters connected with the business of his art.

He must have been fully occupied on the Last Judgment during 1536 and 1537. Paul III. was still in correspondence with the Duke of Urbino, who showed himself not only willing to meet the Pope's wishes with regard to the Tomb of Julius, but also very well disposed toward the sculptor. In July 1537, Hieronimo Staccoli wrote to the Duke of Camerino about a silver salt-cellar which Michelangelo had designed at his request.[1] This prince, Guidobaldo della Rovere, when he afterwards succeeded to the Duchy of Urbino, sent a really warm-hearted despatch to his "dearest Messer Michelangelo." He begins by saying that, though he still cherishes the strongest wish to see the monument of his uncle completed, he does not like to interrupt the fresco in the Sistine Chapel, upon which his Holiness has set his heart. He thoroughly trusts in Michelangelo's loyalty, and is assured that his desire to finish the tomb, for the honour of his former patron's memory, is keen

---

[1] Gotti, ii. 125. Guidobaldo della Rovere, the son of the Duke of Urbino, held the title of Duke of Camerino at this time, by right of his marriage with the heiress of the Varani family. It is probable that the compliance shown by the Della Roveres in the matter of the tomb was due in some measure to their difficulties with the Papal Curia in the matter of the fief of Camerino. See Dennistoun, *Dukes of Urbino*, vol. iii. chaps. 41, 42.

and sincere. Therefore, he hopes that when the picture of the Last Judgment is terminated, the work will be resumed and carried to a prosperous conclusion. In the meantime, let Buonarroti attend to his health, and not put everything again to peril by overstraining his energies.[1]

Signor Gotti quotes a Papal brief, issued on the 18th of September 1537, in which the history of the Tomb of Julius up to date is set forth, and Michelangelo's obligations toward the princes of Urbino are recited. It then proceeds to declare that Clement VII. ordered him to paint the great wall of the Sistine, and that Paul desires this work to be carried forward with all possible despatch. He therefore lets it be publicly known that Michelangelo has not failed to perform his engagements in the matter of the tomb through any fault or action of his own, but by the express command of his Holiness. Finally, he discharges him and his heirs from all liabilities, pecuniary or other, to which he may appear exposed by the unfulfilled contracts.[2]

---

[1] Gotti, i. 265. Francesco Maria della Rovere died in 1538. The letter (preserved in the Arch. Buon., Cod. vii. No. 225) is dated September 7, 1539. It is therefore written by Guidobaldo II. Gotti seems to me to have confused the two Dukes.

[2] Gotti, i. 263. The text of the brief is not published in his Appendix. Milanesi (Vasari, xii. 388) seems to allude to it under the date December 18, 1537.

III.

While thus engaged upon his fresco, Michelangelo received a letter, dated Venice, September 15, 1537, from that rogue of genius, Pietro Aretino.[1] It opens in the strain of hyperbolical compliment and florid rhetoric which Aretino affected when he chose to flatter. The man, however, was an admirable stylist, the inventor of a new epistolary manner. Like a volcano, his mind blazed with wit, and buried sound sense beneath the scoriæ and ashes it belched forth. Gifted with a natural feeling for rhetorical contrast, he knew the effect of some simple and impressive sentence, placed like a gem of value in the midst of gimcrack conceits. Thus: "I should not venture to address you, had not my name, accepted by the ears of every prince in Europe, outworn much of its native indignity. And it is but meet that I should approach you with this reverence; for the world has many kings, and one only Michelangelo. Strange miracle, that Nature, who cannot place aught so high but that you explore it with your art, should be impotent to stamp upon her works that majesty which she contains within herself, the immense power of your style and your chisel! Wherefore, when we gaze on you, we regret no longer that we may not meet with Pheidìas, Apelles, or Vitruvius, whose spirits

[1] *Le Lettere di M. Pietro Aretino*, Parigi, 1609, vol. i. p. 154.

were the shadow of your spirit." He piles the
panegyric up to its climax, by adding it is fortunate
for those great artists of antiquity that their masterpieces cannot be compared with Michelangelo's,
since, " being arraigned before the tribunal of our
eyes, we should perforce proclaim you unique as
sculptor, unique as painter, and as architect unique."
After the blare of this exordium, Aretino settles
down to the real business of his letter, and com-
municates his own views regarding the Last Judgment, which he hears that the supreme master of
all arts is engaged in depicting. " Who would not
quake with terror while dipping his brush into the
dreadful theme? I behold Antichrist in the midst
of thronging multitudes, with an aspect such as only
you could limn. I behold affright upon the forehead of the living; I see the signs of the extinction of the sun, the moon, the stars; I see the
breath of life exhaling from the elements; I see
Nature abandoned and apart, reduced to barrenness,
crouching in her decrepitude; I see Time sapless
and trembling, for his end has come, and he is seated
on an arid throne; and while I hear the trumpets of
the angels with their thunder shake the hearts of
all, I see both Life and Death convulsed with horrible
confusion, the one striving to resuscitate the dead,
the other using all his might to slay the living; I
see Hope and Despair guiding the squadrons of
the good and the cohorts of the wicked; I see the
theatre of clouds, blazing with rays that issue from

the purest fires of heaven, upon which among his hosts Christ sits, ringed round with splendours and with terrors; I see the radiance of his face, coruscating flames of light both glad and awful, filling the blest with joy, the damned with fear intolerable. Then I behold the satellites of the abyss, who with horrid gestures, to the glory of the saints and martyrs, deride Cæsar and the Alexanders; for it is one thing to have trampled on the world, but more to have conquered self. I see Fame, with her crowns and palms trodden under foot, cast out among the wheels of her own chariots. And to conclude all, I see the dread sentence issue from the mouth of the Son of God. I see it in the form of two darts, the one of salvation, the other of damnation; and as they hustle down, I hear the fury of its onset shock the elemental frame of things, and, with the roar of thunderings and voices, smash the universal scheme to fragments. I see the vault of ether merged in gloom, illuminated only by the lights of Paradise and the furnaces of hell. My thoughts, excited by this vision of the Day of Doom, whisper: ' If we quake in terror before the handiwork of Buonarroti, how shall we shake and shrink affrighted when He who shall judge passes sentence on our souls?' "

This description of the Last Day, in which it is more than doubtful whether a man like Aretino had any sincere faith, possesses considerable literary interest. In the first place, it is curious as coming from one who lived on terms of closest intimacy with painters, and who certainly appreciated art; for this reason, that nothing less pictorial than the images evoked could be invented. Then, again, in the first half of the sixteenth century it anticipated the rhetoric of the *barocco* period—the eloquence of seventeenth-century divines, Dutch poets, Jesuit pulpiteers. Aretino's originality consisted in his precocious divination of a whole new age of taste and style, which was destined to supersede the purer graces of the Renaissance.

The letter ends with an assurance that if anything could persuade him to break a resolution he had formed, and to revisit Rome, it would be his great anxiety to view the Last Judgment of the Sistine Chapel with his own eyes.[1]

Michelangelo sent an answer which may be cited as an example of his peculiar irony. Under the form of elaborate compliment it conceals the scorn he must have conceived for Aretino and his insolent advice. Yet he knew how dangerous the man could be, and felt obliged to humour him.[2]

" Magnificent Messer Pietro, my lord and brother,— The receipt of your letter gave me both joy and

---

[1] If Aretino begged for drawings in this letter, he omitted the passage when he sent the manuscript to press. Michelangelo's answer looks as though he had. We know that G. Vasari sent a present of a head modelled in wax and a sketch for S. Catherine by Michelangelo as a present to Aretino, September 7, 1535. See Bottari, *Lett. Pitt.*, vol. iii. p. 190.

[2] *Lettere*, No. cdxxi.

sorrow. I rejoiced exceedingly, since it came from you, who are without peer in all the world for talent. Yet at the same time I grieved, inasmuch as, having finished a large part of the fresco, I cannot realise your conception, which is so complete, that if the Day of Judgment had come, and you had been present and seen it with your eyes, your words could not have described it better. Now, touching an answer to my letter, I reply that I not only desire it, but I entreat you to write one, seeing that kings and emperors esteem it the highest favour to be mentioned by your pen. Meanwhile, if I have anything that you would like, I offer it with all my heart. In conclusion, do not break your resolve of never revisiting Rome on account of the picture I am painting, for this would be too much."

Aretino's real object was to wheedle some priceless sketch or drawing out of the great master. This appears from a second letter written by him on the 20th of January 1538.[1] "Does not my devotion deserve that I should receive from you, the prince of sculpture and of painting, one of those cartoons which you fling into the fire, to the end that during life I may enjoy it, and in death carry it with me to the tomb?" After all, we must give Aretino credit for genuine feelings of admiration toward illustrious artists like Titian, Sansovino, and Michelangelo. Writing many years after the date of these letters, when he has seen an engraving of the Last

[1] *Lettere di M. P. A., op. cit.,* vol. ii. p. 10.

Judgment, he uses terms, extravagant indeed, but apparently sincere, about its grandeur of design.[1] Then he repeats his request for a drawing. " Why will you not repay my devotion to your divine qualities by the gift of some scrap of a drawing, the least valuable in your eyes? I should certainly esteem two strokes of the chalk upon a piece of paper more than all the cups and chains which all the kings and princes gave me."[2]   It seems that Michelangelo continued to correspond with him, and that Benvenuto Cellini took part in their exchange of letters.[3]   But no drawings were sent; and in course of time the ruffian got the better of the virtuoso in Aretino's rapacious nature.   Without ceasing to fawn and flatter Michelangelo, he sought occasion to damage his reputation.   Thus we find him writing in January 1546 to the engraver Enea Vico, bestowing high praise upon a copper-plate which a certain Bazzacco had made from the Last Judgment, but criticising the picture as " licentious and likely to cause scandal with the Lutherans, by

---

[1] *Op. cit.*, vol. iii. p. 46, April 1544.

[2] Guasti prints a manuscript sonnet from the Arch. Buon., which has no author's name.   He calls attention to the resemblance between this passage in Aretino's letter and the following lines :—

> Humil ti prega con voce suave,
> Che la tua sancta man sovr'esso giri,
> Se non con altro, con carbone spento.
> Due line' in croce almen che tu vi tiri
> Assai li fia.—*Rime*, p. lii.

[3] *Op. cit.*, vol. iii. p. 123, date April 1545 ; vol. iv. p. 37, date April 1546.

reason of its immodest exposure of the nakedness of persons of both sexes in heaven and hell."[1] It is not clear what Aretino expected from Enea Vico. A reference to the Duke of Florence seems to indicate that he wished to arouse suspicions among great and influential persons regarding the religious and moral quality of Michelangelo's work.

This malevolent temper burst out at last in one of the most remarkable letters we possess of his. It was obviously intended to hurt and insult Michelangelo as much as lay within his power of innuendo and direct abuse. The invective offers so many points of interest with regard to both men, that I shall not hesitate to translate it here in full.[2]

"Sir, when I inspected the complete sketch of the whole of your Last Judgment, I arrived at recognising the eminent graciousness of Raffaello in its agreeable beauty of invention.

"Meanwhile, as a baptized Christian, I blush before the license, so forbidden to man's intellect, which you have used in expressing ideas connected with the highest aims and final ends to which our faith aspires. So, then, that Michelangelo stupendous in his fame, that Michelangelo renowned for prudence,

---

[1] *Op. cit.*, vol. iii. p. 328. Springer (ii. 268) has misconstrued, I think, the allusion to the Lutherans.

[2] Gaye, ii. 332. Gaye says: "It is original. The signature and postscript are in Aretino's hand." The date of the document is Venice, November 1565. Since Aretino died in 1557 and Michelangelo in 1564, this date is clearly wrong. Gaye conjectures the year may have been 1545; but Aretino wrote one of his begging letters to Michelangelo in 1546, and published it in his *Epistolarium*.

that Michelangelo whom all admire, has chosen to display to the whole world an impiety of irreligion only equalled by the perfection of his painting! Is it possible that you, who, since you are divine, do not condescend to consort with human beings, have done this in the greatest temple built to God, upon the highest altar raised to Christ, in the most sacred chapel upon earth, where the mighty hinges of the Church, the venerable priests of our religion, the Vicar of Christ, with solemn ceremonies and holy prayers, confess, contemplate, and adore his body, his blood, and his flesh?

"If it were not infamous to introduce the comparison, I would plume myself upon my virtue when I wrote *La Nanna*.[1] I would demonstrate the superiority of my reserve to your indiscretion, seeing that I, while handling themes lascivious and immodest, use language comely and decorous, speak in terms beyond reproach and inoffensive to chaste ears. You, on the contrary, presenting so awful a subject, exhibit saints and angels, these without earthly decency, and those without celestial honours.[2]

"The pagans, when they modelled a Diana, gave her clothes; when they made a naked Venus, hid the parts which are not shown with the hand of modesty. And here there comes a Christian, who, because he rates art higher than the faith, deems it

---

[1] Aretino's dialogue upon the art of prostitution.

[2] All the figures in the Last Judgment were simple nudes, with the exception (possibly) of Christ and the Madonna.

a royal spectacle to portray martyrs and virgins in improper attitudes, to show men dragged down by their shame, before which things houses of ill-fame would shut the eyes in order not to see them. Your art would be at home in some voluptuous bagnio, certainly not in the highest chapel of the world. Less criminal were it if you were an infidel, than, being a believer, thus to sap the faith of others. Up to the present time the splendour of such audacious marvels hath not gone unpunished; for their very superexcellence is the death of your good name. Restore them to repute by turning the indecent parts of the damned to flames, and those of the blessed to sunbeams; or imitate the modesty of Florence, who hides your David's shame beneath some gilded leaves. And yet that statue is exposed upon a public square, not in a consecrated chapel.

"As I wish that God may pardon you, I do not write this out of any resentment for the things I begged of you.[1] In truth, if you had sent me what you promised, you would only have been doing what you ought to have desired most eagerly to do in your own interest; for this act of courtesy would silence the envious tongues which say that only certain Gerards and Thomasses dispose of them.[2]

"Well, if the treasure bequeathed you by Pope Julius, in order that you might deposit his ashes in

---

[1] An allusion to his wish to have some of Michelangelo's drawings.

[2] A malevolent allusion, as we shall see in the next chapter, to Tommaso dei Cavalieri and Gherardo Perini.

an urn of your own carving, was not enough to make
you keep your plighted word, what can I expect
from you ?   It is not your ingratitude, your avarice,
great painter, but the grace and merit of the
Supreme Shepherd, which decides his fame.[1]   God
wills that Julius should live renowned for ever in a
simple tomb, inurned in his own merits, and not in
some proud monument dependent on your genius.
Meantime, your failure to discharge your obligations
is reckoned to you as an act of thieving.

"Our souls need the tranquil emotions of piety
more than the lively impressions of plastic art.
May God, then, inspire his Holiness Paul with the
same thoughts as he instilled into Gregory of blessed
memory, who rather chose to despoil Rome of the
proud statues of the Pagan deities than to let their
magnificence deprive the humbler images of the
saints of the devotion of the people.[2]

"Lastly, when you set about composing your picture of the universe and hell and heaven, if you had
steeped your heart with those suggestions of glory,
of honour, and of terror proper to the theme, which I
sketched out and offered to you in the letter I wrote
you and the whole world reads, I venture to assert
that not only would nature and all kind influences
cease to regret the illustrious talents they endowed
you with, and which to-day render you, by virtue of

---

[1] The Italian is obscure and defective here, perhaps because the
body of the letter was dictated.

[2] That is, he hopes Paul will destroy the fresco.

your art, an image of the marvellous : but Provi-
dence, who sees all things, would herself continue
to watch over such a masterpiece, so long as order
lasts in her government of the hemispheres.

        " Your servant,

                " THE ARETINE.

" Now that I have blown off some of the rage I
feel against you for the cruelty you used to my
devotion, and have taught you to see that, while
you may be divine, I am not made of water, I bid you
tear up this letter, for I have done the like,[1] and do
not forget that I am one to whose epistles kings
and emperors reply.

"To the great MICHELANGELO BUONARROTI in Rome."

The malignancy of this letter is only equalled by
its stylistic ingenuity. Aretino used every means
he could devise to wound and irritate a sensitive
nature. The allusion to Raffaello, the comparison
of his own pornographic dialogues with the Last
Judgment in the Sistine, the covert hint that folk
gossiped about Michelangelo's relations to young
men, his sneers at the great man's exclusiveness, his
cruel insinuations with regard to the Tomb of Julius,
his devout hope that Paul will destroy the fresco,
and the impudent eulogy of his precious letter on
the Last Day, were all nicely calculated to annoy.

---

[1] Apparently a promise not to print it. It did in effect not appear
in Aretino's published edition of his letters.

Whether the missive was duly received by Buonarroti we do not know. Gaye asserts that it appears to have been sent through the post. He discovered it in the Archives of the Strozzi Palace.

The virtuous Pietro Aretino was not the only one to be scandalised by the nudities of the Last Judgment; and indeed it must be allowed that when Michelangelo treated such a subject in such a manner, he was pushing the principle of art for art's sake to its extremity.[1] One of the most popular stories told about this work shows that it early began to create a scandal.[2] When it was three fourths finished, Pope Paul went to see the fresco,

---

[1] Gaye (vol. ii. p. 500) prints a curious criticism written by some Florentine when Nanni di Baccio Bigio's copy of the Madonna della Febbre was erected at S. Spirito. It will serve to show that even before the Tridentine Council a reaction was going on against the artistic license of the Cinque Cento. After abusing "the filthy and disgusting" statues of Adam and Eve which had been placed in the Duomo upon the 19th of March 1549, the man proceeds : "In the same month a Pietà was uncovered at S. Spirito, which a Florentine (probably Luigi del Riccio) sent to that church. It is said that the original was the work of that inventor of filthinesses, who cared more for art than for devotion, Michelangelo. All the modern painters and sculptors, by imitating Lutheran caprices of this kind, have brought matters to such a pitch, that nowadays the only figures which are made for holy churches seem intended to bury the faith and devotion of Christianity. I hope that God will one day send His saints and dash to earth idolatrous images like these." It was probably a Piagnone who wrote this invective. One hardly understands why he should have been so angry with what is certainly Michelangelo's most religious work in marble. It is also comic to talk of the neo-paganism of the Italian Renaissance as Lutheran ; but Lutheran then meant only heretical or blasphemous. Aretino came nearer to the point when he hinted that the Last Judgment would cause scandal among the Lutherans.

[2] Vasari, xii. p. 220.

attended by Messer Biagio da Cesena, his Master of the Ceremonies. On being asked his opinion of the painting, Messer Biagio replied that he thought it highly improper to expose so many naked figures in a sacred picture, and that it was more fit for a place of debauchery than for the Pope's chapel. Michelangelo, nettled by this, drew the prelate's portrait to the life, and placed him in hell with horns on his head and a serpent twisted round his loins. Messer Biagio, finding himself in this plight, and being no doubt laughed at by his friends, complained to the Pope, who answered that he could do nothing to help him. "Had the painter sent you to Purgatory, I would have used my best efforts to get you released; but I exercise no influence in hell; *ubi nulla est redemptio.*" Before Michelangelo's death, his follower, Daniele da Volterra, was employed to provide draperies for the most obnoxious figures, and won thereby the name of *Il Braghettone*, or the breeches-maker. Paul IV. gave the painter this commission, having previously consulted Buonarroti on the subject. The latter is said to have replied to the Pope's messenger: "Tell his Holiness that this is a small matter, and can easily be set straight. Let him look to setting the world in order: to reform a picture costs no great trouble." [1] Later on, during the Pontificate of Pio V., a master named Girolamo da Fano continued the process begun by Daniele da Volterra. As a necessary con-

[1] Vasari, xii. p. 245.

sequence of this tribute to modesty, the scheme of Michelangelo's colouring and the balance of his masses have been irretrievably damaged.

IV.

Vasari says that not very long before the Last Judgment was finished, Michelangelo fell from the scaffolding, and seriously hurt his leg. The pain he suffered and his melancholy made him shut himself up at home, where he refused to be treated by a doctor. There was a Florentine physician in Rome, however, of capricious humour, who admired the arts, and felt a real affection for Buonarroti. This man contrived to creep into the house by some privy entrance, and roamed about it till he found the master. He then insisted upon remaining there on watch and guard until he had effected a complete cure. The name of this excellent friend, famous for his skill and science in those days, was Baccio Rontini.

After his recovery Michelangelo returned to work, and finished the Last Judgment in a few months. It was exposed to the public on Christmas Day in 1541.

Time, negligence, and outrage, the dust of centuries, the burned papers of successive conclaves, the smoke of altar-candles, the hammers and the hangings of upholsterers, the brush of the breeches-

maker and restorer, have so dealt with the Last
Judgment that it is almost impossible to do it justice
now. What Michelangelo intended by his scheme
of colour is entirely lost. Not only did Daniele da
Volterra, an execrable colourist, dab vividly tinted
patches upon the modulated harmonies of flesh-tones
painted by the master; but the whole surface has
sunk into a bluish fog, deepening to something like
lamp-black around the altar. Nevertheless, in its
composition the fresco may still be studied; and
after due inspection, aided by photographic repro-
ductions of each portion, we are not unable to
understand the enthusiasm which so nobly and profoundly planned a work of art aroused among contemporaries.

It has sometimes been asserted that this enormous
painting, the largest and most comprehensive in the
world, is a tempest of contending forms, a hurly-
burly of floating, falling, soaring, and descending
figures. Nothing can be more opposed to the truth.
Michelangelo was sixty-six years of age when he
laid his brush down at the end of the gigantic task.
He had long outlived the spontaneity of youthful
ardour. His experience through half a century in
the planning of monuments, the painting of the
Sistine vault, the designing of façades and sacristies
and libraries, had developed the architectonic sense
which was always powerful in his conceptive faculty.
Consequently, we are not surprised to find that,
intricate and confused as the scheme may appear to

an unpractised eye, it is in reality a design of mathematical severity, divided into four bands or planes of
grouping. The wall, since it occupies one entire end
of a long high building, is naturally less broad than
lofty. The pictorial divisions are therefore horizontal
in the main, though so combined and varied as to
produce the effect of multiplied curves, balancing
and antiphonally inverting their lines of sinuosity.
The pendentive upon which the prophet Jonah sits,
descends and breaks the surface at the top, leaving
a semicircular compartment on each side of its
corbel. Michelangelo filled these upper spaces with
two groups of wrestling angels, the one bearing a
huge cross, the other a column, in the air. The
cross and whipping-post are the chief emblems of
Christ's Passion. The crown of thorns is also there,
the sponge, the ladder, and the nails. It is with no
merciful intent that these signs of our Lord's suffering are thus exhibited. Demonic angels, tumbling
on clouds like Leviathans, hurl them to and fro in
brutal wrath above the crowd of souls, as though to
demonstrate the justice of damnation. In spite of
a God's pain and shameful death, mankind has gone
on sinning. The Judge is what the crimes of the
world and Italy have made him. Immediately below
the corbel, and well detached from the squadrons of
attendant saints, Christ rises from His throne. His
face is turned in the direction of the damned, His
right hand is lifted as though loaded with thunder-
bolts for their annihilation. He is a ponderous

young athlete; rather say a mass of hypertrophied
muscles, with the features of a vulgarised Apollo.
The Virgin sits in a crouching attitude at His right
side, slightly averting her head, as though in painful expectation of the coming sentence.   The saints
and martyrs who surround Christ and His Mother,
while forming one of the chief planes in the composition, are arranged in four unequal groups of
subtle and surprising intricacy. All bear the emblems of their cruel deaths, and shake them in the
sight of Christ as though appealing to His judgment-
seat.   It has been charitably suggested that they
intend to supplicate for mercy.   I cannot, however,
resist the impression that they are really demanding
rigid justice. S. Bartholomew flourishes his flaying-
knife and dripping skin with a glare of menace.
S. Catherine struggles to raise her broken wheel.
S. Sebastian frowns down on hell with a sheaf of
arrows quivering in his stalwart arm. The saws, the
carding-combs, the crosses, and the gridirons, all
subserve the same purpose of reminding Christ that,
if He does not damn the wicked, confessors will
have died with Him in vain.   It is singular that,
while Michelangelo depicted so many attitudes of
expectation, eagerness, anxiety, and astonishment in
the blest, he has given to none of them the expression of gratitude, or love, or sympathy, or shrinking
awe.   Men and women, old and young alike, are
human beings of Herculean build.   Paradise, according to Buonarroti's conception, was not meant

for what is graceful, lovely, original, and tender.
The hosts of heaven are adult and over-developed
gymnasts. Yet, while we record these impressions,
it would be unfair to neglect the spiritual beauty of
some souls embracing after long separation in the
grave, with folding arms, and clasping hands, and
clinging lips. While painting these, Michelangelo
thought peradventure of his father and his brother.

The two planes which I have attempted to describe occupy the upper and the larger portion of
the composition. The third in order is made up
of three masses. In the middle floats a band of
Titanic cherubs, blowing their long trumpets over
earth and sea to wake the dead. Dramatically,
nothing can be finer than the strained energy and
superhuman force of these superb creatures. Their
attitudes compel our imagination to hear the crash-
ing thunders of the trump of doom. To the left of
the spectator are souls ascending to be judged,
some floating through vague ether, enwrapped with
graveclothes, others assisted by descending saints
and angels, who reach a hand, a rosary, to help the
still gross spirit in its flight. To the right are the
condemned, sinking downwards to their place of
torment, spurned by seraphs, cuffed by angelic
grooms, dragged by demons, hurling, howling,
huddled in a mass of horror. It is just here, and
still yet farther down, that Michelangelo put forth
all his power as a master of expression. While the
blessed display nothing which is truly proper to

their state of holiness and everlasting peace, the
damned appear in every realistic aspect of most
stringent agony and terror. The colossal forms of
flesh with which the multitudes of saved and damned
are equally endowed, befit that extremity of physical
and mental anguish more than they suit the serenity
of bliss eternal. There is a wretch, twined round
with fiends, gazing straight before him as he sinks;
one half of his face is buried in his hand, the other
fixed in a stony spasm of despair, foreshadowing
perpetuity of hell. Nothing could express with
sublimity of a higher order the sense of irreme-
diable loss, eternal pain, a future endless without
hope, than the rigid dignity of this not ignoble
sinner's dread. Just below is the place to which
the doomed are sinking. Michelangelo reverted to
Dante for the symbolism chosen to portray hell.
Charon, the demon, with eyes of burning coal, compels a crowd of spirits in his ferryboat. They land
and are received by devils, who drag them before
Minos, judge of the infernal regions. He towers at
the extreme right end of the fresco, indicating that
the nether regions yawn infinitely deep, beyond our
ken; just as the angels above Christ suggest a
region of light and glory, extending upward through
illimitable space. The scene of judgment on which
attention is concentrated forms but an episode in
the universal, sempiternal scheme of things. Balancing hell, on the left hand of the spectator, is brute
earth, the grave, the forming and the swallowing

clay, out of which souls, not yet acquitted or condemned, emerge with difficulty, in varied forms
of skeletons or corpses, slowly thawing into life
eternal.

Vasari, in his description of the Last Judgment,
seized upon what after all endures as the most
salient aspect of this puzzling work, at once so
fascinating and so repellent.[1] " It is obvious," he
says, " that the peerless painter did not aim at anything but the portrayal of the human body in perfect
proportions and most varied attitudes, together with
the passions and affections of the soul. That was
enough for him, and here he has no equal. He
wanted to exhibit the grand style : consummate
draughtsmanship in the nude, mastery over all
problems of design. He concentrated his power
upon the human form, attending to that alone, and
neglecting all subsidiary things, as charm of colour,
capricious inventions, delicate devices and novelties
of fancy." Vasari might have added that Michelangelo also neglected what ought to have been a
main object of his art : convincing eloquence, the
solemnity proper to his theme, spirituality of earthly
grossness quit. As a collection of athletic nudes in
all conceivable postures of rest and action, of fore-
shortening, of suggested movement, the Last Judgment remains a stupendous miracle. Nor has the
aged master lost his cunning for the portrayal of
divinely simple faces, superb limbs, masculine beauty,

[1] Vasari, xii. 220.

in the ideal persons of young men. The picture, when we dwell long enough upon its details, emerges into prominence, moreover, as indubitably awe-inspiring, terrifying, dreadful in its poignant expression of wrath, retaliation, thirst for vengeance, cruelty, and helpless horror. But the supreme point even of Doomsday, of the Dies Iræ, has not been seized. We do not hear the still small voice of pathos and of human hope which thrills through Thomas a Celano's hymn :—

> Quærens me sedisti lassus,
> Redemisti crucem passus :
> Tantus labor non sit cassus.

The note is one of sustained menace and terror, and the total scheme of congregated forms might be compared to a sense-deafening solo on a trombone. While saying this, we must remember that it was the constant impulse of Michelangelo to seize one moment only, and what he deemed the most decisive moment, in the theme he had to develop. Having selected the instant of time at which Christ, half risen from His judgment-seat of cloud, raises an omnific hand to curse, the master caused each fibre of his complex composition to thrill with the tremendous passion of that coming sentence. The long series of designs for Crucifixions, Depositions from the Cross, and Pietàs which we possess, all of them belonging to a period of his life not much later than 1541, prove that his nature was quite as sensitive to pathos as to terror; only, it was not in him to attempt a combination of terror and pathos.

"He aimed at the portrayal of the human body. He wanted to exhibit the grand style." So says Vasari, and Vasari is partly right. But we must not fall into the paradox, so perversely maintained by Ruskin in his lecture on Tintoretto and Michelangelo, that the latter was a cold and heartless artist, caring chiefly for the display of technical skill and anatomical science. Partial and painful as we may find the meaning of the Last Judgment, that meaning has been only too powerfully and personally felt. The denunciations of the prophets, the woes of the Apocalypse, the invectives of Savonarola, the tragedies of Italian history, the sense of present and indwelling sin, storm through and through it. Technically, the masterpiece bears signs of fatigue and discontent, in spite of its extraordinary vigour of conception and execution. The man was old and tired, thwarted in his wishes and oppressed with troubles. His very science had become more formal, his types more arid and schematic, than they used to be. The thrilling life, the divine afflatus, of the Sistine vault have passed out of the Last Judgment. Wholly admirable, unrivalled, and unequalled by any other human work upon a similar scale as this fresco may be in its command over the varied resources of the human body, it does not strike our mind as the production of a master glorying in carnal pride and mental insolence, but rather as that of one discomfited and terrified, upon the point of losing heart.

Henri Beyle, jotting down his impressions in the Sistine Chapel, was reminded of the Grand Army's flight after the burning of Moscow. "When, in our disastrous retreat from Russia, it chanced that we were suddenly awakened in the middle of the dark night by an obstinate cannonading, which at each moment seemed to gain in nearness, then all the forces of a man's nature gathered close around his heart; he felt himself in the presence of fate, and having no attention left for things of vulgar interest, he made himself ready to dispute his life with destiny. The sight of Michelangelo's picture has brought back to my consciousness that almost forgotten sensation." This is a piece of just and sympathetic criticism, and upon its note I am fain to close.

V.

It is probable that the fame of the Last Judgment spread rapidly abroad through Italy, and that many visits to Rome were made for the purpose of inspecting it.[1] Complimentary sonnets must also have been

---

[1] It was frequently copied in whole or in part. The finest reproduction in oils is that which Marcello Venusti executed at Michelangelo's orders for the Cardinal Farnese. The picture is now at Naples. Of the numerous drawings ascribed to Michelangelo, many are obviously studies by young painters. The Last Judgment was engraved over

addressed to the painter. I take it that Niccolò Martelli sent some poems on the subject from Florence, for Michelangelo replied upon the 20th of January 1542 in the following letter of singular modesty and urbane kindness : [1]—

"I received from Messer Vincenzo Perini your letter with two sonnets and a madrigal. The letter and the sonnet addressed to me are so marvellously fine, that if a man should find in them anything to castigate, it would be impossible to castigate him as thoroughly as they are castigated. It is true they praise me so much, that had I Paradise in my bosom, less of praise would suffice. I perceive that you suppose me to be just what God wishes that I were. I am a poor man and of little merit, who plod along in the art which God gave me, to lengthen out my life as far as possible. Such as I am, I remain your servant and that of all the house of Martelli. I thank you for your letter and the poems, but not as much as duty bids, for I cannot soar to such heights of courtesy."

When the Last Judgment was finished, Michelangelo not unreasonably hoped that he might resume his work upon the Tomb of Julius. But this was not to be. Antonio da San Gallo had just completed the Chapel of the Holy Sacrament in the Vatican, which

and over again. I have counted nineteen separate engravings before the date 1700 in Passerini's *Bibliografia di Michelangelo Buonarroti,* Firenze : Cellini, 1875. The finest was that of Martino Rota,

[1] *Lettere,* No. cdxxii,

is known as the Cappella Paolina, and the Pope resolved that its frescoes should be painted by Buonarroti. The Duke of Urbino, yielding to his wishes,
wrote to Michelangelo upon the 6th of March 1542,
saying that he should be quite satisfied if the three
statues by his hand, including the Moses, were
assigned to the tomb, the execution of the rest being
left to competent workmen under his direction.[1]

In effect, we possess documents proving that the
tomb was consigned to several masters during this
year, 1542. The first is a contract dated February
27, whereby Raffaello da Montelupo undertakes to
finish three statues, two of these being the Active
Life and the Contemplative.[2] The second is a contract dated May 16, in which Michelangelo assigns
the architectural and ornamental portion of the
monument conjointly to Giovanni de' Marchesi and
Francesco d' Amadore, called Urbino, providing that
differences which may arise between them shall be
referred to Donato Giannotti.[3] There is a third contract, under date June 1, about the same work in-
trusted to the same two craftsmen, prescribing details
with more exactitude.[4] It turned out that the appre-

---

[1] Gaye, ii. 289. This letter seems to have been the result of negotiations between Paul III. and the Duke during the winter. Gaye (ibid.,
p. 290) publishes a despatch from Cardinal Ascanio Parisani to the
Duke, dated November 23, 1541, in which he speaks of the Pope's
wishes with regard to the Cappella Paolina, and the assignment of the
tomb to other masters.

[2] Lettere, p. 709. (All the documents here cited were collected by
Gaye, ii. pp. 289–309.)

[3] Ibid., p. 710.   [4] Ibid., p. 712.

hension of disagreement between the masters about the division of their labour was not unfounded, for Michelangelo wrote twice in July to his friend Luigi del Riccio, complaining bitterly of their dissensions, and saying that he has lost two months in these trifles.[1] He adds that one of them is covetous,.the other mad, and he fears their quarrel may end in wounds or murder. The matter disturbs his mind greatly, chiefly on account of Urbino, because he has brought him up, and also because of the time wasted over "their ignorance and bestial stupidity." The dispute was finally settled by the intervention of three master-masons (acting severally for Michelangelo, Urbino, and Giovanni), who valued the respective portions of the work.[2]

I must interrupt this narrative of the tomb to explain who some of the persons just mentioned were, and how they came to be connected with Buonarroti. Donato Giannotti was the famous writer upon political and literary topics, who, after playing a conspicuous part in the revolution of Florence against the Medici, now lived in exile at Rome. His dialogues on Dante, and Francesco d'Olanda's account of the meetings at S. Silvestro, prove that he formed a member of that little circle which included Michelangelo and Vittoria Colonna. Luigi del Riccio was a Florentine merchant, settled in the

---

[1] Ibid., Lettere, Nos. cdxxxi., cdxxxii. Compare a letter from Del Riccio to Michelangelo, Gaye, ii. 291, July 11, 1542.

[2] Ibid., p. 714.

banking-house of the Strozzi at Rome. For many
years he acted as Michelangelo's man of business;
but their friendship was close and warm in many
other ways. They were drawn together by a common
love of poetry, and by the charm of a rarely gifted
youth called Cecchino dei Bracci. Urbino was the
great sculptor's servant and man of all work, the last
and best of that series, which included Stefano
Miniatore, Pietro Urbano, Antonio Mini. Michelangelo made Urbino's fortune, mourned his death,
and undertook the guardianship of his children, as
will appear in due course. All through his life the
great sculptor was dependent upon some trusted
servant, to whom he became personally attached, and
who did not always repay his kindness with gratitude. After Urbino's death, Ascanio Condivi filled
a similar post, and to this circumstance we owe the
most precious of our contemporary biographies.

Our most important document with regard to the
Tomb of Julius is an elaborate petition addressed by
Michelangelo to Paul III. upon the 20th of July.[1]
It begins by referring to the contract of April 18,
1532, and proceeds to state that the Pope's new
commission for the Cappella Paolina has interfered
once more with the fulfilment of the sculptor's engagements. Then it recites the terms suggested by
the Duke of Urbino in his letter of March 6, 1542,
according to which three of the statues of the tomb
may be assigned to capable craftsmen, while the

---

[1] Ibid., Lettere, No. cdxxxiii.

other three, including the Moses, will have to be finished by Michelangelo himself. Raffaello da Montelupo has already undertaken the Madonna and Child, a Prophet, and a Sibyl.[1] Giovanni de' Marchese and Francesco da Urbino are at work upon the architecture. It remains for Michelangelo to furnish the Moses and two Captives, all three of which are nearly completed. The Captives, however, were designed for a much larger monument, and will not suit the present scheme. Accordingly, he has blocked out two other figures, representing the Active and Contemplative Life. But even these he is unable to finish, since the painting of the chapel absorbs his time and energy. He therefore prays the Pope to use his influence with the Duke of Urbino, so that he may be henceforward wholly and absolutely freed from all obligations in the matter of the tomb. The Moses he can deliver in a state of perfection, but he wishes to assign the Active and Contemplative Life to Raffaello or to any other sculptor who may be preferred by the Duke. Finally, he is prepared to deposit a sum of 1200 crowns for the total costs, and to guarantee that the work shall be efficiently executed in all its details.

It· is curious that in this petition and elsewhere no mention is made of what might be considered the most important portion of the tomb—namely, the portrait statue of Julius.

[1] This shows that the contract with Raffaello quoted above had been altered. See p. 69.

The document was presented to Messer Piero Giovanni Aliotti, Bishop of Forlì, and keeper of the wardrobe to Pope Paul. Accordingly, the final contract regarding the tomb was drawn up and signed upon the 20th of August.[1] I need not recapitulate its terms, for I have already printed a summary of them in a former chapter of this work.[2] Suffice it to say that Michelangelo was at last released from all active responsibility with regard to the tomb, and that the vast design of his early manhood now dwindled down to the Moses. To Raffaello da Montelupo was left the completion of the remaining five statues.[3]

This lamentable termination to the cherished scheme of his lifetime must have preyed upon Michelangelo's spirits. The letters in which he alludes to it, after the contract had been signed, breathe a spirit of more than usual fretfulness. Moreover, the Duke of Urbino now delayed to send his ratification, by which alone the deed could become valid. In October, writing to Del Riccio, Michelangelo complains that Messer Aliotti is urging him to begin painting in the chapel;[4] but the plaster is not yet fit to work on. Meanwhile, although he has deposited 1400 crowns, "which would have kept him working for seven years, and would have enabled him to finish two tombs," the

---

[1] Lettere, p. 715.   [2] Vol. i. ch. 4.

[3] Eventually, as we shall see, he found time to finish the two Lives and the Madonna.

[4] Lettere, No. cdxxxiv.

Duke's ratification does not come. " It is easy enough to see what that means without writing it in words ! Enough ; for the loyalty of thirty-six years, and for having given myself of my own free will to others, I deserve no better. Painting and sculpture, labour and good faith, have been my ruin, and I go continually from bad to worse. Better would it have been for me if I had set myself to making matches in my youth ! I should not be in such distress of mind. . . . I will not remain under this burden, nor be vilified every day for a swindler by those who have robbed my life and honour. Only death or the Pope can extricate me." It appears that at this time the Duke of Urbino's agents were accusing him of having lent out moneys which he had received on account for the execution of the monument. Then follows, in the same month of October, that stormy letter to some prelate, which is one of the most weighty autobiographical documents from the hand of Michelangelo in our possession.[1]

" Monsignore,—Your lordship sends to tell me that I must begin to paint, and have no anxiety. I answer that one paints with the brain and not with the hands; and he who has not his brains at his command produces work that shames him. Therefore, until my business is settled, I can do nothing good. The ratification of the last contract

---

[1] Lettere, No. cdxxxv. It was first published by Sebastiano Ciampi, Firenze, Passigli, 1834. People have disputed who the prelate was. I should suggest the Bishop of Forlì, that Messer P. F. Aliotti who kept urging him to paint, and to whom he sent the petition in July.

does not come.   On the strength of the other, made
before Clement, I am daily stoned as though I had
crucified Christ. . . . My whole youth and manhood have been lost, tied down to this tomb. . . .
I see multitudes with incomes of 2000 or 3000
crowns lying in bed, while I with all my immense
labour toil to grow poor. . . . I am not a thief and
usurer, but a citizen of Florence, noble, the son of
an honest man, and do not come from Cagli."
(These and similar outbursts of indignant passion,
scattered up and down the epistle, show to what
extent the sculptor's irritable nature had been ex-
asperated by calumnious reports.   As he openly
declares, he is being driven mad by pin-pricks.
Then follows the detailed history of his dealings
with Julius, which, as I have already made copious
use of it, may here be given in outline.)   "In the
first year of his pontificate, Julius commissioned
me to make his tomb, and I stayed eight months
at Carrara quarrying marbles and sending them to
the Piazza of S. Peter's, where I had my lodgings
behind S. Caterina.   Afterward the Pope decided not
to build his tomb during his lifetime, and set me
down to painting.   Then he kept me two years at
Bologna casting his statue in bronze, which has
been destroyed.   After that I returned to Rome
and stayed with him until his death, always keeping
my house open without post or pension, living on
the money for the tomb, since I had no other income.   After the death of Julius, Aginensis wanted

me to go on with it, but on a larger scale. So I brought the marbles to the Macello dei Corvi, and got that part of the mural scheme finished which is now walled in at S. Pietro in Vincoli, and made the figures which I have at home still. Meanwhile, Leo, not wishing me to work at the tomb, pretended that he wanted to complete the façade of S. Lorenzo at Florence, and begged me of the Cardinal.

"To continue my history of the Tomb of Julius, I say that when he changed his mind about building it in his lifetime, some shiploads of marble came to the Ripa, which I had ordered a short while before from Carrara, and as I could not get money from the Pope to pay the freightage, I had to borrow 150 or 200 ducats from Baldassare Balducci—that is, from the bank of Jacopo Gallo. At the same time workmen came from Florence, some of whom are still alive; and I furnished the house which Julius gave me behind S. Caterina with beds and other furniture for the men, and what was wanted for the work of the tomb. All this being done without money, I was greatly embarrassed. Accordingly, I urged the Pope with all my power to go forward with the business, and he had me turned away by a groom one morning when I came to speak upon the matter." (Here intervenes the story of the flight to Florence, which has been worked up in the course of Chapter IV.) "Later on, while I was at Florence, Julius sent three briefs to the Signory. At last the latter sent for me and said: 'We do not want to go to war with Pope Julius because of you. You must return; and if you do so, we will write you letters of such authority that if he does you harm, he will be doing it to this Signory.' Accordingly, I took the letters, and went back to the Pope, and what followed would be long to tell!

"All the dissensions between Pope Julius and me arose from the envy of Bramante and Raffaello da Urbino; and this was the cause of my not finishing the tomb in his lifetime. They wanted to ruin me. Raffaello had indeed good reason, for all he had of art, he had from me."

Twice again in October Michelangelo wrote to Luigi del Riccio about the ratification of his contract.[1] "I cannot live, far less paint." "I am resolved to stop at home and finish the three figures, as I agreed to do. This would be better for me than to drag my limbs daily to the Vatican. Let him who likes get angry. If the Pope wants me to paint, he must send for the Duke's ambassador and procure the ratification."

What happened at this time about the tomb can be understood by help of a letter written to Salvestro da Montauto on the 3rd of February 1545.[2] Michelangelo refers to the last contract, and says that the Duke of Urbino ratified the deed. Accordingly, five

[1] Lettere, Nos. cdxxxvi., cdxxxvii.
[2] Ibid., No. cdxlv. I will add here that the terminal figures on the lower half of the tomb were carved by Giacomo del Duca, the coat of arms of Della Rovere by Battista Benti of Pietrasanta, and the Pope himself by Maso del Bosco.

statues were assigned to Raffaello da Montelupo. "But while I was painting the new chapel for Pope Paul III., his Holiness, at my earnest prayer, allowed me a little time, during which I finished two of them, namely, the Active and Contemplative Life, with my own hand."

With all his good-will, however, Michelangelo did not wholly extricate himself from the anxieties of this miserable affair. As late as the year 1553, Annibale Caro wrote to Antonio Gallo entreating him to plead for the illustrious old man with the Duke of Urbino.[1] "I assure you that the extreme distress caused him by being in disgrace with his Excellency is sufficient to bring his grey hairs to the grave before his time."

VI.

The Tomb of Julius, as it now appears in the Church of S. Pietro in Vincoli in Rome, is a monument composed of two discordant parts, by inspecting which a sympathetic critic is enabled to read the dreary history of its production. As Condivi allows, it was a thing "rattoppata e rifatta," patched together and hashed up.

The lower half represents what eventually sur-

[1] Bottari, *Lett. Pitt.*, iii. 196. This letter contains an interesting reference to Condivi's Life, which was on the point of coming out.

vived from the grandiose original design for one façade of that vast mount of marble which was to have been erected in the Tribune of St. Peter's.[1] The socles, upon which captive Arts and Sciences were meant to stand, remain; but instead of statues, inverted consoles take their places, and lead lamely up to the heads and busts of terminal old men. The pilasters of these terms have been shortened. There are four of them, enclosing two narrow niches, where beautiful female figures, the Active Life and the Contemplative Life, still testify to the enduring warmth and vigour of the mighty sculptor's genius. As single statues duly worked into a symmetrical scheme, these figures would be admirable, since grace of line and symbolical contrast of attitude render both charming. In their present position they are reduced to comparative insignificance by heavy architectural surroundings. The space left free between the niches and the terms is assigned to the seated statue of Moses, which forms the main attraction of the monument, and of which, as a masterpiece of Michelangelo's best years, I shall have to speak later on.

[1] The different size and scale of the statues on this monument are very striking. Moses, of course, overbalances the whole, and suffers greatly from being hardly raised at all above the ground. Michelangelo designed him to be seen at a considerable height above the eye. The Sibyl looks larger and heavier than the Prophet; is certainly bulkier than the Madonna and the two Lives. Michelangelo and his school do not appear to have been particular about keeping relative proportions in their monuments. Leone Leoni's tomb for Gian Giacomo de' Medici at Milan is extravagantly wilful and capricious in this respect.

The architectural plan and the surface decoration of this lower half are conceived in a style belonging to the earlier Italian Renaissance. Arabesques and masks and foliated patterns adorn the flat slabs. The recess of each niche is arched with a concave shell. The terminal busts are boldly modelled, and impose upon the eye. The whole is rich in detail, and though somewhat arid in fanciful invention, it carries us back to the tradition of Florentine work by Mino da Fiesole and Desiderio da Settignano.

When we ascend to the upper portion, we seem to have passed, as indeed we do pass, into the region of the new manner created by Michelangelo at S. Lorenzo. The orders of the pilasters are immensely tall in proportion to the spaces they enclose. Two of these spaces, those on the left and right side, are filled in above with meaningless rectangular recesses, while seated statues occupy less than a whole half in altitude of the niches. The architectural design is nondescript, corresponding to no recognised style, unless it be a bastard Roman Doric. There is absolutely no decorative element except four shallow masks beneath the abaci of the pilasters. All is cold and broad and dry, contrasting strangely with the accumulated details of the lower portion. In the central niche, immediately above the Moses, stands a Madonna of fine sculptural quality, beneath a shallow arch, which repeats the shell-pattern. At her feet lies the extended figure of Pope Julius II., crowned with the tiara, raising himself in a half-recumbent attitude upon his right arm.[1]

Of the statues in the upper portion, by far the finest in artistic merit is the Madonna. This dignified and gracious lady, holding the Divine Child in her arms, must be reckoned among Buonarroti's triumphs in dealing with the female form. There is more of softness and sweetness here than in the Madonna of the Medicean sacristy, while the infant playing with a captured bird is full of grace. Michelangelo left little in this group for the chisel of Montelupo to deform by alteration. The seated female, a Sibyl, on the left, bears equally the stamp of his design. Executed by himself, this would have been a masterpiece for grandeur of line and dignified repose. As it is, the style, while seeming to aim at breadth, remains frigid and formal. The so-called Prophet on the other side counts among the signal failures of Italian sculpture. It has neither beauty nor significance. Like a heavy Roman consul of the Decadence, the man sits there, lumpy and meaningless; we might take it for a statue-portrait erected by some provincial municipality to celebrate a local magnate; but of prophecy or inspiration

---

[1] It has occurred to me that this awkward pose of Julius—"with his hand under his cheek, as if he died of the toothache"—may have been intentionally so ordered by the family, in reminiscence of the two fine monuments by the hand of Andrea Sansovino, which the Pope himself erected in S. Maria del Popolo to the memories of the Cardinals Ascanio Sforza and Hieronymo Basso. These are remarkable for the adoption of the half-recumbent pensive attitude I have described.

there is nothing to detect in this inert figure. We wonder why he should be placed so near a Pope.

It is said that Michelangelo expressed dissatisfaction with Montelupo's execution of the two statues finally committed to his charge, and we know from documents that the man was ill when they were finished. Still we can hardly excuse the master himself for the cold and perfunctory performance of a task which had such animated and heroic beginnings. Competent judges, who have narrowly surveyed the monument, say that the stones are badly put together, and the workmanship is defective in important requirements of the sculptor-mason's craft.[1] Those who defend Buonarroti must fall back upon the theory that weariness and disappointment made him at last indifferent to the fate of a design which had cost him so much anxiety, pecuniary difficulties, and frustrated expectations in past years. He let the Tomb of Julius, his first vast dream of art, be botched up out of dregs and relics by ignoble hands, because he was heart-sick and out of pocket.

As artist, Michelangelo might, one thinks, have avoided the glaring discord of styles between the upper and the lower portions of the tomb; but sensitiveness to harmony of manner lies not in the nature of men who rapidly evolve new forms of thought and feeling from some older phase. Probably he felt the width and the depth of that gulf which divided himself in 1505 from the same self

[1] Heath Wilson, p. 449.

in 1545, less than we do. Forty years in a creative nature introduce subtle changes, which react upon the spirit of the age, and provoke subsequent criticism to keen comments and comparisons. The individual and his contemporaries are not so well aware of these discrepancies as posterity.

The Moses, which Paul and his courtiers thought sufficient to commemorate a single Pope, stands as the eminent jewel of this defrauded tomb. We may not be attracted by it. We may even be repelled by the goat-like features, the enormous beard, the ponderous muscles, and the grotesque garments of the monstrous statue. In order to do it justice, let us bear in mind that the Moses now remains detached from a group of environing symbolic forms which Michelangelo designed. Instead of taking its place as one among eight corresponding and counter-balancing giants, it is isolated, thrust forward on the eye; whereas it was intended to be viewed from below in concert with a scheme of balanced figures, male and female, on the same colossal scale.

Condivi writes not amiss, in harmony with the gusto of his age, and records what a gentle spirit thought about the Moses then:[1] "Worthy of all admiration is the statue of Moses, duke and captain of the Hebrews. He sits posed in the attitude of a thinker and a sage, holding beneath his right arm the tables of the law, and with the left hand giving support to his chin, like one who is tired and full of

[1] Condivi, p. 59.

anxious cares.   From the fingers of this hand escape
long flowing lines of beard, which are very beautiful
in their effect upon the eye.   The face is full of
vivid life and spiritual force, fit to inspire both love
and terror, as perhaps the man in truth did.   He
bears, according to the customary wont of artists while
portraying Moses, two horns upon the head, not far
removed from the summit of the brows.   He is
robed and girt about the legs with hosen, the arms
bare, and all the rest after the antique fashion.   It
is a marvellous work, and full of art : mostly in this,
that underneath those subtleties of raiment one can
perceive the naked form, the garments detracting
nothing from the beauty of the body ; as was the
universal way of working with this master in all his
clothed figures, whether painted or sculptured."

Except that Condivi dwelt too much upon the
repose of this extraordinary statue, too little upon
its vivacity and agitating unrest, his description
serves our purpose as well as any other.   He does
not seem to have felt the turbulence and carnal
insolence which break our sense of dignity and
beauty now.

Michelangelo left the Moses incomplete in many
details, after bringing the rest of the figure to a high
state of polish.   Tooth-marks of the chisel are ob-
servable upon the drapery, the back, both hands,
part of the neck, the hair, and the salient horns.
It seems to have been his habit, as Condivi and
Cellini report, to send a finished statue forth with

some sign-manual of roughness in the final touches. That gave his work the signature of the sharp tools he had employed upon it. And perhaps he loved the marble so well that he did not like to quit the good white stone without sparing a portion of its clinging strength and stubbornness, as symbol of the effort of his brain and hand to educe live thought from inert matter.

In the century after Michelangelo's death a sonnet was written by Giovanni Battista Felice Zappi upon this Moses. It is famous in Italian literature, and expresses adequately the ideas which occur to ordinary minds when they approach the Moses. For this reason I think that it is worthy of being introduced in a translation here :—

> Who is the man who, carved in this huge stone,
>   Sits giant, all renownèd things of art
>   Transcending? he whose living lips, that start,
>   Speak eager words? I hear, and take their tone.
> He sure is Moses. That the chin hath shown
>   By its dense honour, the brows' beam bipart:
>   'Tis Moses, when he left the Mount, with part,
>   A great part, of God's glory round him thrown.
> Such was the prophet when those sounding vast
>   Waters he held suspense about him; such
>   When he the sea barred, made it gulph his foe.
> And you, his tribes, a vile calf did you cast?
>   Why not an idol worth like this so much?
>   To worship that had wrought you lesser woe.

VII.

Before quitting the Tomb of Julius, I must discuss the question of eight scattered statues, partly unfinished, which are supposed, on more or less good grounds, to have been designed for this monument.[1] About two of them, the bound Captives in the Louvre, there is no doubt. Michelangelo mentions these in his petition to Pope Paul, saying that the change of scale implied by the last plan obliged him to abstain from using them. We also know their history. When the sculptor was ill at Rome in 1544, Luigi del Riccio nursed him in the palace of the Strozzi. Gratitude for this hospitality induced him to make a present of the statues to Ruberto degli Strozzi, who took them to France and offered them to the King. Francis gave them to the Constable de Montmorenci; and he placed them in his country-house of Ecouen. In 1793 the Republic offered them for sale, when they were bought for the French nation by M. Lenoir.

One of these Captives deserves to be called the most fascinating creation of the master's genius. Together with the Adam, it may be taken as fixing his standard of masculine beauty. He is a young man,

[1] There is an interesting pen-drawing at Oxford for six bound Captives, none of which exactly correspond in attitude to the eight statues above alluded to. It deserves to be studied attentively in connection with the subject treated in this section. (Reproduced in Springer's *Raffael und Michelangelo*, vol. ii. p. 25.)

with head thrown back, as though in swoon or slumber; the left arm raised above the weight of massy curls, the right hand resting on his broad full bosom. There is a divine charm in the tranquil face, tired but not fatigued, sad but not melancholy, suggesting that the sleeping mind of the immortal youth is musing upon solemn dreams. Praxiteles might have so expressed the Genius of Eternal Repose; but no Greek sculptor would have given that huge girth to the thorax, or have exaggerated the mighty hand with such delight in sinewy force. These qualities, peculiar to Buonarroti's sense of form, do not detract from the languid pose and supple rhythm of the figure, which flows down, a sinuous line of beauty, through the slightly swelling flanks, along the finely moulded thighs, to loveliest feet emerging from the marble. It is impossible, while gazing on this statue, not to hear a strain of intellectual music. Indeed, like melody, it tells no story, awakes no desire, but fills the soul with something beyond thought or passion, subtler and more penetrating than words.

The companion figure has not equal grace. Athletically muscular, though adolescent, the body of this young man, whose hands are tied behind his back, is writhed into an attitude of vehement protest and rebellion. He raises his face with appealing pain to heaven. The head, which is only blocked out, overweighs the form, proving that Michelangelo, unlike the Greeks, did not observe a fixed canon of proportion for the human frame. This statue bears a strong resemblance in feeling and conception to the Apollo designed for Baccio Valori.

There are four rough-hewn male figures, eccentrically wrought into the rock-work of a grotto in the Boboli Gardens, which have been assigned to the Tomb of Julius. This attribution involves considerable difficulties. In the first place, the scale is different, and the stride of one of them, at any rate, is too wide for the pedestals of that monument. Then their violent contortions and ponderous adult forms seem to be at variance with the spirit of the Captives. Mr. Heath Wilson may perhaps be right in his conjecture that Michelangelo began them for the sculptural decoration on the façade of S. Lorenzo. Their incompleteness baffles criticism; yet we feel instinctively that they were meant for the open air and for effect at a considerable distance. They remind us of Deucalion's men growing out of the stones he threw behind his back. We could not wish them to be finished, or to lose their wild attraction, as of primeval beings, the remnants of dim generations nearer than ourselves to elemental nature. No better specimens of Buonarroti's way of working in the marble could be chosen. Almost savage hatchings with the point blend into finer touches from the toothed chisel; and here and there the surface has been treated with innumerable smoothing lines that round it into skin and muscle. To a man who chiselled thus, marble must have yielded like softest freestone beneath his tools ; and how recklessly he wrought is clear from the defective proportions of one old man's figure, whose leg below the knee is short beyond all excuse.

A group of two figures, sometimes called the Victory, now in the Bargello Palace, was catalogued without hesitation by Vasari among the statues for the tomb. A young hero, of gigantic strength and height, stands firmly poised upon one foot, while his other leg, bent at the knee, crushes the back of an old man doubled up beneath him. In the face of the vanquished warrior critics have found a resemblance to Michelangelo. The head of the victorious youth seems too small for his stature, and the features are almost brutally vacuous, though burning with an insolent and carnal beauty. The whole forcible figure expresses irresistible energy and superhuman litheness combined with massive strength. This group cannot be called pleasing, and its great height renders it almost inconceivable that it was meant to range upon one monument with the Captives of the Louvre. There are, however, so many puzzles and perplexities connected with that design in its several stages, that we dare affirm or deny nothing concerning it. M. Guillaume, taking it for granted that the Victory was intended for the tomb, makes the plausible suggestion that some of the peculiarities which render it in composition awkward, would have been justified by the addition of bronze wings.[1] Mr. Heath Wilson, seeking after an allegory, is fain to believe that it represents Michelangelo's own state of subjection while employed upon the Serravezza quarries.[2]

Last comes the so-called Adonis of the Bargello Palace, which not improbably was designed for one of the figures prostrate below the feet of a victorious Genius. It bears, indeed, much resemblance to a roughly indicated nude at the extreme right of the sketch for the tomb.[3] Upon this supposition, Michelangelo must have left it in a very unfinished state, with an unshaped block beneath the raised right thigh. This block has now been converted into a boar. Extremely beautiful as the Adonis undoubtedly is, the strained, distorted attitude seems to require some explanation. That might have been given by the trampling form and robes of a Genius. Still it is

[1] *L'Œuvre et la Vie*, p. 78. Michelangelo put wings to his Victories in the first sketch for the tomb.

[2] The group is in Serravezza marble. See Heath Wilson, p. 243. We have no right to construct allegories in order to explain difficulties in works of art. Yet, if I were to seek one here, and to recognise Michelangelo's self in the old man, I should prefer to think that he had heard the story of a Greek sculptor who, loving a beautiful young man, depicted himself as the youth's captive, or the captive to eternal beauty incarnated in him :—

> Methought in dreams I wrestled yester-morn,
> A greybeard with a youngster, I with thee :
> I stumbled and was bound, a bruisèd man,
> Thy captive, glorying in captivity.
> This is a parable which I will plan,
> For men of after-time to muse upon,
> In Parian marble or Pentelican.

[3] Just below the Moses.

difficult to comprehend why the left arm and hand, finished, I feel almost sure, by Michelangelo, should have been so carefully executed. The Genius, if draped, would have hidden nearly the whole of that part of the statue. The face of this Adonis displays exactly the same type as that of the so-called Victory and of Giuliano de' Medici. Here the type assumes singular loveliness.

CHAPTER XII.

painfully elaborated.—Michelangelo the younger's falsified edition
of the poems.—Specific qualities to be traced in them.—Varchi's
peroration to his Discourse upon a Sonnet of Michelangelo.

I.

AFTER the death of Clement VII. Michelango never
returned to reside at Florence. The rest of his life
was spent in Rome. In the year 1534 he had
reached the advanced age of fifty-nine, and it is
possible that he first became acquainted with the
noble lady Vittoria Colonna about 1538. Recent
students of his poetry and friendships have suggested that their famous intimacy began earlier,
during one of his not infrequent visits to Rome.
But we have no proof of this. On the contrary,
the only letters extant which he sent to her, two in
number, belong to the year 1545.[1] It is certain that
anything like friendship between them grew up at
some considerable time after his final settlement in
Rome.

Vittoria was the daughter of Fabrizio Colonna,
Grand Constable of Naples, by his marriage with
Agnesina di Montefeltro, daughter of Federigo, Duke
of Urbino. Blood more illustrious than hers could
not be found in Italy. When she was four years
old, her parents betrothed her to Ferrante Francesco
d'Avalos, a boy of the same age, the only son of the
Marchese di Pescara. In their nineteenth year the

---

[1] Since he was born in 1475, he must have been then about seventy
years of age.

affianced couple were married at Ischia, the fief and residence of the house of D'Avalos. Ferrante had succeeded to his father's title early in boyhood, and was destined for a brilliant military career. On the young bride's side at least it was a love-match. She was tenderly attached to her handsome husband, ignorant of his infidelities, and blind to his fatal faults of character. Her happiness proved of short duration. In 1512 Pescara was wounded and made prisoner at the battle of Ravenna, and, though he returned to his wife for a short interval, duty called him again to the field of war in Lombardy in 1515. After this date Vittoria saw him but seldom. The last time they met was in October 1522. As general of the Imperial forces, Pescara spent the next years in perpetual military operations. Under his leadership the battle of Pavia was won in 1525, and King Francis became his master's prisoner. So far, nothing but honour, success, and glory waited on the youthful hero. But now the tide turned. Pescara, when he again settled down at Milan, began to plot with Girolamo Morone, Grand Chancellor of Francesco Sforza's duchy. Morone had conceived a plan for reinstating his former lord in Milan by the help of an Italian coalition. He offered Pescara the crown of Naples if he would turn against the Emperor. The Marquis seems at first to have lent a not unwilling ear to these proposals, but seeing reason to doubt the success of the scheme, he finally resolved to betray Morone to Charles V., and did this with cold-blooded ingenuity. A few months afterwards, on November 25, 1525, he died, branded as a traitor, accused of double treachery, both to his sovereign and his friend.

If suspicions of her husband's guilt crossed Vittoria's mind, as we have some reason to believe they did, these were not able to destroy her loyalty and love. Though left so young a widow and childless, she determined to consecrate her whole life to his memory and to religion. His nephew and heir, the Marchese del Vasto, became her adopted son. The Marchioness survived Pescara two-and-twenty years, which were spent partly in retirement at Ischia, partly in journeys, partly in convents at Orvieto and Viterbo, and finally in a semi-monastic seclusion at Rome. The time spared from pious exercises she devoted to study, the composition of poetry, correspondence with illustrious men of letters, and the society of learned persons. Her chief friends belonged to that group of earnest thinkers who felt the influences of the Reformation without ceasing to be loyal children of the Church. With Vittoria's name are inseparably connected those of Gasparo Contarini, Reginald Pole, Giovanni Morone, Jacopo Sadoleto, Marcantonio Flaminio, Pietro Carnesecchi, and Fra Bernardino Ochino. The last of these avowed his Lutheran principles, and was severly criticised by Vittoria Colonna for doing so. Carnesecchi was burned for heresy. Vittoria never adopted Protestantism, and died an orthodox Catholic. Yet her intimacy with men of liberal opinions exposed her to mistrust and censure in old age. The movement of the Counter-Reformation had begun, and any kind of speculative freedom aroused suspicion. This saintly princess was accordingly placed under the supervision of the Holy Office, and to be her friend was slightly dangerous.[1] It is obvious that Vittoria's religion was of an evangelical type, inconsistent with the dogmas developed by the Tridentine Council; and it is probable that, like her friend Contarini, she advocated a widening rather than a narrowing of Western Christendom. To bring the Church back to purer morals and sincerity of faith was their aim. They yearned for a reformation and regeneration from within.

In all these matters, Michelangelo, the devout student of the Bible and the disciple of Savonarola, shared Vittoria's sentiments. His nature, profoundly and simply religious from the outset, assumed a tone of deeper piety and habitual devotion during the advance of years. Vittoria Colonna's influence at this period strengthened his Christian emotions, which remained untainted by asceticism or superstition.[2] They were further united by another bond, which was their common interest in poetry. The

---

[1] See Ferrero and Müller, *op. cit.*, pp. 331-346, for extracts from documents relating to Vittoria and the Roman Inquisition.

[2] I may here call attention to a note in which Guasti brings together a series of passages illustrating the religious bias of Buonarroti's character. *Rime*, pp. xxxvi., xxxvii., note 4 to p. xxxvii.

Marchioness of Pescara was justly celebrated during her lifetime as one of the most natural writers of Italian verse. Her poems consist principally of sonnets consecrated to the memory of her husband, or composed on sacred and moral subjects. Penetrated by genuine feeling, and almost wholly free from literary affectation, they have that dignity and sweetness which belong to the spontaneous utterances of a noble heart. Whether she treats of love or of religion, we find the same simplicity and sincerity of style. There is nothing in her pious meditations that a Christian of any communion may not read with profit, as the heartfelt outpourings of a soul athirst for God and nourished on the study of the gospel.

Michelangelo preserved a large number of her sonnets, which he kept together in one volume. Writing to his nephew Lionardo in 1554, he says:[1] "Messer Giovan Francesco (Fattucci) asked me about a month ago if I possessed any writings of the Marchioness. I have a little book bound in parchment, which she gave me some ten years ago. It has one hundred and three sonnets, not counting another forty she afterwards sent on paper from Viterbo. I had these bound into the same book, and at that time I used to lend them about to many persons, so that they are all of them now in print. In addition to these poems I have many letters which she wrote from Orvieto and Viterbo. These

---

[1] Lettere, No. ccxliii. The first edition of Vittoria Colonna's verses was that of Parma, 1538.

then are the writings I possess of the Marchioness."
He composed several pieces, madrigals and sonnets,
under the genial influence of this exchange of
thoughts.   It was a period at which his old love
of versifying revived with singular activity.   Other
friends, like Tommaso Cavalieri, Luigi del Riccio,
and afterwards Vasari, enticed his Muse to frequent
utterance.[1]   Those he wrote for the Marchioness
were distributed in manuscript among his private
friends, and found their way into the first edition
of his collected poems.[2]   But it is a mistake to
suppose that she was the sole or even the chief
source of his poetical inspiration.

We shall see that it was his custom to mark his
feeling for particular friends by gifts of drawings
as well as of poems.   He did this notably in the
case of both Vittoria Colonna and Tommaso dei
Cavalieri.   For the latter he designed subjects from
Greek mythology; for the former, episodes in the
Passion of our Lord.   "At the request of this lady,"
says Condivi, "he made a naked Christ, at the
moment when, taken from the cross, our Lord would
have fallen like an abandoned corpse at the feet of
his most holy Mother, if two angels did not support
him in their arms.   She sits below the cross with a
face full of tears and sorrow, lifting both her wide-
spread arms to heaven, while on the stem of the

[1] See, for example, the series of quatrains poured forth to please Del
Riccio on the occasion of Cecchino de' Bracci's death.

[2] See Lettere, No. cdlxvii., where he sends some of them to a friend in
Florence.

tree above is written this legend, 'Non vi si pensa quanto sangue costa.' The cross is of the same kind as that which was carried in procession by the White Friars at the time of the plague of 1348, and afterwards deposited in the Church of S. Croce at Florence. He also made, for love of her, the design of a Jesus Christ upon the cross, not with the aspect of one dead, as is the common wont, but in a divine attitude, with face raised to the Father, seeming to exclaim, 'Eli! Eli!' In this drawing the body does not appear to fall, like an abandoned corpse, but as though in life to writhe and quiver with the agony it feels."

Of these two designs we have several more or less satisfactory mementoes. The Pietà was engraved by Giulio Bonasoni and Tudius Bononiensis (date 1546), exactly as Condivi describes it. The Crucifixion survives in a great number of pencil-drawings, together with one or two pictures painted by men like Venusti, and many early engravings of the drawings. One sketch in the Taylor Museum at Oxford is generally supposed to represent the original designed for Vittoria.

II.

What remains of the correspondence between Michelangelo and the Marchioness opens with a letter referring to their interchange of sonnets and drawings. It is dated Rome, 1545.[1] Vittoria had evidently sent him poems, and he wishes to make her a return in kind: "I desired, lady, before I accepted the things which your ladyship has often expressed the will to give me—I desired to produce something for you with my own hand, in order to be as little as possible unworthy of this kindness. I have now come to recognise that the grace of God is not to be bought, and that to keep it waiting is a grievous sin. Therefore I acknowledge my error, and willingly accept your favours. When I possess them, not indeed because I shall have them in my house, but for that I myself shall dwell in them, the place will seem to encircle me with Paradise. For which felicity I shall remain ever more obliged to your ladyship than I am already, if that is possible.

"The bearer of this letter will be Urbino, who lives in my service. Your ladyship may inform him when you would like me to come and see the head you promised to show me."

This letter is written under the autograph copy of a sonnet which must have been sent with it, since it expresses the same thought in its opening quatrain. My translation of the poem runs thus:[2]—

> Seeking at least to be not all unfit
> For thy sublime and boundless courtesy,
> My lowly thoughts at first were fain to try
> What they could yield for grace so infinite.

---

[1] Lettere, No. cdliv.
[2] Sonnet, No. xiii. p. 43. It may be compared with Sonnet, No. 69, where the idea is not very different.

BRUTUS, marble, about 1540. Museo Nazionale, Florence.
Alinari/Art Resource, NY.

But now I know my unassisted wit
  Is all too weak to make me soar so high,
  For pardon, lady, for this fault I cry,
  And wiser still I grow, remembering it.
Yea, well I see what folly 'twere to think
  That largess dropped from thee like dews from heaven
  Could e'er be paid by work so frail as mine !
To nothingness my art and talent sink ;
  He fails who from his mortal stores hath given
  A thousandfold to match one gift divine.

Michelangelo's next letter refers to the design for the Crucified Christ, described by Condivi. It is pleasant to find that this was sent by the hand of Cavalieri :[1] " Lady Marchioness,—Being myself in Rome, I thought it hardly fitting to give the Crucified Christ to Messer Tommaso, and to make him an intermediary between your ladyship and me, your servant ; especially because it has been my earnest wish to perform more for you than for any one I ever knew upon the world. But absorbing occupations, which still engage me, have prevented my informing your ladyship of this. Moreover, knowing that you know that love needs no task-master, and that he who loves doth not sleep, I thought the

[1] Lettere, No. cdlv., date Rome 1545.   I have read the original autograph of this letter in the Codex Vaticanus, p. 99, *a tergo*.   At the foot of it is written a version of the Madrigal beginning—

$$\text{" Ora in su l'uno } \left.\begin{matrix} \text{destro} \\ \end{matrix}\right\}$$
$$\text{Ora in sul altro } \left.\begin{matrix} \text{manco} \\ \end{matrix}\right\} \text{piede."}$$

Early in the same manuscript (p. 37) we find this madrigal copied out with the superscription : " A la Marchesa di Pescara," in Michelangelo's writing.

less of using go-betweens. And though I seemed
to have forgotten, I was doing what I did not talk
about in order to effect a thing that was not looked
for. My purpose has been spoiled : *He sins who
faith like this so soon forgets.*"

A sonnet which may or may not have been written
at this time, but seems certainly intended for the
Marchioness, shall here be given as a pendant to
the letter : [1]—

> Blest spirit, who with loving tenderness
>   Quickenest my heart, so old and near to die,
>   Who 'mid thy joys on me dost bend an eye,
>   Though many nobler men around thee press !
> As thou wert erewhile wont my sight to bless,
>   So to console my mind thou now dost fly ;
>   Hope therefore stills the pangs of memory,
>   Which, coupled with desire, my soul distress.
> So finding in thee grace to plead for me—
>   Thy thoughts for me sunk in so sad a case—
>   He who now writes returns thee thanks for these.
> Lo ! it were foul and monstrous usury
>   To send thee ugliest paintings in the place
>   Of thy fair spirit's living phantasies.

Unfortunately we possess no other document in
prose addressed immediately to Vittoria. But four of
her letters to him exist, and from these I will select
some specimens reflecting light upon the nature of
the famous intimacy.[2] The Marchioness writes

---

[1] Sonnets, No. xii. p. 42 of my translation.
[2] Grimm, Guasti, and Campori (*Lettere Artistiche Inedite*, Modena,
Sogliani, 1866) have printed a few addressed to Michelangelo. The
Arch. Buon. (Cod. ix. 507–510) contains four without dates. Ferrero
and Müller collect these four, and add one from the British Museum.

always in the tone and style of a great princess, adding that peculiar note of religious affectionateness which the French call "*onction*," and marking her strong admiration of the illustrious artist. The letters are not dated; but this matters little, since they only turn on literary courtesies exchanged, drawings presented, and pious interests in common.

"Unique Master Michelangelo, and my most singular friend,—I have received your letter, and examined the crucifix, which truly hath crucified in my memory every other picture I ever saw. Nowhere could one find another figure of our Lord so well executed, so living, and so exquisitely finished. Certes, I cannot express in words how subtly and marvellously it is designed. Wherefore I am resolved to take the work as coming from no other hand but yours, and accordingly I beg you to assure me whether this is really yours or another's. Excuse the question. If it is yours, I must possess it under any conditions. In case it is not yours, and you want to have it carried out by your assistant, we will talk the matter over first. I know how extremely difficult it would be to copy it, and therefore I would rather let him finish something else than this. But if it be in fact yours, rest assured, and make the best of it, that it will never come again into your keeping. I have examined it minutely in full light and by the lens and mirror, and never saw anything more perfect.—Yours to command,

"THE MARCHIONESS OF PESCARA."

Like many grand ladies of the highest rank, even though they are poetesses, Vittoria Colonna did not always write grammatically or coherently. I am not therefore sure that I have seized the exact meaning of this diplomatical and flattering letter. It would appear, however, that Michelangelo had sent her the drawing for a crucifix, intimating that, if she liked it, he would intrust its execution to one of his workmen, perhaps Urbino. This, as we know, was a common practice adopted by him in old age, in order to avoid commissions which interfered with his main life-work at S. Peter's. The noble lady, fully aware that the sketch is an original, affects some doubt upon the subject, declines the intervention of a common crafts-man, and declares her firm resolve to keep it, leaving an impression that she would gladly possess the crucifix if executed by the same hand which had supplied the masterly design.[1]

Another letter refers to the drawing of a Christ upon the cross between two angels.

"Your works forcibly stimulate the judgment of all who look at them. My study of them made me speak of adding goodness to things perfect in them-selves, and I have seen now that 'all is possible to him who believes.' I had the greatest faith in God that He would bestow upon you supernatural grace for the making of this Christ. When I came to

---

[1] Grimm takes the same view as I do of Vittoria's meaning in this letter. Von Scheffler thinks she was not sure whether the crucifix had not become the property of some third person.

examine it, I found it so marvellous that it surpasses all my expectations.   Wherefore, emboldened
by your miracles, I conceived a great desire for that
which I now see marvellously accomplished : I
mean that the design is in all parts perfect and
consummate, and one could not desire more, nor
could desire attain to demanding so much.   I tell
you that I am mighty pleased that the angel on the
right hand is by far the fairer, since Michael will
place you, Michelangelo, upon the right hand of
our Lord at that last day.   Meanwhile, I do not
know how else to serve you than by making orisons
to this sweet Christ, whom you have drawn so well
and exquisitely, and praying you to hold me yours
to command as yours in all and for all."

The admiration and the good-will of the great
lady transpire in these somewhat incoherent and
studied paragraphs.   Their verbiage leaves much
to be desired in the way of logic and simplicity.
It is pleasanter perhaps to read a familiar note,
sent probably by the hand of a servant to Buonarroti's
house in Rome.

"I beg you to let me have the crucifix a short
while in my keeping, even though it be unfinished.
I want to show it to some gentlemen who have
come from the Most Reverend the Cardinal of
Mantua.   If you are not working, will you not come
to-day at your leisure and talk with me ?—Yours to
command,

"THE MARCHIONESS OF PESCARA."

It seems that Michelangelo's exchange of letters and poems became at last too urgent. We know it was his way (as in the case of Luigi del Riccio) to carry on an almost daily correspondence for some while, and then to drop it altogether when his mood changed. Vittoria, writing from Viterbo, gives him a gentle and humorous hint that he is taking up too much of her time :[1]—

"Magnificent Messer Michelangelo,—I did not reply earlier to your letter, because it was, as one might say, an answer to my last : for I thought that if you and I were to go on writing without inter-mission according to my obligation and your courtesy, I should have to neglect the Chapel of S. Catherine here, and be absent at the appointed hours for company with my sisterhood, while you would have to leave the Chapel of S. Paul, and be absent from morning through the day from your sweet usual colloquy with painted forms, the which with their natural accents do not speak to you less clearly than the living persons round me speak to me. Thus we should both of us fail in our duty, I to the brides, you to the vicar of Christ. For these reasons, inas-much as I am well assured of our steadfast friend-ship and firm affection, bound by knots of Christian kindness, I do not think it necessary to obtain the proof of your good-will in letters by writing on my

---

[1] The superscription to this epistle, which exists in the Arch. Buon., Cod. ix. No. 510, is couched in very flattering terms : " Al mio più che magnifico e più che carissimo M. Michelagnolo Buonarroti."

side, but rather to await with well-prepared mind
some substantial occasion for serving you.   Meanwhile I address my prayers to that Lord of whom
you spoke to me with so fervent and humble a heart
when I left Rome, that when I return thither I may
find you with His image renewed and enlivened by
true faith in your soul, in like measure as you have
painted it with perfect art in my Samaritan.   Believe
me to remain always yours and your Urbino's."

This letter must have been written when Michelangelo was still working on the frescoes of the
Cappella Paolina, and therefore before 1549.[1] The
check to his importunacy, given with genial tact
by the Marchioness, might be taken, by those who
believe their *liaison* to have had a touch of passion
in it, as an argument in favour of that view.   The
great age which Buonarroti had now reached renders
this, however, improbable ; while the general tenor
of their correspondence is that of admiration for a
great artist on the lady's side, and of attraction to
a noble nature on the man's side, cemented by
religious sentiment and common interests in serious
topics.

III.

All students of Michelangelo's biography are well
acquainted with the Dialogues on Painting, com-

[1] Before he had completed his seventy-fourth year.

posed by the Portuguese miniature artist, Francis
of Holland.[1] Written in the quaint style of the
sixteenth century, which curiously blent actual circumstance and fact with the author's speculation,
these essays present a vivid picture of Buonarroti's
conferences with Vittoria Colonna and her friends.
The dialogues are divided into four parts, three of
which profess to give a detailed account of three
several Sunday conversations in the Convent of S.
Silvestro on Monte Cavallo. After describing the
objects which brought him to Rome, Francis says:[2]
"Above all, Michelangelo inspired me with such
esteem, that when I met him in the palace of the
Pope or on the streets, I could not make my mind
up to leave him until the stars forced us to retire.'
Indeed, it would seem from his frank admissions
in another place that the Portuguese painter had
become a little too attentive to the famous old man,
and that Buonarroti " did all he could to shun his
company, seeing that when they once came together,
they could not separate." [3] It happened one Sunday
that Francis paid a visit to his friend Lattanzio
Tolomei, who had gone abroad, leaving a message
that he would be found in the Church of S. Silvestro,
where he was hoping to hear a lecture by Brother
Ambrose of Siena on the Epistles of S. Paul, in

---

[1] The original is inedited, but a French translation of the larger
part was published by Count A. Raczynski in his *Les Arts en Portugal*.
Paris : Renouard, 1846. The manuscript is dated Lisbon, S. Luke's
Day, 1538.

[2] *Op. cit.*, p. 7.   [3] Ibid., p. 9.

company with the Marchioness. Accordingly he
repaired to this place, and was graciously received
by the noble lady. She courteously remarked that
he would probably enjoy a conversation with Michelangelo more than a sermon from Brother Ambrose,
and after an interval of compliments a servant was
sent to find him. It chanced that Buonarroti was
walking with the man whom Francis of Holland calls
"his old friend and colour-grinder," Urbino, in the
direction of the Thermae. So the lackey, having
the good chance to meet him, brought him at once
to the convent. The Marchioness made him sit between her and Messer Tolomei, while Francis took
up his position at a little distance. The conversation then began, but Vittoria Colonna had to use the
tact for which she was celebrated before she could
engage the wary old man on a serious treatment of
his own art.

He opened his discourse by defending painters
against the common charge of being "eccentric in
their habits, difficult to deal with, and unbear-
able; whereas, on the contrary, they are really most
humane."[1] Common people do not consider, he
remarked, that really zealous artists are bound to
abstain from the idle trivialities and current compliments of society, not because they are haughty or
intolerant by nature, but because their art imperi-
ously claims the whole of their energies. "When
such a man shall have the same leisure as you

[1] *Op. cit.*, pp. 11, 12. I have condensed the argument.

enjoy, then I see no objection to your putting him
to death if he does not observe your rules of
etiquette and ceremony. You only seek his company and praise him in order to obtain honour
through him for yourselves, nor do you really mind
what sort of man he is, so long as kings and
emperors converse with him. I dare affirm that any
artist who tries to satisfy the better vulgar rather
than men of his own craft, one who has nothing
singular, eccentric, or at least reputed to be so, in
his person, will never become a superior talent. For
my part, I am bound to confess that even his
Holiness sometimes annoys and wearies me by
begging for too much of my company. I am most
anxious to serve him, but, when there is nothing
important going forward, I think I can do so better
by studying at home than by dancing attendance
through a whole day on my legs in his reception-
rooms. He allows me to tell him so ; and I may
add that the serious occupations of my life have
won for me such liberty of action that, in talking to
the Pope, I often forget where I am, and place my
hat upon my head. He does not eat me up on that
account, but treats me with indulgence, knowing
that it is precisely at such times that I am working
hard to serve him. As for solitary habits, the world
is right in condemning a man who, out of pure
affectation or eccentricity, shuts himself up alone,
loses his friends, and sets society against him. Those,
however, who act in this way naturally, because

their profession obliges them to lead a recluse life, or because their character rebels against feigned politenesses and conventional usage, ought in common justice to be tolerated. What claim by right have you on him? Why should you force him to take part in those vain pastimes, which his love for a quiet life induces him to shun? Do you not know that there are sciences which demand the whole of a man, without leaving the least portion of his spirit free for your distractions?" This apology for his own life, couched in a vindication of the artistic temperament, breathes an accent of sincerity, and paints Michelangelo as he really was, with his somewhat haughty sense of personal dignity. What he says about his absence of mind in the presence of great princes might be illustrated by a remark attributed to Clement VII. "When Buonarroti comes to see me, I always take a seat and bid him to be seated, feeling sure that he will do so without leave or license."

The conversation passed by natural degrees to a consideration of the fine arts in general. In the course of this discussion, Michelangelo uttered several characteristic opinions, strongly maintaining the superiority of the Italian to the Flemish and German schools, and asserting his belief that, while all objects are worthy of imitation by the artist, the real touchstone of excellence lies in his power to represent the human form.[1] His theory of the arts

[1] *Op. cit.*, pp. 14-16. Compare p. 40.

in their reciprocal relations and affinities throws interesting light upon the qualities of his own genius
and his method in practice.[1] " The science of design,
or of line-drawing, if you like to use this term, is
the source and very essence of painting, sculpture,
architecture, and of every form of representation, as
well too as of all the sciences. He who has made
himself a master in this art possesses a great treasure. Sometimes, when I meditate upon these topics,
it seems to me that I can discover but one art or
science, which is design, and that all the works of
the human brain and hand are either design itself,
or a branch of that art." This theme he develops
at some length, showing how a complete mastery of
drawing is necessary not only to the plastic arts of
painting and sculpture, but also to the constructive
and mechanical arts of architecture, fortification,
gun-foundry, and so forth, applying the same principle to the minutest industries.

With regard to the personal endowments of the
artist, he maintained that " a lofty style, grave and
decorous, was essential to great work.[2] Few artists
understand this, and endeavour to appropriate these
qualities. Consequently we find many members of
the confraternity who are only artists in name. The
world encourages this confusion of ideas, since few
are capable of distinguishing between a fellow who
has nothing but his colour-box and brushes to make

[1] *Op. cit.*, pp. 39, 24, 31.
[2] Ibid., pp. 36–38.

him a painter, and the really gifted natures who appear only at wide intervals." He illustrates the position that noble qualities in the artist are indispensable to nobility in the work of art, by a digression on religious painting and sculpture. " In order to represent in some degree the adored image of our Lord, it is not enough that a master should be great and able. I maintain that he must also be a man of good conduct and morals, if possible a saint, in order that the Holy Ghost may rain down inspiration on his understanding.[1] Ecclesiastical and secular princes ought, therefore, to permit only the most illustrious among the artists of their realm to paint the benign sweetness of our Saviour, the purity of our Lady, and the virtues of the saints. It often happens that ill-executed images distract the minds of worshippers and ruin their devotion, unless it be firm and fervent. Those, on the contrary, which are executed in the high style I have described, excite the soul to contemplation and to tears, even among the least devout, by inspiring reverence and fear through the majesty of their aspect." This doctrine is indubitably sound. To our minds, nevertheless, it rings a little hollow on the lips of the great

[1] Ammanati, in a letter addressed to the Florentine Academy of Design, date August 22, 1582, says that "Michelangelo once spoke to me as thus : ' Good Christians always make good and beautiful figures.' " —*Lettere Pittoriche*, vol. iii. p. 539. The letter in itself is very interesting, since Ammanati vehemently attacks the indecency of the nude, and expresses the strongest remorse for his own fountain of Neptune on the Piazza della Signoria.

master who modelled the Christ of the Minerva and painted the Christ and Madonna of the Last Judgment. Yet we must remember that, at the exact period when these dialogues took place, Buonarroti, under the influence of his friendship with Vittoria Colonna, was devoting his best energies to the devout expression of the Passion of our Lord. It is deeply to be regretted that, out of the numerous designs which remain to us from this endeavour, all of them breathing the purest piety, no monumental work except the Pietà at Florence emerged for perpetuity.

Many curious points, both of minute criticism and broad opinion, might still be gleaned from the dialogues set down by Francis of Holland. It must suffice here to resume what Michelangelo maintained about the artist's method. One of the interlocutors begged to be informed whether he thought that a master ought to aim at working slowly or quickly.[1] " I will tell you plainly what I feel about this matter. It is both good and useful to be able to work with promptitude and address. We must regard it as a special gift from God to be able to do that in a few hours which other men can only perform in many days of labour. Consequently, artists who paint rapidly, without falling in quality below those who paint but slowly, deserve the highest commendation. Should this rapidity of execution, however, cause a man to transgress the limits of sound art, it would

---

[1] *Lettere Pittoriche*, p. 41.

have been better to have proceeded with more
tardiness and study. A good artist ought never to
allow the impetuosity of his nature to overcome his
sense of the main end of art, perfection. Therefore
we cannot call slowness of execution a defect, nor
yet the expenditure of much time and trouble, if
this be employed with the view of attaining greater
perfection. The one unpardonable fault is bad work.
And here I would remind you of a thing essential to
our art, which you will certainly not ignore, and to
which I believe you attach the full importance it
deserves. In every kind of plastic work we ought
to strive with all our might at making what has
cost time and labour look as though it had been
produced with facility and swiftness. It sometimes
happens, but rarely, that a portion of our work turns
out excellent with little pains bestowed upon it.
Most frequently, however, it is the expenditure of
care and trouble which conceals our toil. Plutarch
relates that a bad painter showed Apelles a picture,
saying : 'This is from my hand; I have just made
it in a moment.' The other replied : 'I should
have recognised the fact without your telling me ;
and I marvel that you do not make a multitude of
such things every day.'" Michelangelo is reported
to have made a similar remark to Vasari when the
latter took him to inspect some frescoes he had
painted, observing that they had been dashed off
quickly.

We must be grateful to Francis of Holland for

this picture of the Sunday-morning interviews at
S. Silvestro. The place was cool and tranquil. The
great lady received her guests with urbanity, and led
the conversation with high-bred courtesy and tact.
Fra Ambrogio, having discoursed upon the spiritual
doctrines of S. Paul's Epistles, was at liberty to
turn an attentive ear to purely æsthetical speculations. The grave and elderly Lattanzio Tolomei
added the weight of philosophy and literary culture
to the dialogue. Michelangelo, expanding in the
genial atmosphere, spoke frankly on the arts which
he had mastered, not dictating *ex cathedra* rules,
but maintaining a note of modesty and common-
sense and deference to the opinion of others. Francis
engaged on equal terms in the discussion. His
veneration for Buonarroti, and the eagerness with
which he noted all the great man's utterances, did
not prevent him from delivering lectures at a somewhat superfluous length. In short, we may fairly
accept his account of these famous conferences as
a truthful transcript from the refined and witty
social gatherings of which Vittoria Colonna formed
the centre.[1]

[1] The Arch. Buon. has one letter written to Michelangelo from
Lisbon, August 15, 1553, by Francesco d'Olanda, Cod. x. No. 583.
It contains nothing of special interest, but displays a strong feeling of
affection and veneration for the great master in his old age. Gotti has
printed it, vol. i. p. 245.

IV.

This friendship with Vittoria Colonna forms a very charming episode in the history of Michelangelo's career, and it was undoubtedly one of the consolations of his declining years. Yet too great stress has hitherto been laid on it by his biographers. Not content with exaggerating its importance in his life, they have misinterpreted its nature. The .world seems unable to take interest in a man unless it can contrive to discover a love-affair in his career. The singular thing about Michelangelo is that, with the exception of Vittoria Colonna, no woman is known to have influenced his heart or head in any way. In his correspondence he never mentions women, unless they be aunts, cousins, grand-nieces, or servants. About his mother he is silent. We have no tradition regarding amours in youth or middle age ; and only two words dropped by Condivi lead us to conjecture that he was not wholly insensible to the physical attractions of the female.[1]   Romancers and legend-makers have, therefore, forced Vittoria Colonna to play the rôle of Juliet in Michelangelo's life-drama. It has not occurred to these critics that there is something essentially disagreeable in the thought of an aged couple entertaining an amorous correspondence. I use these words deliberately, because poems which breathe obvious passion of no merely

[1] " La continenza sua, tanto nel coito, quanto nel cibo." Condivi, p. 84.

spiritual character have been assigned to the number he composed for Vittoria Colonna. This, as we shall see, is chiefly the fault of his first editor, who printed all the sonnets and madrigals as though they were addressed to one woman or another. It is also in part due to the impossibility of determining their exact date in the majority of instances. Verses, then, which were designed for several objects of his affection, male or female, have been indiscriminately referred to Vittoria Colonna, whereas we can only attribute a few poems with certainty to her series.[1]

This mythus of Michelangelo's passion for the Marchioness of Pescara has blossomed and brought forth fruit abundantly from a single and pathetic passage in Condivi.[2] "In particular, he greatly loved the Marchioness of Pescara, of whose divine spirit he was enamoured, being in return dearly beloved by her. He still preserves many of her letters, breathing honourable and most tender affection, and such as were wont to issue from a heart like hers. He also wrote to her a great number of sonnets, full of wit and sweet longing. She frequently removed from Viterbo and other places, whither she had gone for solace or to pass the summer, and came to Rome with the sole object of seeing Michelangelo. He for his part, loved her so, that I remember to have

---

[1] See above, p. 101, note, for the autograph dedication of one madrigal to the Marchesa di Pescara.

[2] Condivi, p. 77. It is rather singular that Vasari, who always steals Condivi's best things, should have omitted the touching anecdote about her deathbed. The rest he has incorporated in his second edition.

heard him say that he regretted nothing except that when he went to visit her upon the moment of her passage from this life, he did not kiss her forehead or her face, as he did kiss her hand. Her death was the cause that oftentimes he dwelt astonied, thinking of it, even as a man bereft of sense."

Michelangelo himself, writing immediately after Vittoria's death, speaks of her thus :[1] "She felt the warmest affection for me, and I not less for her. Death has robbed me of a great friend." It is curious that he here uses the masculine gender : " un grande amico." He also composed two sonnets, which were in all probability inspired by the keen pain of this bereavement. To omit them here would be unjust to the memory of their friendship :[2]—

---

[1] Lettere, No. cdlxvii.

[2] *Rime*, Sonnets Nos. lxi. and lxii. It must be said that, so far as I know, we have no autograph authority for ascribing them to her. The same must be said about No. lxiii., which Guasti also places among sonnets written "In Morte di Vittoria Colonna." The autograph in Cod. Vat., p. 85, has no superscription. The curious play upon the words *Febo* and *poggio* in lines 2, 9, 10, might raise a suspicion that this sonnet was composed after his rupture with Febo di Poggio, about whom something will be said later on in this chapter. This suspicion is confirmed by the fragment of a sonnet (No. xciii.), which plays on the name Febo di Poggio. In Guasti's *Rime* it is numbered xciii., and seems to allude in covert language to Febo's preference for some other friend. I will give the original and a translation, premising that the person addressed as *tu* in the first quatrain is Febo, and is different from the person addressed in the second (under the metaphor of an eagle perhaps) as *felice uccello.*

> Ben fu, temprando il ciel tuo vivo raggio
> Solo a du' occhi, a me di pietà voto,
> Allor che con veloce eterno moto
> A noi dette la luce, a te 'l viaggio.

When my rude hammer to the stubborn stone
 Gives human shape, now that, now this, at will,
 Following his hand who wields and guides it still,
 It moves upon another's feet alone :
But that which dwells in heaven, the world doth fill
 With beauty by pure motions of its own ;
 And since tools fashion tools which else were none,
 Its life makes all that lives with living skill.
Now, for that every stroke excels the more
 The higher at the forge it doth ascend,
 Her soul that fashioned mine hath sought the skies ;
Wherefore unfinished I must meet my end,
 If God, the great Artificer, denies
 That aid which was unique on earth before.

————

When she who was the source of all my sighs
 Fled from the world, herself, my straining sight,
 Nature, who gave us that unique delight,
 Was sunk in shame, and we had weeping eyes.
Yet shall not vauntful Death enjoy the prize,
 This sun of suns which then he veiled in night ;
 For Love hath triumphed, lifting up her light
 On earth and 'mid the saints in Paradise.

———

Felice *uccello*, che con tal vantaggio
 Da noi, t'è *Febo* e 'l suo bel viso noto,
 E più c' al gran veder t'è bene arroto
 Volare al *poggio*, ond' io rovino e caggio.

————

Certes the heavens, by tempering thy live ray
 For twain eyes only, proved toward me their spite ;
 Then when, with swift eternal motion, light
 Was given to us, to thee the path of day.
Happy the bird who with such vantage may,
 Transcending ours, know Febo and his bright
 Visage ! beyond that vision too may light,
 Winged on the hill whence ruined I fall away.

It is significant that Michelangelo the younger made no use either of
Sonnet lxiii., or fragment xciii., in his version.   Lastly, I may say that
the poets frequently used *poggio* as a metaphor for the bosom.

What though remorseless and impiteous doom
  Deemed that the music of her deeds would die,
  And that her splendour would be sunk in gloom ?
The poet's page exalts her to the sky
  With life more living in the lifeless tomb,
  And Death translates her soul to reign on high.

It will not, perhaps, be out of place here to offer English versions of three madrigals, one of which was certainly written for Vittoria Colonna in her life-time, while another may have been composed after her death. I may introduce them by remarking that when Michelangelo adopted this form of lyric, looser than the sonnet, he was wont to indulge in even more extravagant conceits. The first proves that he regarded the Marchioness as his Egeria in the spiritual life, and that the gathering clouds of old age were making him reflect upon the final issues of man's soul :[1]—

Now to the right, now to the left hand driven,
Wander my steps, seeking eternal weal.
Both vice and virtue make appeal
Unto my heart perplexed, which tires me still :—
Like one who sees not heaven,
But blunders on distraught o'er vale and hill.
I send you paper, beg you take a quill,
And with your sacred ink
Make love give light, and mercy truth impart ;
So that my soul, delivered, purged of ill,
Shall not be drawn to error's brink,
Through life's brief remnant, by a blinded heart.
I ask of thee, that goddess art,
Lady, if up in heaven doth lower dwell
A contrite sin than virtue, lord o'er hell.

---

[1] *Rime*, Madrigal No. v. The autograph in Cod. Vat. has a super-scription to the Marchioness of Pescara. See p. 101, note.

The second is interesting for the light it seems to throw upon Vittoria Colonna's influence. Michelangelo describes her as a woman through whose lips a man, or rather a god, speaks to him, causing a complete change in his moral nature, and luring him from previous emotions of which he now repents :[1]—

A man within a woman, nay, a god,
Speaks through her spoken word :
I therefore, who have heard,
Must suffer change, and shall be mine no more.
She lured me from the paths I whilom trod.
Borne from my former state by her away,
I stand aloof, and mine own self deplore.
Above all vain desire
The beauty of her face doth lift my clay ;
All lesser loveliness seems charnel mire.
O lady, who through fire
And water leadest souls to joys eterne,
Let me no more unto myself return.

The third illustrates in a singular manner that custom of sixteenth-century literature which Shakespeare followed in his sonnets, of weaving poetical images out of thoughts borrowed from law and business. It is also remarkable in this respect, that Michelangelo has here employed precisely the same conceit for Vittoria Colonna which he found serviceable when at an earlier date he wished to deplore the death of the Florentine, Cecchino dei Bracci. For both of them he says that Heaven bestowed upon the beloved object all its beauties, instead of scatter-

---

[1] *Rime*, Madr. No. lvii. p. 94.

ing these broad-cast over the human race,[1] which, had it done so, would have entailed the bankruptcy and death of all :—

> So that high heaven should have not to distrain
> From several that vast beauty ne'er yet shown,
> To one exalted dame alone
> The total sum was lent in her pure self :—
> Heaven had made sorry gain,
> Recovering from the crowd its scattered pelf.
> Now in a puff of breath,
> Nay, in one second, God
> Hath ta'en her back through death,
> Back from the senseless folk and from our eyes.
> Yet earth's oblivious sod,
> Albeit her body dies,
> Will bury not her live words fair and holy.
> Ah, cruel mercy ! Here thou showest solely
> How, had heaven lent us ugly what she took,
> And death the debt reclaimed, all men were broke.

Without disputing the fact that a very sincere emotion underlay these verses, it must be submitted that, in the words of Samuel Johnson about "Lycidas," "he who thus grieves will excite no sympathy; he who thus praises will confer no honour." This conviction will be enforced when we reflect that the thought upon which the madrigal above translated has been woven (1547) had been already used for Cecchino dei Bracci in 1544. It is clear that, in dealing with Michelangelo's poetical compositions, we have to accept a mass of conven-

---

[1] *Rime*, Madrigal No. vi., compare in particular the epitaph on Cecchino, No. viii.

tional utterances, penetrated with a few firmly grasped Platonical ideas. It is only after long familiarity with his work that a man may venture to distinguish between the accents of the heart and the head-notes in the case of so great a master using an art he practised mainly as an amateur. I shall have to return to these considerations when I discuss the value of his poetry taken as a whole.

The union of Michelangelo and Vittoria was beautiful and noble, based upon the sympathy of ardent and high-feeling natures. Nevertheless we must remember that when Michelangelo lost his old servant Urbino, his letters and the sonnet written upon that occasion express an even deeper passion of grief.

Love is an all-embracing word, and may well be used to describe this exalted attachment, as also to qualify the great sculptor's affection for a faithful servant or for a charming friend. We ought not, however, to distort the truth of biography or to corrupt criticism, from a personal wish to make more out of his feeling than fact and probability warrant. This is what has been done by all who approached the study of Michelangelo's life and writings. Of late years, the determination to see Vittoria Colonna through every line written by him which bears the impress of strong emotion, and to suppress other aspects of his sensibility, has been so deliberate, that I am forced to embark upon a discussion which might otherwise have not been brought so prominently forward. For the understanding of his character, and for a proper estimate of his poetry, it has become indispensable to do so.

V.

Michelangelo's best friend in Rome was a young nobleman called Tommaso Cavalieri. Speaking of his numerous allies and acquaintances, Vasari writes : "Immeasurably more than all the rest, he loved Tommaso dei Cavalieri, a Roman gentleman, for whom, as he was young and devoted to the arts, Michelangelo made many stupendous drawings of superb heads in black and red chalk, wishing him to learn the method of design. Moreover, he drew for him a Ganymede carried up to heaven by Jove's eagle, a Tityos with the vulture feeding on his heart, the fall of Phaethon with the sun's chariot into the river Po, and a Bacchanal of children ; all of them things of the rarest quality, and drawings the like of which were never seen. Michelangelo made a cartoon portrait of Messer Tommaso, life-size, which was the only portrait that he ever drew, since he detested to imitate the living person, unless it was one of incomparable beauty."[1] Several of Michel-

[1] In the Louvre there is a fine study for the head of Minos (Last Judgment), which looks like a faithful portrait of Messer Biagio da Cesena. Chatsworth has a large drawing of Leo the Tenth's face, attributed (but with insufficient reason, I think) to Michelangelo.

angelo's sonnets are addressed to Tommaso Cavalieri.
Benedetto Varchi, in his commentary, introduces two
of them with these words:[1] "The first I shall
present is one addressed to M. Tommaso Cavalieri,
a young Roman of very noble birth, in whom I
recognised, while I was sojourning at Rome, not
only incomparable physical beauty, but so much
elegance of manners, such excellent intelligence,
and such graceful behaviour, that he well deserved,
and still deserves, to win the more love the better he
is known." Then Varchi recites the sonnet:[2]—

> Why should I seek to ease intense desire
>   With still more tears and windy words of grief,
>   When heaven, or late or soon, sends no relief
>   To souls whom love hath robed around with fire?
> Why need my aching heart to death aspire,
>   When all must die? Nay, death beyond belief
>   Unto these eyes would be both sweet and brief,
>   Since in my sum of woes all joys expire!
> Therefore, because I cannot shun the blow
>   I rather seek, say who must rule my breast,
>   Gliding between her gladness and her woe?
> If only chains and bands can make me blest,
>   No marvel if alone and bare I go,
>   An armèd KNIGHT's captive and slave confessed.

"The other shall be what follows, written perhaps
for the same person, and worthy, in my opinion, not
only of the ripest sage, but also of a poet not un-
exercised in writing verse:—

---

[1] *Rime*, p. cviii.
[2] They are respectively Nos. xxxi. and xxx.

With your fair eyes a charming light I see,
    For which my own blind eyes would peer in vain;
    Stayed by your feet, the burden I sustain
    Which my lame feet find all too strong for me;
Wingless upon your pinions forth I fly;
    Heavenward your spirit stirreth me to strain;
    E'en as you will, I blush and blanch again,
    Freeze in the sun, burn 'neath a frosty sky.
Your will includes and is the lord of mine;
    Life to my thoughts within your heart is given;
    My words begin to breathe upon your breath;
Like to the moon am I, that cannot shine
    Alone; for, lo! our eyes see naught in heaven
    Save what the living sun illumineth."

The frank and hearty feeling for a youth of singular distinction which is expressed in these sonnets, gave no offence to society during the period of the earlier Renaissance; but after the Tridentine Council social feeling altered upon this and similar topics. While morals remained what they had been, language and manners grew more nice and hypocritical. It happened thus that grievous wrong was done to the text of Michelangelo's poems, with the best intentions, by their first editor. Grotesque misconceptions, fostered by the same mistaken zeal, are still widely prevalent.

When Michelangelo the younger arranged his granduncle's poems for the press, he was perplexed by the first of the sonnets quoted by Varchi. The last line, which runs in the Italian thus—

Resto prigion d'un Cavalier armato,

has an obvious play of words upon Cavalieri's sur-
name.   This he altered into

Resto prigion d'un cor di virtù armato.

The reason was that, if it stood unaltered, "the
ignorance of men would have occasion to murmur."
"Varchi," he adds, "did wrong in printing it according to the text." "Remember well," he observes,
"that this sonnet, as well as the preceding number
and some others, are concerned, as is manifest, with
a masculine love of the Platonic species."[1]   Michelangelo the younger's anxiety for his granduncle's
memory induced him thus to corrupt the text of his
poems.   The same anxiety has led their latest editor
to explain away the obvious sense of certain words.
Signor Guasti approves of the first editor's pious
fraud, on the ground that morality has higher claims
than art; but he adds that the expedient was not
necessary: "for these sonnets do not refer to masculine love, nor yet do any others.   In the first (xxxi.)
the lady is compared to an armed knight, because
she carries the weapons of her sex and beauty;
and while I think on it, an example occurs to my
mind from Messer Cino in support of the argument.
As regards the second (lxii.), those who read these
pages of mine will possibly remember that Michelangelo, writing of the dead Vittoria Colonna, called

[1] *Rime*, p. 45.   I have read these autograph annotations to Michelangelo the younger's transcript of the Rime in the Archivio Buonarroti.
He altered the word *amici* in No. lii. into *animi*.

her *amico;* and on reflection, this sounds better than *amica,* in the place where it occurs. Moreover, there are not wanting in these poems instances of the term *signore,* or lord, applied to the beloved lady; which is one of the many periphrastical expressions used by the Romance poets to indicate their mistress."[1] It is true that Cino compares his lady in one sonnet to a knight who has carried off the prize of beauty in the lists of love and grace by her elegant dancing.[2] But he never calls a lady by the name of *cavaliere.* It is also indubitable that the Tuscans occasionally addressed the female or male object of their adoration under the title of *signore,* lord of my heart and soul.[3] But such instances weigh nothing against the direct testimony of a contemporary like Varchi, into whose hands Michelangelo's poems came at the time of their composition, and who was well acquainted with the circumstances of their composition. There is, moreover, a fact of singular importance bearing on this question, to which Signor Guasti has not attached the value it deserves. In a letter belonging to the year 1549, Michelangelo thanks Luca Martini for a copy of Varchi's commentary on his sonnet, and begs him to

[1] *Rime,* ibid. The reference to Cino is borrowed from a note of Carducci's, which I shall refer to lower down.

[2] *Vita e Poesie di Messer Cino da Pistoja.* Pisa: Capurro, 1813, p. 115.

[3] Carducci, in his edition of Poliziano's poems (*Le Stanze,* &c., Firenze, Barbèra, 1863, p. 204), gives a note upon this use of the word *Signore* in love-poetry, of which Guasti availed himself, as appears by the context. But that Michelangelo by the *Signore* always or frequently

express his affectionate regards and hearty thanks to that eminent scholar for the honour paid him.[1] In a second letter addressed to G. F. Fattucci, under date October 1549, he conveys "the thanks of Messer Tomao de' Cavalieri to Varchi for a certain little book of his which has been printed, and in which he speaks very honourably of himself, and not less so of me."[2] In neither of these letters does Michelangelo take exception to Varchi's interpretation of Sonnet xxxi. Indeed, the second proves that both he and Cavalieri were much pleased with it. Michelangelo even proceeds to inform Fattucci that Cavalieri "has given me a sonnet which I made for him in those same years, begging me to send it on as a proof and witness that he really is the man intended.

meant a woman can be disproved in many ways. I will only adduce the fragment of one sonnet (No. lxxxiii.)

> Oltre qui fu dove 'l *Signior* mi tolse,
>   Suo mercè, il core, e vie più la vita :
>   Qui co' begli occhi mi promisse aita,
>   E co' medesmi qui tor me la volse.
> Quince oltre mi legò, quivi mi sciolse ;
>   Per me qui piansi, e con doglia infinita
>   Da questo sasso vidi far partita
>   *Colui,* c' a me mi tolse, e non mi volse.

> Hereby was where my *Master* from me took
>   By grace my heart, nay more, the life of me ;
>   Here with his beauteous eyes he swore to be
>   My help, and with those eyes that promise broke.
> Just there he found me, here aside me shook ;
>   Here I bewept my fate, most miserably
>   From this stone saw *him* take departure, he
>   Who robbed me from myself, me would not brook.

[1] Lettere, No. cdlxiii. p. 524. [2] Ibid., No. cdlxvi. p. 527.

This I will enclose in my present letter." Furthermore, we possess an insolent letter of Pietro Aretino,
which makes us imagine that the " ignorance of the
vulgar" had already begun to "murmur."[1] After
complaining bitterly that Michelangelo refused to
send him any of his drawings, he goes on to remark
that it would be better for the artist if he did so,
" inasmuch as such an act of courtesy would quiet
the insidious rumours which assert that only Gerards
and Thomases can dispose of them." We have
seen from Vasari that Michelangelo executed some
famous designs for Tommaso Cavalieri. The same
authority asserts that he presented " Gherardo Perini,
a Florentine gentleman, and his very dear friend,"
with three splendid drawings in black chalk.[2]
Tommaso Cavalieri and Gherardo Perini were, therefore, the "Gerards and Thomases" alluded to by
Aretino.[3]

Michelangelo the younger's and Cesare Guasti's
method of defending Buonarroti from a malevolence
which was only too well justified by the vicious

[1] Gaye, vol. ii. p. 332. Its date is November 1565 ; see above, p. 51,
a mistake possibly for 1545. Aretino died in 1557. It may be added
here that Condivi tells us expressly that Michelangelo in his lifetime
was calumniated because of his friendships. This makes Condivi's
treatment of Michelangelo's emotions and of the Vittoria Colonna
episode apologetical. See Condivi, pp. 79, 80.

[2] Vasari, xii. p. 277. One of these was the famous "Damned Soul"
of the Uffizi, as is proved by Michelangelo's inscription on it.

[3] There is one letter by Michelangelo to Perini couched in terms of
warm affection. Lettere, No. ccclxxvi. p. 418. Compare the terms
in which Michelangelo writes about Pier Francesco Borgherini to his
brother. Lettere, No. cix.

manners of the time, seems to me so really injurious
to his character, that I feel bound to carry this investigation further.   First of all, we ought to bear
in mind what Buonarroti admitted concerning his
own temperament.[1]   " You must know that I am, of
all men who were ever born, the most inclined to
love persons.   Whenever I behold some one who
possesses any talent or displays any dexterity of
mind, who can do or say something more appro-
priately than the rest of the world, I am compelled
to fall in love with him; and then I give myself
up to him so entirely that I am no longer my own
property, but wholly his."   He mentions this as a
reason for not going to dine with Luigi del Riccio
in company with Donato Giannotti and Antonio
Petrejo.   "If I were to do so, as all of you are
adorned with talents and agreeable graces, each of
you would take from me a portion of myself, and
so would the dancer, and so would the lute-player,
if men with distinguished gifts in those arts were
present.   Each person would filch away a part of
me, and instead of being refreshed and restored to
health and gladness, as you said, I should be utterly
bewildered and distraught, in such wise that for
many days to come I should not know in what
world I was moving."   This passage serves to explain the extreme sensitiveness of the great artist to
personal charm, grace, accomplishments, and throws
light upon the self-abandonment with which he

---

[1] In Donato Giannotti's Dialogue.   See Guasti, *Rime*, p. xxxi.

sometimes yielded to the attractions of delightful people.[1]

We possess a series of Michelangelo's letters addressed to or concerned with Tommaso Cavalieri, the tone of which is certainly extravagant.[2] His biographer, Aurelio Gotti, moved by the same anxiety as Michelangelo the younger and Guasti, adopted the extraordinary theory that they were really directed to Vittoria Colonna, and were meant to be shown to her by the common friend of both, Cavalieri.[3] "There is an epistle to this young man," he says, "so studied in its phrases, so devoid of all naturalness, that we cannot extract any rational sense from it without supposing that Cavalieri was himself a friend of the Marchioness, and that Michelangelo, while writing to him, intended rather to address his words to the Colonna." Of this letter, which bears the date January 1, 1533, three drafts exist, proving the great pains taken by Michelangelo in its composition.[4]

---

[1] Among the inedited correspondence of the Arch. Buon. (Cod. x. Nos. 610–612) are to be found three letters from a certain Pier Antonio, who describes himself as "familiare di Mssere Revsmo di Ridolfi." They have no great biographical importance, except that they seem to point at an acquaintance, formed in this light-hearted and irreflective manner, with a youth distinguished for some special accomplishment.

[2] Lettere, Nos. cdxi.–cdxviii.

[3] Gotti, vol. i. pp. 231–234. That Cavalieri was a member of Vittoria Colonna's circle appears from Lettere No. cdlv. Milanesi either started or adopted the above hypothesis in a note appended to p. 468 of the Lettere.

[4] Lettere, Nos. cdxi., cdxii., cdxiii. pp. 462–464. It is extremely difficult to translate the involved and laboured conceits of the text.

"Without due consideration, Messer Tomao, my very dear lord, I was moved to write to your lordship, not by way of answer to any letter received from you, but being myself the first to make advances, as though I felt bound to cross a little stream with dry feet, or a ford made manifest by paucity of water. But now that I have left the shore, instead of the trifling river I expected, the ocean with its towering waves appears before me, so that, if it were possible, in order to avoid drowning, I would gladly retrace my steps to the dry land whence I started. Still, as I am here, I will e'en make of my heart a rock, and proceed farther; and if I shall not display the art of sailing on the sea of your powerful genius, that genius itself will excuse me, nor will be disdainful of my inferiority in parts, nor desire from me that which I do not possess, inasmuch as he who is unique in all things can have peers in none. Therefore your lordship, the light of our century without paragon upon this world, is unable to be satisfied with the productions of other men, having no match or equal to yourself.[1] And if, peradventure, something of mine, such as I hope and promise to perform, give pleasure to your mind, I shall esteem it more fortunate than excellent; and should I be ever sure of pleasing your lordship, as

---

[1] He calls young Cavalieri *luce* here, as he calls Febo di Poggio by the same title. "Light," I think, with Michelangelo was a favourite image when he wished to express the radiance of an amiable nature shining through a specially attractive form.

is said, in any particular, I will devote the present time and all my future to your service ; indeed, it will grieve me much that I cannot regain the past, in order to devote a longer space to you than the future only will allow, seeing I am now too old.   I have no more to say.   Read the heart, and not the letter, because ' the pen toils after man's good-will in vain.'

"I have to make excuses for expressing in my first letter a marvellous astonishment at your rare genius ; and thus I do so, having recognised the error I was in ; for it is much the same to wonder at God's working miracles as to wonder at Rome producing divine men.   Of this the universe confirms us in our faith."

It is clear that Michelangelo alludes in this letter to the designs which he is known to have made for Cavalieri, and the last paragraph has no point except as an elaborate compliment addressed to a Roman gentleman.   It would be quite out of place if applied to Vittoria Colonna.   Gotti finds the language strained and unnatural.   We cannot deny that it differs greatly from the simple diction of the writer's ordinary correspondence.   But Michelangelo did sometimes seek to heighten his style, when he felt that the occasion demanded a special effort ; and then he had recourse to the laboured images in vogue at that period, employing them with something of the ceremonious cumbrousness displayed in his poetry.   The letters to Pietro Aretino, Niccolò

Martelli, Vittoria Colonna, Francis I., Luca Martini, and Giorgio Vasari might be quoted as examples.[1]

As a postscript to this letter, in the two drafts which were finally rejected, the following enigmatical sentence is added :—

" It would be permissible to give the name of the things a man presents, to him who receives them ; but proper sense of what is fitting prevents it being done in this letter."

Probably Michelangelo meant that he should have liked to call Cavalieri his friend, since he had already given him friendship. The next letter, July 28, 1533, begins thus :—

" My dear Lord,—Had I not believed that I had made you certain of the very great, nay, measureless love I bear you, it would not have seemed strange to me nor have roused astonishment to observe the great uneasiness you show in your last letter, lest, through my not having written, I should have forgotten you. Still it is nothing new or marvellous when so many other things go counter, that this also should be topsy-turvy. For what your lordship says to me, I could say to yourself : nevertheless, you do this perhaps to try me, or to light a new and stronger flame, if that indeed were possible : but be it as it wills : I know well that, at this hour, I could as easily forget your name as the food by which I live ; nay, it were easier to forget the food, which only nourishes my body miserably, than your

---

[1] Lettere, Nos. cdxxi., cdxxii., cdlvi., cdlix., cdlxiii., cdlxviii.

name, which nourishes both body and soul, filling the one and the other with such sweetness that neither weariness nor fear of death is felt by me while memory preserves you to my mind. Think, if the eyes could also enjoy their portion, in what condition I should find myself."

This second letter has also been extremely laboured; for we have three other turns given in its drafts to the image of food and memory. That these two documents were really addressed to Cavalieri, without any thought of Vittoria Colonna, is proved by three letters sent to Michelangelo by the young man in question. One is dated August 2, 1533, another September 2, and the third bears no date. The two which I have mentioned first belong to the summer of 1533; the third seems to be the earliest. It was clearly written on some occasion when both men were in Rome together, and at the very beginning of their friendship.[1] I will translate them in their order.[2] The first undated letter was sent to Michelangelo in Rome, in answer to some writing of the illustrious sculptor which we do not possess :—

[1] It is much to be regretted that this letter is undated, since it would fix the exact period when Michelangelo first met Cavalieri. I conjecture that this happened in the spring or summer of 1532, when the sculptor was on a visit to Rome. The splendid sonnet (No. xxxii.) which opens on the words "Se un casto amor" is written at the foot of a letter addressed by Giuliano Bugiardini to Michelangelo in Rome, and dated the 5th of August 1532. The sonnet can be referred with strong probability to the Cavalieri series.

[2] Extracted from the Archivio Buonarroti, Cod. vii. 141 et seq. See the originals in the Appendix.

"I have received from you a letter, which is the more acceptable because it was so wholly unexpected. I say unexpected, because I hold myself unworthy of such condescension in a man of your eminence. With regard to what Pierantonio spoke to you in my praise, and those things of mine which you have seen, and which you say have aroused in you no small affection for me,[1] I answer that they were insufficient to impel a man of such transcendent genius, without a second, not to speak of a peer, upon this earth, to address a youth who was born but yesterday, and therefore is as ignorant as it is possible to be. At the same time I cannot call you a liar. I rather think then, nay, am certain, that the love you bear me is due to this, that you, being a man most excellent in art, nay, art itself, are forced to love those who follow it and love it, among whom am I; and in this, according to my capacity, I yield to few. I promise you truly that you shall receive from me for your kindness affection equal, and perhaps greater, in exchange; for I never loved a man more than I do you, nor desired a friendship more than I do yours. About this, though my judgment may fail in other things, it is unerring; and you shall see the proof, except only

---

[1] Cavalieri studied the arts of design, and lived to carry on Michelangelo's work at the Capitol of Rome after his friend's death in 1564. I do not know who this Pierantonio is, unless it be the young man mentioned in a note to p. 133 above. He was certainly a member of Cavalieri's circle, for he mentions him very particularly in a letter without date. Arch. Buon., Cod. x. No. 610. This letter will be quoted in full lower down.

that fortune is adverse to me in that now, when I might enjoy you, I am far from well. I hope, however, if she does not begin to trouble me again, that within a few days I shall be cured, and shall come to pay you my respects in person. Meanwhile I shall spend at least two hours a day in studying two of your drawings, which Pierantonio brought me : the more I look at them, the more they delight me ; and I shall soothe my complaint by cherishing the hope which Pierantonio gave me, of letting me see other things of yours. In order not to be troublesome, I will write no more. Only I beg you remember, on occasion, to make use of me ; and recommend myself in perpetuity to you.—Your most affectionate servant, "THOMAO CAVALIERE."

The next letters were addressed to Michelangelo in Florence :—

"Unique, my Lord,—I have received from you a letter, very acceptable, from which I gather that you are not a little saddened at my having written to you about forgetting. I answer that I did not write this for either of the following reasons : to wit, because you have not sent me anything, or in order to fan the flame of your affection. I only wrote to jest with you, as certainly I think I may do. Therefore, do not be saddened, for I am quite sure you will not be able to forget me.[1] Regarding what you

---

[1] Springer, *Raffael und Michelangelo*, vol. ii. p. 300, calls special attention to this phrase, " not be able to forget me."

write to me about that young Nerli, he is much my
friend, and having to leave Rome, he came to ask
whether I needed anything from Florence. I said
no, and he begged me to allow him to go in my
name to pay you my respects, merely on account of
his own desire to speak with you. I have nothing
more to write, except that I beg you to return
quickly. When you come you will deliver me from
prison, because I wish to avoid bad companions;
and having this desire, I cannot converse with any
one but you. I recommend myself to you a thousand times.—Yours more than his own,

"THOMAO CAVALIERE.

"ROME, *August* 2, 1533."

It appears from the third letter, also sent to
Florence, that during the course of the month
Michelangelo had despatched some of the draw-
ings he made expressly for his friend :—

"Unique, my Lord,—Some days ago I received
a letter from you, which was very welcome, both
because I learned from it that you were well, and
also because I can now be sure that you will soon
return. I was very sorry not to be able to answer
at once. However, it consoles me to think that,
when you know the cause, you will hold me excused. On the day your letter reached me, I was
attacked with vomiting and such high fever that
I was on the point of death ; and certainly I should
have died, if it (*i.e.*, the letter) had not somewhat

revived me. Since then, thank God, I have been always well. Messer Bartolomeo (Angiolini) has now brought me a sonnet sent by you, which has made me feel it my duty to write. Some three days since I received my Phaethon, which is exceedingly well done. The Pope, the Cardinal de' Medici, and every one, have seen it; I do not know what made them want to do so. The Cardinal expressed a wish to inspect all your drawings, and they pleased him so much that he said he should like to have the Tityos and Ganymede done in crystal. I could not manage to prevent him from using the Tityos, and it is now being executed by Maestro Giovanni. Hard I struggled to save the Ganymede. The other day I went, as you requested, to Fra Sebastiano. He sends a thousand messages, but only to pray you to come back.—Your affectionate,

"THOMAO CAVALIERE.

"ROME, *September 6.*"

All the drawings mentioned by Vasari as having been made for Cavalieri are alluded to here, except the Bacchanal of Children. Of the Phaethon we have two splendid examples in existence, one at Windsor, the other in the collection of M. Emile Galichon.[1] They differ considerably in details, but have the same almost mathematical exactitude of pyramidal composition. That belonging to M. Galichon must

[1] Engraved in *L'Œuvre et la Vie,* p. 266. It is said that all Michelangelo's drawings in the possession of Cavalieri passed for the sum of 500 crowns into the hands of Cardinal Farnese. Vasari, xii. p. 272, note 4.

have been made in Rome, for it has this rough
scrawl in Michelangelo's hand at the bottom,
"Tomao, se questo scizzo non vi piace, ditelo a
Urbino." He then promises to make another. Perhaps Cavalieri sent word back that he did not like
something in the sketch — possibly the women
writhing into trees—and that to this circumstance
we owe the Windsor drawing, which is purer in
style. There is a fine Tityos with the vulture
at Windsor, so exquisitely finished and perfectly
preserved that one can scarcely believe it passed
through the hands of Maestro Giovanni. Windsor,
too, possesses a very delicate Ganymede, which
seems intended for an intaglio.[1] The subject is
repeated in an unfinished pen-design at the Uffizi,
incorrectly attributed to Michelangelo, and is represented by several old engravings. The Infant
Bacchanals again exist at Windsor, and fragmentary
jottings upon the margin of other sketches intended for the same theme survive.

VI.

A correspondence between Bartolommeo Angelini
in Rome and Michelangelo in Florence during the

[1] There is another pen-and-ink sketch of Jupiter, embracing Cupid,
at Oxford, which Mr. Fagan, in his *Catalogue of Drawings in Great
Britain*, identifies with the one designed for Cavalieri. But, as Vasari
distinctly talks of a Rape of Ganymede in black or red chalk, preference
must be given to the Windsor drawing.

summers of 1532 and 1533 throws some light upon the latter's movements, and also upon his friendship for Tommaso Cavalieri.[1] The first letter of this series, written on the 21st of August 1532, shows that Michelangelo was then expected in Rome. "Fra Sebastiano says that you wish to dismount at your own house. Knowing then that there is nothing but the walls, I hunted up a small amount of furniture, which I have had sent thither, in order that you may be able to sleep and sit down and enjoy some other conveniences. For eating, you will be able to provide yourself to your own liking in the neighbourhood."[2] From the next letter (September 18, 1532) it appears that Michelangelo was then in Rome.[3] There ensues a gap in the

[1] There are eleven autograph letters from Angelini belonging to this epoch in the Museo Buonarroti. Unfortunately, we possess only the fragment of one of Michelangelo's in reply. In the Appendix I shall print all Angelini's letters, which were transcribed for me by the great kindness of my friend Cavaliere Biagi.

[2] Compare the amusing letter from Sebastiano del Piombo (*Les Correspondants*, p. 102) about Michelangelo's empty house at Rome. It appears that a *sbirro* was put in charge of it, just as we put in a policeman as caretaker. Pierantonio also, in one of his inedited letters, speaks of having mellowed this *sbirro's* heart with wine, in order to get something carried out about the marbles in the workshop.

[3] I gather this because the autograph is neither dated nor addressed as though to be sent through the post. This is almost a sure sign that it was composed by its writer in Rome to Michelangelo in Rome, and sent by a messenger. Guasti refers to a letter from Bugiardini to Michelangelo in Rome, dated August 5, 1532, on the back of which is written the Sonnet "Se un casto amor," *Rime*, p. 190. This date, which is, however, correct, hardly agrees with Angelini's letter above quoted, and is at variance with Sebastiano's above quoted, which is dated August 13, 1532. Michelangelo was in Florence then, and his house in Rome empty.

correspondence, which is not resumed until July
12, 1533. It now appears that Buonarroti had
recently left Rome at the close of another of his
visits. Angelini immediately begins to speak of
Tommaso Cavalieri. "I gave that soul you wot of
to M. Tommao, who sends you his very best regards,
and begs me to communicate any letters I may receive from you to him. Your house is watched
continually every night, and I often go to visit it by
day. The hens and master cock are in fine feather,
and the cats complain greatly over your absence,
albeit they have plenty to eat." Angelini never
writes now without mentioning Cavalieri. Since
this name does not occur in the correspondence
before the date of July 12, 1533, it is possible that
Michelangelo made the acquaintance during his residence at Rome in the preceding winter. His letters
to Angelini must have conveyed frequent expressions of anxiety concerning Cavalieri's affection ; for
the replies invariably contain some reassuring words
(July 26) : "Yours makes me understand how great
is the love you bear him; and in truth, so far as I
have seen, he does not love you less than you love
him." Again (August 11, 1533) : "I gave your letter
to M. Thomao, who sends you his kindest remem-
brances, and shows the very strongest desire for
your return, saying that when he is with you, then
he is really happy, because he possesses all that he
wishes for upon this world. So then, it seems to
me that, while you are fretting to return, he is burn-

ing with desire for you to do so. Why do you not begin in earnest to make plans for leaving Florence? It would give peace to yourself and all of us, if you were here. I have seen your soul, which is in good health and under good guardianship. The body waits for your arrival."

This mysterious reference to the soul, which Angelini gave, at Buonarroti's request, to young Cavalieri, and which he now describes as prospering, throws some light upon the passionate phrases of the following mutilated letter, addressed to Angelini by Michelangelo upon the 11th of October.[1] The writer, alluding to Messer Tommao, says that, having given him his heart, he can hardly go on living in his absence: "And so, if I yearn day and night without intermission to be in Rome, it is only in order to return again to life, which I cannot enjoy without the soul." This conceit is carried on for some time, and the letter winds up with the following sentence: "My dear Bartolommeo, although you may think that I am joking with you, this is not the case. I am talking sober sense, for I have grown twenty years older and twenty pounds lighter since I have been here." This epistle, as we shall see in due course, was acknowledged. All Michelangelo's intimates in Rome became acquainted with the details of this friendship. Writing to Sebastiano from Florence in this year, he says:[2] "I beg you, if you see Messer T. Cavalieri, to recommend me to him

[1] Lettere, No. cdxviii. p. 469.   [2] Ibid., No. cdxv.

infinitely ; and when you write, tell me something about him to keep him in my memory ; for if I were to lose him from my mind, I believe that I should fall down dead straightway." In Sebastiano's letters there is one allusion to Cavalieri, who had come to visit him in the company of Bartolommeo Angelini, when he was ill.[1]

It is not necessary to follow all the references to Tommaso Cavalieri contained in Angelini's letters.[2] They amount to little more than kind messages and warm wishes for Michelangelo's return. Soon, however, Michelangelo began to send poems, which Angelini acknowledges (September 6): " I have received the very welcome letter you wrote me, together with your graceful and beautiful sonnet, of which I kept a copy, and then sent it on to M. Thomao. He was delighted to possess it, being thereby assured that God has deigned to bestow upon him the friendship of a man endowed with so many noble gifts as you are." Again he writes (October 18): " Yours of the 12th is to hand, together with M. Thomao's letter and the most beautiful sonnets. I have kept copies, and sent them on to him for whom they were intended, because I know with what affection he regards all things that pertain to you. He promised to send an answer which shall be enclosed in this I now am writing. He is counting not the days merely, but the hours, till you return." In another letter, without date, Angelini says, " I

---

[1] *Les Correspondants*, p. 114.   [2] Dates, August 21, 23, 30, 1533.

gave your messages to M. Thomao, who replied that your presence would be dearer to him than your writing, and that if it seems to you a thousand years, to him it seems ten thousand, till you come. I received your gallant (galante) and beautiful sonnet; and though you said nothing about it, I saw at once for whom it was intended, and gave it to him. Like everything of yours, it delighted him. The tenor of the sonnet shows that love keeps you perpetually restless. I do not think this ought to be the effect of love, and so I send you one of my poor performances to prove the contrary opinion." We may perhaps assume that this sonnet was the famous No. xxxi., from the last line of which every one could perceive that Michelangelo meant it for Tommaso Cavalieri.

VII.

It is significant that, while Michelangelo's affection for the young Roman was thus acquiring force, another friendship, which must have once been very dear to him, sprang up and then declined, but not apparently through his own fault or coldness. We hear of Febo di Poggio in the following autumn for the first and last time. Before proceeding to speak of him, I will wind up what has to be said about Tommaso Cavalieri. Not long after the date of the last letter quoted above, Michelangelo returned to

Rome, and settled there for the rest of his life. He
continued to the end of his days in close friendship
with Cavalieri, who helped to nurse him during his
last illness, who took charge of his effects after his
death, and who carried on the architectural work he
had begun at the Capitol.

Their friendship seems to have been uninterrupted
by any disagreement, except on one occasion when
Michelangelo gave way to his suspicious irritability,
quite at the close of his long life. This drew forth
from Cavalieri the following manly and touching
letter :—

" Very magnificent, my Lord,—I have noticed during several days past that you have some grievance—
what, I do not know—against me. Yesterday I became certain of it when I went to your house. As I
cannot imagine the cause, I have thought it best to
write this, in order that, if you like, you may inform
me. I am more than positive that I never offended
you. But you lend easy credence to those whom
perhaps you ought least to trust ; and some one has
possibly told you some lie, for fear I should one day
reveal the many knaveries done under your name,
the which do you little honour ; and if you desire
to know about them, you shall. Only I cannot,
nor, if I could, should I wish to force myself—but
I tell you frankly that if you do not want me for
a friend, you can do as you like, but you cannot
compel me not to be a friend to you. I shall always
try to do you service ; and only yesterday I came to

show you a letter written by the Duke of Florence, and to lighten your burdens, as I have ever done until now. Be sure you have no better friend than me ; but on this I will not dwell. Still, if you think otherwise, I hope that in a short time you will explain matters ; and I know that you know I have always been your friend without the least interest of my own. Now I will say no more, lest I should seem to be excusing myself for something which does not exist, and which I am utterly unable to imagine. I pray and conjure you, by the love you bear to God, that you tell me what you have against me, in order that I may disabuse you. Not having more to write, I remain your servant,

"THOMAO DE' CAVALIERI.

"From my house, *November* 15, 1561." [1]

It is clear from this letter, and from the relations which subsisted between Michelangelo and Cavalieri up to the day of his death, that the latter was a gentleman of good repute and honour, whose affection did credit to his friend. I am unable to see that anything but an injury to both is done by explaining away the obvious meaning of the letters and the sonnets I have quoted. The supposition that Michelangelo intended the Cavalieri letters to reach Vittoria Colonna through that friend's hands does not, indeed, deserve the complete refutation

---

[1] See Appendix for the original.

which I have given it. I am glad, however, to be able to adduce the opinion of a caustic Florentine scholar upon this topic, which agrees with my own, and which was formed without access to the original documents which I have been enabled to make use of.[1] Fanfani says: "I have searched, but in vain, for documentary proofs of the passion which Michelangelo is supposed to have felt for Vittoria Colonna, and which she returned with ardour according to the assertion of some critics. My own belief, concurring with that of better judges than myself, is that we have here to deal with one of the many baseless stories told about him. Omitting the difficulties presented by his advanced age, it is wholly contrary to all we know about the Marchioness, and not a little damaging to her reputation for austerity, to suppose that this admirable matron, who, after the death of her husband, gave herself up to God, and abjured the commerce of the world, should, later in life, have carried on an intrigue, as the saying is, upon the sly, particularly when a third person is imposed on our credulity, acting the part of go-between and cloak in the transaction, as certain biographers of the great artist, and certain commentators of his poetry, are pleased to assert, with how much common-sense and what seriousness I will not ask."

---

[1] *Spigolatura Michelangiolesca*, P. Fanfani. Pistoja : Tip. Cino, 1876, p. x.

VIII.

The history of Luigi del Riccio's affection for a lad of Florence called Cecchino dei Bracci, since this is interwoven with Michelangelo's own biography and the criticism of his poems, may be adduced in support of the argument I am developing. Cecchino was a youth of singular promise and personal charm. His relative, the Florentine merchant, Luigi del Riccio, one of Buonarroti's most intimate friends and advisers, became devotedly attached to the boy. Michelangelo, after his return to Rome in 1534, shared this friend Luigi's admiration for Cecchino; and the close intimacy into which the two elder men were drawn, at a somewhat later period of Buonarroti's life, seems to have been cemented by their common interest in poetry, and their common feeling for a charming personality. We have a letter of uncertain date, in which Michelangelo tells Del Riccio that he has sent him a madrigal, begging him, if he thinks fit, to commit the verses "to the fire—that is, to what consumes me."[1] Then he asks him to resolve a certain problem which has occurred to his mind during the night, "for while I was saluting *our idol* in a dream, it seemed to me that he laughed, and in the same instant threatened me; and not knowing which of these two moods I have to abide by, I beg you to find out from him; and on

[1] Lettere, cdxxiii. p. 474.

Sunday, when we meet again, you will inform me."
Cecchino, who is probably alluded to in this letter,[1]
died at Rome on the 8th of January 1542, and was
buried in the Church of Araceli.[2] Luigi felt the
blow acutely. Upon the 12th of January he wrote
to his friend Donato Giannotti, then at Vicenza, in
the following words :—

" Alas, my friend Donato ! Our Cecchino is dead.
All Rome weeps. Michelangelo is making for me
the design of a decent sepulture in marble ; and I
pray you to write me the epitaph, and to send it to
me with a consolatory letter, if time permits, for my
grief has distraught me. Patience ! I live with a
thousand and a thousand deaths each hour. O
God ! How has Fortune changed her aspect ! "[3]
Giannotti replied, enclosing three fine sonnets, the
second of which, beginning—

> Messer Luigi mio, di noi che fia
> Che sian restati senza il nostro sole ?

seems to have taken Michelangelo's fancy.[4] Many
good pens in Italy poured forth laments on this
occasion. We have verses written by Giovanni Aldo-

---

[1] In a sonnet of lamentation written after Cecchino's death, Luigi
addressed him as " Idol mio."

[2] " D.O.M. Francisco Braccio Florentino, nobili adolescenti, imma-
tura morte prærepto, annos agenti xvi., die viii. Jan. mdlxiv. M.M.V.
Aloysius del Riccio affini et alumno dulcissimo D.

> Invida fata, puer, mihi te rapuere ; sed ipse
> Do tumulum et lacrymas, quæ dare debueras."

—*Op. di Donato Giannotti*, Firenze : Le Monnier, vol. i. p. l.

[3] D. Giannotti, ibid., p. 382.

[4] Lettere, cdxliv. The manuscript is in the Arch. Buon., Cod. xiii. 187.

brandini, Carlo Gondi, Fra Paolo del Rosso, and
Anton Francesco Grazzini, called Il Lasca.[1] Not
the least touching is Luigi's own threnody, which
starts upon this note :—

> Idol mio, che la tua leggiadra spoglia
> Mi lasciasti anzi tempo.

Michelangelo, seeking to indulge his own grief and
to soothe that of his friend Luigi, composed no less
than forty-two epigrams of four lines each, in which
he celebrated the beauty and rare personal sweetness of Cecchino in laboured philosophical conceits.
They rank but low among his poems, having too
much of scholastic trifling and too little of the
accent of strong feeling in them. Certainly these
pieces did not deserve the pains which Michelangelo
the younger bestowed, when he altered the text of
a selection from them so as to adapt their Platonic
compliments to some female.[2] Far superior is a
sonnet written to Del Riccio upon the death of the
youth, showing how recent had been Michelangelo's
acquaintance with Cecchino, and containing an unfulfilled promise to carve his portrait :[3]—

> Scarce had I seen for the first time his eyes,
>   Which to your living eyes were life and light,
>   When, closed at last in death's injurious night,
>   He opened them on God in Paradise.

---

[1] Lettere, cdxliv. pp. 385–387.

[2] *Rime di Michelangelo Buonarroti*, ed. Barbèra, p. 342.

[3] My version, Sonnet viii. There is an autograph copy of the sonnet
in the Cod. Vat., p. 33. Underneath it is written, "Cechin Bracci amato
da luigi del riccio."

I know it, and I weep—too late made wise :
   Yet was the fault not mine ; for death's fell spite
   Robbed my desire of that supreme delight
   Which in your better memory never dies.
Therefore, Luigi, if the task be mine
   To make unique Cecchino smile in stone
   For ever, now that earth hath made him dim,
If the beloved within the lover shine,
   Since art without him cannot work alone,
   You must I carve to tell the world of him.

The strange blending of artificial conceits with
spontaneous feeling in these poetical effusions, the
deep interest taken in a mere lad like Cecchino by
so many eminent personages, and the frank publicity
given to a friendship based apparently upon the
beauty of its object, strike us now as almost unintelligible.   Yet we have the history of Shakespeare's
Sonnets, and the letters addressed by Languet to
young Sidney, in evidence that fashion at the end
of the sixteenth century differed widely from that
which prevails at the close of the nineteenth.

IX.

Some further light may here be thrown upon
Michelangelo's intimacy with young men by two
fragments extracted independently from the Buonarroti Archives by Milanesi and Guasti.   In the
collection of the letters we find the following sorrow-

ful epistle, written in December 1533, upon the eve
of Michelangelo's departure from Florence.   It is
addressed to a certain Febo : [1]—

"FEBO,—Albeit you bear the greatest hatred toward my person—I know not why—I scarcely believe,
because of the love I cherish for you, but probably
through the words of others, to which you ought to
give no credence, having proved me—yet I cannot
do otherwise than write to you this letter.   I am
leaving Florence to-morrow, and am going to Pescia
to meet the Cardinal di Cesis and Messer Baldassare.
I shall journey with them to Pisa, and thence to
Rome, and I shall never return again to Florence.
I wish you to understand that, so long as I live,
wherever I may be, I shall always remain at your
service with loyalty and love, in a measure unequalled by any other friend whom you may have
upon this world.

"I pray God to open your eyes from some other
quarter, in order that you may come to comprehend
that he who desires your good more than his own
welfare, is able to love, not to hate like an enemy."

Milanesi prints no more of the manuscript in his edition of the Letters.   But Guasti, conscientiously collecting fragments of Michelangelo's verses, gives six
lines, which he found at the foot of the epistle : [2]—

[1] Lettere, cdxx. p. 471.

[2] Rime, p. 309. Surprised by the tone of these verses and the letter,
Guasti suggests that, under Febo, Michelangelo may have intended to
address Florence. Ibid., p. xix. Of course we must suppose that Guasti
had not seen Febo's answer to the letter, dated January 14, 1534, which

Vo' sol del mie morir contento veggio :
　　La terra piange, e 'l ciel per me si muove ;
　　E vo' men pietà stringe ov' io sto peggio.
O sol che scaldi il mondo in ogni dove,
　　O Febo, o luce eterna de' mortali,
　　Perchè a me sol ti scuri e non altrove ?

Naught comforts you, I see, unless I die :
　　Earth weeps, the heavens for me are moved to woe ;
　　You feel of grief the less, the more grieve I.
O sun that warms the world where'er you go,
　　O Febo, light eterne for mortal eyes !
　　Why dark to me alone, elsewhere not so ?

These verses seem to have been written as part of a long Capitolo which Michelangelo himself, the elder, used indifferently in addressing Febo and his abstract " donna." [1] Who Febo was, we do not

will be cited below. W. Lang, the German exponent of Michelangelo's poetry, adopted the hypothesis. Von Scheffler, who also had no access to the Arch. Buon., thinks that Cavalieri was here addressed under the *alias* of Febo. These evasions of a difficulty which does not really exist are even more grotesque than the hypothesis about the Cavalieri correspondence, which I have exploded.

[1] In the autograph collection of Michelangelo's poems (Arch. Buon.) we have three separate handlings of the opening stanzas. One is addressed directly to Febo di Poggio, and begins, as above—

" Vo' sol del mie morir contento veggio."

Another preserves five rhymes out of the first six, with this alteration—

" Contenta del mie mal te sola veggio."

It is written on the back of a letter from Il Topolino, April 4, 1524, Arch. Buon., Cod. vii. No. 205, and may possibly be the earliest draft. I may add here that the Cod. Vat. (p. 4) contains the same first line, " Te sola del mio male contenta veggio," at the beginning of a madrigal. The third runs thus :—

" Te sola del mie mal contenta veggio."

Michelangelo junior, in his copy of the third variant, writes upon the

know. But the sincere accent of the letter and the lyric cry of the rough lines leave us to imagine that he was some one for whom Michelangelo felt very tenderly in Florence.

Milanesi prints this letter to Febo with the following title, "*A Febo (di Poggio).*" This proves that he at any rate knew it had been answered by some one signing "Febo di Poggio." The autograph, in an illiterate hand and badly spelt, is preserved among the Buonarroti Archives, and bears date January 14, 1534.[1] Febo excuses himself for not having been able to call on Michelangelo the night before he left Florence, and professes to have come the next day and found him already gone. He adds that he is in want of money, both to buy clothes and to go to see the games upon the Monte. He prays for a gratuity, and winds up : " Vostro da figliuolo (yours like a son), Febo di Poggio." I will add a full translation here, and print the original in the Appendix :—

" Magnificent M. Michelangelo, to be honoured as

margin the lines to Febo, with this comment, "Altrimente e peggio." His own *rifacimento* of the Capitolo starts with a new line and rhyme :—

" Poi che d' ogni mia speme il verde è spento."

Accepted in its latest and altered fashion, it has of course been assigned to the Vittoria Colonna series. Michelangelo's own habit of changing the sex occasionally in his poems makes their criticism, as regards this point, difficult. The stanzas, for instance, entitled " Alla sua Donna" (*Rime*, p. 329) start, according to all appearance, as an address to a man, and then change.

[1] Codex, viii. c. 303. The date, according to Florentine reckoning, corresponds to our Jan. 14, 1535.

a father,—I came back yesterday from Pisa, whither I had gone to see my father. Immediately upon my arrival, that friend of yours at the bank put a letter from you into my hands, which I received with the greatest pleasure, having heard of your well-being. God be praised, I may say the same about myself. Afterwards I learned what you say about my being angry with you. You know well I could not be angry with you, since I regard you in the place of a father. Besides, your conduct toward me has not been of the sort to cause in me any such effect. That evening when you left Florence, in the morning I could not get away from M. Vincenzo, though I had the greatest desire to speak with you.[1] Next morning I came to your house, and you were already gone, and great was my disappointment at your leaving Florence without my seeing you.

"I am here in Florence ; and when you left, you told me that if I wanted anything, I might ask it of that friend of yours ; and now that M. Vincenzo is away, I am in want of money, both to clothe myself, and also to go to the Monte, to see those people fighting, for M. Vincenzo is there. Accordingly, I went to visit that friend at the bank, and he told me that he had no commission whatsoever from you ; but that a messenger was starting to-night for Rome, and that an answer could come back within five days. So then, if you give him

---

[1] We may perhaps conjecture that this was Vincenzo Perini.

orders, he will not fail. I beseech you, then, to
provide and assist me with any sum you think fit,
and do not fail to answer.

"I will not write more, except that with all my
heart and power I recommend myself to you, praying
God to keep you from harm.—Yours in the place of
a son,   "FEBO DI POGGIO.

"FLORENCE, *January* 4, 1534."

X.

In all the compositions I have quoted as illustrative of Michelangelo's relations with young men,
there is a singular humility which gives umbrage to
his editors. The one epistle to Gerardo Perini, cited
above, contains the following phrases: "I do not
feel myself of force enough to correspond to your
kind letter;" "Your most faithful and poor friend."[2]
Yet there was nothing extraordinary in Cavalieri,
Cecchino, Febo, or Perini, except their singularity
of youth and grace, good parts and beauty. The
vulgar are offended when an illustrious man pays
homage to these qualities, forgetful of Shakespeare's self-abasement before Mr. W. H. and of
Languet's prostration at the feet of Sidney. In

---

[1] See above, p. 119, note 2, for the poems which seem to have been
addressed to this Febo.

[2] Lettere, No. ccclxxvi. p. 418.

the case of Michelangelo, we may find a solution
of this problem, I think, in one of his sonnets.
He says, writing a poem belonging very probably to
the series which inspired Michelangelo the younger
with alarm : [1]—

> As one who will re-seek her home of light,
>   Thy form immortal to this prison-house
>   Descended, like an angel piteous,
>   To heal all hearts and make the whole world bright.
> 'Tis this that thralls my soul in love's delight,
>   Not thy clear face of beauty glorious;
>   For he who harbours virtue still will choose
>   To love what neither years nor death can blight.
> So fares it ever with things high and rare
>   Wrought in the sweat of nature; heaven above
>   Showers on their birth the blessings of her prime:
> Nor hath God deigned to show Himself elsewhere
>   More clearly than in human forms sublime,
>   Which, since they image Him, alone I love.

It was not, then, to this or that young man, to this
or that woman, that Michelangelo paid homage, but
to the eternal beauty revealed in the mortal image
of divinity before his eyes. The attitude of the
mind, the quality of passion, implied in these poems,
and conveyed more clumsily through the prose of
the letters, may be difficult to comprehend. But
until we have arrived at seizing them we shall fail
to understand the psychology of natures like Michel-

[1] No. lvi. in my version of the sonnets; this and the four which
precede it, and those which follow down to lxi., ought to be carefully
studied by those who do not comprehend the reverent sense of physical
beauty felt by men like Michelangelo.

angelo.   No language of admiration is too strong,
no self-humiliation too complete, for a soul which
has recognised deity made manifest in one of its
main attributes, beauty.   In the sight of a philo-
sopher, a poet, and an artist, what are kings, popes,
people of importance, compared with a really perfect
piece of God's handiwork ?

> From thy fair face I learn, O my loved lord,
>   That which no mortal tongue can rightly say ;
>   The soul imprisoned in her house of clay,
>   Holpen by thee, to God hath often soared.
> And though the vulgar, vain, malignant horde
>   Attribute what their grosser wills obey,
>   Yet shall this fervent homage that I pay,
>   This love, this faith, pure joys for us afford.
> Lo, all the lovely things we find on earth,
>   Resemble for the soul that rightly sees
>   That source of bliss divine which gave us birth :
> Nor have we first-fruits or remembrances
>   Of heaven elsewhere.   Thus, loving loyally,
>   I rise to God, and make death sweet by thee.

We know that, in some way or other, perhaps
during those early years at Florence among the
members of the Platonic Academy, Michelangelo
absorbed the doctrines of the *Phædrus* and *Symposium*.   His poems abound in references to the contrast between Uranian and Pandemic, celestial and
vulgar, Eros.   We have even one sonnet in which
he distinctly states the Greek opinion that the love
of women is unworthy of a soul bent upon high
thoughts and virile actions.   It reads like a verse

transcript from the main argument of the *Sym posium* :[1]—

> Love is not always harsh and deadly sin,
> > When love for boundless beauty makes us pine;
> > The heart, by love left soft and infantine,
> > Will let the shafts of God's grace enter in.
> Love wings and wakes the soul, stirs her to win
> > Her flight aloft, nor e'er to earth decline;
> > 'Tis the first step that leads her to the shrine
> > Of Him who slakes the thirst that burns within.
> The love of that whereof I speak ascends:
> > Woman is different far ; the love of her
> > But ill befits a heart manly and wise.
> The one love soars, the other earthward tends;
> > The soul lights this, while that the senses stir;
> > And still lust's arrow at base quarry flies.

The same exalted Platonism finds obscure but impassioned expression in this fragment of a sonnet (No. lxxix.) :—

> For Love's fierce wound, and for the shafts that harm,
> > True medicine 'twould have been to pierce my heart;
> > But my soul's Lord owns only one strong charm,
> > Which makes life grow where grows life's mortal smart.
> My Lord dealt death, when with his powerful arm
> > He bent Love's bow.   Winged with that shaft, from Love
> > An angel flew, cried, " Love, nay Burn !   Who dies,
> > Hath but Love's plumes whereby to soar above !

---

[1] *Rime,* Sonnet liii.   The terzets in the Italian are as follows :—

> L'amor di quel ch' io parlo in alto aspira ;
> > Donna è dissimil troppo, e mal conviensi
> > Arder di quella al cor saggio e virile.
> L'un tira al cielo, e l'altro in terra tira ;
> > Nell' alma l'un, l'altro abita ne' sensi,
> > E l'arco tira a cose basse e vile.

Lo, I am He who from thine earliest years
Toward heaven-born Beauty raised thy faltering eyes.
Beauty alone lifts live man to heaven's spheres."

Feeling like this, Michelangelo would have been justly indignant with officious relatives and critics, who turned his *amici* into *animi*, redirected his Cavalieri letters to the address of Vittoria Colonna, discovered Florence in Febo di Poggio, and ascribed all his emotional poems to some woman.

There is no doubt that both the actions and the writings of contemporaries justified a considerable amount of scepticism regarding the purity of platonic affections. The words and lives of many illustrious persons gave colour to what Segni stated in his History of Florence, and what Savonarola found it necessary to urge upon the people from his pulpit.[1] But we have every reason to feel certain that, in a malicious age, surrounded by jealous rivals, with the fierce light of his transcendent glory beating round his throne, Buonarroti suffered from no scandalous reports, and maintained an untarnished character for sobriety of conduct and purity of morals.

The general opinion regarding him may be gathered

---

[1] See my *Renaissance in Italy*, vol. i. p. 435, vol. v. p. 365. A singular example of Italian sentiment and custom might be quoted from one of Michelangelo's own letters, addressed in 1518 to his friend Niccolò Quarantesi, Lettere, No. cccliii. It refers to a man who was very anxious that his son should be taken into the great sculptor's service. He did not want him, and told the father so : " E lui non la intese, ma rispose, che se io lo vedessi, che non che in casa, io me lo caccerei nel letto. Io vi dico che rinunzio a questa consolazione, e non la voglio tòrre a lui."

from Scipione Ammirati's History (under the year
1564). This annalist records the fact that "Buonarroti having lived for ninety years, there was never
found through all that length of time, and with
all that liberty to sin, any one who could with right
and justice impute to him a stain or any ugliness of
manners."

How he appeared to one who lived and worked
with him for a long period of intimacy, could not be
better set forth than in the warm and ingenuous
words of Condivi: "He has loved the beauty of
the human body with particular devotion, as is
natural with one who knows that beauty so com-
pletely; and has loved it in such wise that certain
carnally minded men, who do not comprehend the
love of beauty, except it be lascivious and indecorous,
have been led thereby to think and to speak evil of
him: just as though Alcibiades, that comeliest young
man, had not been loved in all purity by Socrates,
from whose side, when they reposed together, he was
wont to say that he arose not otherwise than from
the side of his own father.   Oftentimes have I
heard Michelangelo discoursing and expounding on
the theme of love, and have afterwards gathered
from those who were present upon these occasions
that he spoke precisely as Plato wrote, and as we
may read in Plato's works upon this subject. I, for
myself, do not know what Plato says; but I know
full well that, having so long and so intimately conversed with Michelangelo, I never once heard issue

from that mouth words that were not of the truest honesty, and such as had virtue to extinguish in the heart of youth any disordered and uncurbed desire which might assail it. I am sure, too, that no vile thoughts were born in him, by this token, that he loved not only the beauty of human beings, but in general all fair things, as a beautiful horse, a beautiful dog, a beautiful piece of country, a beautiful plant, a beautiful mountain, a beautiful wood, and every site or thing in its kind fair and rare, admiring them with marvellous affection. This was his way; to choose what is beautiful from nature, as bees collect the honey from flowers, and use it for their purpose in their workings: which indeed was always the method of those masters who have acquired any fame in painting. That old Greek artist, when he wanted to depict a Venus, was not satisfied with the sight of one maiden only. On the contrary, he sought to study many; and culling from each the particular in which she was most perfect, to make use of these details in his Venus. Of a truth, he who imagines to arrive at any excellence without following this system (which is the source of a true theory in the arts), shoots very wide indeed of his mark." [1]

Condivi perhaps exaggerated the influence of lovely nature, horses, dogs, flowers, hills, woods, &c., on Michelangelo's genius. His work, as we know, is singularly deficient in motives drawn from any province but human beauty; and his poems

[1] Condivi, lxiv. pp. 79–81.

and letters contain hardly a trace of sympathy with
the external world. Yet, in the main contention,
Condivi told the truth. Michelangelo's poems and
letters, and the whole series of his works in fresco
and marble, suggest no single detail which is
sensuous, seductive, enfeebling to the moral principles. Their tone may be passionate; it is indeed
often red-hot with a passion like that of Lucretius
and Beethoven; but the genius of the man trans-
ports the mind to spiritual altitudes, where the lust
of the eye and the longings of the flesh are left
behind us in a lower region. Only a soul attuned
to the same chord of intellectual rapture can
breathe in that fiery atmosphere and feel the vibra-
tions of its electricity.[1]

[1] The views which I have expressed in this chapter regarding the
real nature of Michelangelo's friendship with Vittoria Colonna, his
emotion for Tommaso Cavalieri, and other topics bearing on these ques-
tions, were formed quite independently. My study of the original
documents made me feel it a duty to dispose of the theories advanced by
Guasti, Milanesi, and Gotti. But when the manuscript of my book was
already in the printer's hands, I further investigated the whole problem.
The fanciful hypotheses of W. Lang, the false interpretations of Anton
Springer, had to be considered. Then I obtained by accident a little
book by Parlagreco, which Lombroso has adopted and condensed, and in
which Michelangelo's peculiar erotic temperament is considered as the
distinct sign of neurotic disease. Finally there fell into my hands a
very subtle and scientific treatise by Ludwig von Scheffler, published
this year in Germany, which strongly corroborates my own opinions.
It would have been ridiculous, in the face of all these writers, to refuse
the examination of the problem discussed in this chapter. In conclusion,
I request those readers who may desire further information to study
the separate essay or excursus which will be printed in the Appendix
immediately before the series of Angelini's, Cavalieri's, and Febo di
Poggio's original letters.

XI.

I have used Michelangelo's poems freely throughout this work as documents illustrative of his opinions and sentiments, and also in their bearing on the events of his life. I have made them reveal the man in his personal relations to Pope Julius II., to Vittoria Colonna, to Tommaso dei Cavalieri, to Luigi del Riccio, to Febo di Poggio. I have let them tell their own tale, when sorrow came upon him in the death of his father and Urbino, and when old age shook his lofty spirit with the thought of approaching death. I have appealed to them for lighter incidents: matters of courtesy, the completion of the Sistine vault, the statue of Night at S. Lorenzo, the subjection of Florence to the Medici, his heart-felt admiration for Dante's genius. Examples of his poetic work, so far as these can be applied to the explanation of his psychology, his theory of art, his sympathies, his feeling under several moods of passion, will consequently be found scattered up and down my volumes. Translation, indeed, is difficult to the writer, and unsatisfactory to the reader. But I have been at pains to direct an honest student to the original sources, so that he may, if he wishes, compare my versions with the text. Therefore I do not think it necessary to load this chapter with voluminous citations. Still, there remains something to be said about Michelangelo as poet, and about the place he occupies as poet in Italian literature.

The value of Michelangelo's poetry is rather psychological than purely literary. He never claimed to be more than an amateur, writing to amuse himself. His style is obscure, crabbed, ungrammatical. Expression only finds a smooth and flowing outlet when the man's nature is profoundly stirred by some powerful emotion, as in the sonnets to Cavalieri, or the sonnets on the deaths of Vittoria Colonna and Urbino, or the sonnets on the thought of his own death. For the most part, it is clear that he found great difficulty in mastering his thoughts and images. This we discover from the innumerable variants of the same madrigal or sonnet which he made, and his habit of returning to them at intervals long after their composition. A good fourth of the Codex Vaticanus consists of repetitions and *rifacimenti*. He was also wont to submit what he wrote to the judgment of his friends, requesting them to alter and improve. He often had recourse to Luigi del Riccio's assistance in such matters.[1] I may here adduce an inedited letter from two friends in Rome, Giovanni Francesco Bini and Giovanni Francesco Stella, who returned a poem they had handled in this manner:[2] "We

[1] See the notes to the madrigals in Guasti's *Rime.*

[2] Arch. Buon., Cod. vi. No. 93. "Noi ci siamo ingegnati di mutare alcune cose del vostro sonetto ma non di acconciarlo, peroche non ne avera molto bisogno. Hora ch' egli sia mutato o pur acconcio bene come per vostra humanità ricercate, questo sarà più giuditio vostro, che

have done our best to alter some things in your
sonnet, but not to set it all to rights, since there
was not much wanting. Now that it is changed
or put in order, according as the kindness of your
nature wished, the result will be more due to your
own judgment than to ours, since you have the true
conception of the subject in your mind. We shall
be greatly pleased if you find yourself as well served
as we earnestly desire that you should command us."
It was the custom of amateur poets to have recourse
to literary craftsmen before they ventured to circulate
their compositions. An amusing instance of this
will be found in Professor Biagi's monograph upon
Tullia d'Aragona, all of whose verses passed through
the crucible of Benedetto Varchi's revision.[1]

The thoughts and images out of which Michelangelo's poetry is woven are characteristically abstract and arid. He borrows no illustrations from
external nature. The beauty of the world and all
that lives in it might have been non-existent so far
as he was concerned. Nor do his octave stanzas in
praise of rural life form an exception to this statement; for these are imitated from Poliziano, so far
as they attempt pictures of the country, and their
chief poetical feature is the masque of vices belonging to human nature in the city.[2] His stock-in-

ne havete il vero soggetto nella mente. Ci sarà ben gran piacere che
voi restiate tanto servito quanto noi desideriamo che ci comandiate."

[1] "Un' Etéra Romana, Tullia d'Aragona." *Nuova Antologia*, vol. iv.,
August 1886.

[2] *Rime*, pp. 317-328.

trade consists of a few Platonic notions and a few
Petrarchan antitheses. In the very large number of
compositions which are devoted to love, this one
idea predominates : that physical beauty is a direct
beam sent from the eternal source of all reality, in
order to elevate the lover's soul and lead him on
the upward path toward heaven. Carnal passion he
regards with the aversion of an ascetic. It is impossible to say for certain to whom these mystical
love-poems were addressed. Whether a man or a
woman is in the case (for both were probably the
objects of his æsthetical admiration), the tone of
feeling, the language, and the philosophy do not
vary. He uses the same imagery, the same conceits,
the same abstract ideas for both sexes, and adapts
the leading motive which he had invented for a person
of one sex to a person of the other when it suits
his purpose. In our absolute incapacity to fix any
amative connection upon Michelangelo, or to link his
name with that of any contemporary beauty, we arrive
at the conclusion, strange as this may be, that the
greater part of his love-poetry is a scholastic exercise upon emotions transmuted into metaphysical
and mystical conceptions. Only two pieces in the
long series break this monotony by a touch of
realism. They are divided by a period of more
than thirty years. The first seems to date from an
early epoch of his life : [1]—

---

[1] *Rime*, Sonnetti Nos. xx., xxi. Compare the " Stanze alla sua Donna,"
ibid., pp. 329–336. Von Scheffler points out that Sonnet xx. was written

What joy hath yon glad wreath of flowers that is
Around her golden hair so deftly twined,
Each blossom pressing forward from behind,
As though to be the first her brows to kiss!
The livelong day her dress hath perfect bliss,
 That now reveals her breast, now seems to bind:
 And that fair woven net of gold refined
Rests on her cheek and throat in happiness!
Yet still more blissful seems to me the band,
 Gilt at the tips, so sweetly doth it ring,
 And clasp the bosom that it serves to lace:
Yea, and the belt, to such as understand,
 Bound round her waist, saith: Here I'd ever cling!
 What would my arms do in that girdle's place?

The second can be ascribed with probability to the year 1534 or 1535. It is written upon the back of a rather singular letter addressed to him by a certain Pierantonio, when both men were in Rome together:[1]—

---

at Bologna, where Michelangelo used to read Petrarch and the other Tuscan poets to his host Aldovrandi. He regards it as a stylistic exercise, not indicative of the author's real emotion.

[1] The conceit of this poem is taken from the silkworm. The letter which I have alluded to above, though it bears no date, having been sent by hand, must be assigned to the first or second year of Michelangelo's final residence in Rome. Pierantonio writes as follows: "Io sono istato il gorno pasato in grandissimo diletto fra quantità di giovani, e o mandato uno pedagogo al magnifico Messer Tomao (Cavalieri) per intendere chome ista, che risposegli mi dicessi istava meglio: del che si si pare una bona nova; et anchora m'a pregato quello de peruschi che io vadia a vedere certe sua pinture, onde io gli risposi che domane dopo magniare m'aspetasi, che averò charo servirlo in altro non chè in quello: che se a voi piacerà venire chome già pensamo, avremo un poco di baia che nesuno se ne potrà accorgere, e vedrete in fatti quello che più volte v'o deto in parole: io vero domattina alla M^{ca} Signoria Vostra e faremo quanto quella avrà choncurso.—Vostro minor servitore Pierantonio."

Kind to the world, but to itself unkind,
　　A worm is born, that, dying noiselessly,
　　Despoils itself to clothe fair limbs, and be
　　In its true worth alone by death divined.
Would I might die for my dear lord to find
　　Raiment in my outworn mortality :
　　That, changing like the snake, I might be free
　　To cast the slough wherein I dwell confined !
Nay, were it mine, that shaggy fleece that stays,
　　Woven and wrought into a vestment fair,
　　Around yon breast so beauteous in such bliss !
All through the day thou'd have me !　Would I were
　　The shoes that bear that burden ! when the ways
　　Were wet with rain, thy feet I then should kiss !

I have already alluded to the fact that we can trace two widely different styles of writing in Michelangelo's poetry. Some of his sonnets, like the two just quoted, and those we can refer with certainty to the Cavalieri series, together with occasional compositions upon the deaths of Cecchino and Urbino, seem to come straight from the heart, and their manuscripts offer few variants to the editor. Others,

Arch. Buon., Cod. x. No. 612. I have already referred to this Pierantonio, p. 133, note 1, above. The sonnet is composed with more than Michelangelo's usual spontaneity, and rings like those he wrote for Tommaso Cavalieri. But who inspired it, and whether it has any reference to Pierantonio himself, cannot be decided. The word *gonna*, which I have translated into *vestment*, probably must be taken in the sense in which it is twice used by Ariosto (*Orl. Fur.*, xvii. 49 and 51), for a doublet of furry skin. The context of the "shaggy fleece," *irsuta pelle*, seems to prove this. In old Italian *gonna* was applied to the tight-fitting jerkin worn by men next the skin. *Rimanere in gonna*, says the Della Crusca dictionary, is equivalent to being stripped to the shirt, *restare in farsetto, essere spogliato*. I am informed on good authority that *gonna* is still used by the Tuscan peasants for a skin pelisse worn by men.

of a different quality, where he is dealing with Platonic subtleties or Petrarchan conceits, have been twisted into so many forms, and tortured by such frequent re-handlings, that it is difficult now to settle a final text. The Codex Vaticanus is peculiarly rich in examples of these compositions. Madrigal lvii. and Sonnet lx., for example, recur with wearisome reiteration. These laboured and scholastic exercises, unlike the more spontaneous utterances of his feelings, are worked up into different forms, and the same conceits are not seldom used for various persons and on divers occasions.[1]

One of the great difficulties under which a critic labours in discussing these personal poems is that their chronology cannot be ascertained in the majority of instances. Another is that we are continually hampered by the false traditions invented by Michelangelo the younger. Books like Lannan Rolland s "Michel-Ange et Vittoria Colonna" have no value whatsoever, because they are based upon that unlucky grand-nephew's deliberately corrupted text.[2] Even Wordsworth's translations, fine as they are, have lost a large portion of their interest since the publication of the autographs by Cesare Guasti in 1863. It is certain that the younger Michelangelo meant well to his illustrious ancestor. He was

[1] See the instances given above regarding Cecchino dei Braccio and Vittoria Colonna (p. 123), Febo di Poggio and the abstract "donna" (p. 156).

[2] Yet this now superseded book was reprinted in 1875, Paris, Didier et Cie.

anxious to give his rugged compositions the elegance
and suavity of academical versification. He wished
also to defend his character from the imputation
of immorality. Therefore he rearranged the order
of stanzas in the longer poems, pieced fragments
together, changed whole lines, ideas, images, ampli-
fied and mutilated, altered phrases which seemed
to him suspicious. Only one who has examined the
manuscripts of the Buonarroti Archives knows what
pains he bestowed upon this ungrateful and disastrous
task. But the net result of his meddlesome benevolence is that now for nearly three centuries the
greatest genius of the Italian Renaissance has worn
a mask concealing the real nature of his emotion,
and that a false legend concerning his relations to
Vittoria Colonna has become inextricably interwoven
with the story of his life.

The extraordinary importance attached by Michelangelo in old age to the passions of his youth is
almost sufficient to justify those psychological inves-
tigators who regard him as the subject of a nervous
disorder. It does not seem to be accounted for
by anything known to us regarding his stern and
solitary life, his aloofness from the vulgar, and his
self-dedication to study. In addition to the splendid
devotional sonnets addressed to Vasari, which will
appear in their proper place, I may corroborate
these remarks by the translation of a set of three
madrigals bearing on the topic.[1]

<hr />

[1] *Rime,* Canzoni iii. pp. 347–349.

Ah me, ah me! how have I been betrayed
By my swift-flitting years, and by the glass,
Which yet tells truth to those who firmly gaze!
Thus happens it when one too long delays,
As I have done, nor feels time fleet and fade :—
One morn he finds himself grown old, alas!
To gird my loins, repent, my path repass,
Sound counsel take, I cannot, now death's near;
Foe to myself, each tear,
Each sigh, is idly to the light wind sent,
For there's no loss to equal time ill-spent.

Ah me, ah me! I wander telling o'er
Past years, and yet in all I cannot view
One day that might be rightly reckoned mine.
Delusive hopes and vain desires entwine
My soul that loves, weeps, burns, and sighs full sore.
Too well I know and prove that this is true,
Since of man's passions none to me are new.
Far from the truth my steps have gone astray,
In peril now I stay,
For, lo! the brief span of my life is o'er.
Yet, were it lengthened, I should love once more.

Ah me! I wander tired, and know not whither:
I fear to sight my goal, the years gone by
Point it too plain; nor will closed eyes avail.
Now Time hath changed and gnawed this mortal veil,
Death and the soul in conflict strive together
About my future fate that looms so nigh.
Unless my judgment greatly goes awry,
Which God in mercy grant, I can but see
Eternal penalty
Waiting my wasted will, my misused mind,
And know not, Lord, where health and hope to find.

After reading these lamentations, it is well to
remember that Michelangelo at times indulged a

sense of humour. As examples of his lighter vein, we might allude to the sonnet on the Sistine and the capitolo in answer to Francesco Berni, written in the name of Fra Sebastiano.[1] Sometimes his satire becomes malignant, as in the sonnet against the people of Pistoja, which breathes the spirit of Dantesque invective.[2] Sometimes the fierceness of it is turned against himself, as in the capitolo upon old age and its infirmities.[3] The grotesqueness of this lurid descant on senility and death is marked by something rather Teutonic than Italian, a "Danse Macabre" intensity of loathing; and it winds up with the bitter reflections, peculiar to him in his latest years, upon the vanity of art. "My much-prized art, on which I relied and which brought me fame, has now reduced me to this. I am poor and old, the slave of others. To the dogs I must go, unless I die quickly."

A proper conclusion to this chapter may be borrowed from the peroration of Varchi's discourse upon the philosophical love-poetry of Michelangelo. This time he chooses for his text the second of those sonnets (No. lii.) which caused the poet's grand-nephew so much perplexity, inducing him to alter the word *amici* in the last line into *animi*. It runs as follows [4] :—

---

[1] *Rime*, Sonnet v., and Capitolo i.
[2] *Rime*, Sonnet vi., p. 160.
[3] *Rime*, Capitolo ii., p. 294.
[4] *Rime*, p. cxi. Varchi's text is our only authority for the sonnet.

I saw no mortal beauty with these eyes
　　When perfect peace in thy fair eyes I found;
　　But far within, where all is holy ground,
　　My soul felt Love, her comrade of the skies:
For she was born with God in Paradise;
　　Else should we still to transient love be bound;
　　But, finding these so false, we pass beyond
　　Unto the Love of loves that never dies.
Nay, things that die cannot assuage the thirst
　　Of souls undying; nor Eternity
　　Serves Time, where all must fade that flourisheth.
Sense is not love, but lawlessness accurst:
　　This kills the soul; while our love lifts on high
　　Our friends on earth—higher in heaven through death.

"From this sonnet," says Varchi, "I think that any man possessed of judgment will be able to discern to what extent this angel, or rather archangel, in addition to his three first and most noble professions of architecture, sculpture, and painting, wherein without dispute he not only eclipses all the moderns, but even surpasses the ancients, proves himself also excellent, nay singular, in poetry, and in the true art of loving; the which art is neither less fair nor less difficult, albeit it be more necessary and more profitable than the other four. Whereof no one ought to wonder: for this reason; that, over and above what is manifest to everybody, namely that nature, desirous of exhibiting her utmost power, chose to fashion a complete man, and (as the Latins say) one furnished in all proper parts; he, in addition to the gifts of nature, of such sort and so liberally scattered, added such study

and a diligence so great that, even had he been by
birth most rugged, he might through these means
have become consummate in all virtue : and supposing he were born, I do not say in Florence and
of a very noble family, in the time too of Lorenzo
the Magnificent, who recognised, willed, knew, and
had the power to elevate so vast a genius ; but in
Scythia, of any stock or stem you like, under some
commonplace barbarian chief, a fellow not disdainful merely, but furiously hostile to all intellectual
ability ; still, in all circumstances, under any star,
he would have been Michelangelo, that is to say,
the unique painter, the singular sculptor, the most
perfect architect, the most excellent poet, and a
lover of the most divinest.   For the which reasons
I (it is now many years ago), holding his name not
only in admiration, but also in veneration, before I
knew that he was architect already, made a sonnet ;
with which (although it be as much below the
supreme greatness of his worth as it is unworthy
of your most refined and chastened ears) I mean
to close this present conference ; reserving the discussion on the arts (in obedience to our Consul's
orders) for another lecture.

Illustrious sculptor, 'twas enough and more,
Not with the chisel and bruised bronze alone,
But also with brush, colour, pencil, tone,
To rival, nay, surpass that fame of yore.
But now, transcending what those laurels bore
Of pride and beauty for our age and zone,

You climb of poetry the third high throne,
   Singing love's strife and peace, love's sweet and sore.
O wise, and dear to God, old man well born,
   Who in so many, so fair ways, make fair
   This world, how shall your dues be duly paid ?
Doomed by eternal charters to adorn
   Nature and art, yourself their mirror are ;
   None, first before, nor second after, made."

In the above translation of Varchi's peroration
I have endeavoured to sustain those long-winded
periods of which he was so perfect and professed a
master.   We must remember that he actually read
this dissertation before the Florentine Academy on
the second Sunday in Lent, in the year 1546, when
Michelangelo was still alive and hearty.   He afterwards sent it to the press ; and the studied trumpet-
tones of eulogy, conferring upon Michelangelo the
quintuple crown of pre-eminence in painting, sculpture, architecture, poetry, and loving, sounded from
Venice down to Naples.   The style of the oration
may strike us as *rococo* now, but the accent of
praise and appreciation is surely genuine.   Varchi's
enthusiastic comment on the sonnets xxx., xxxi., and
lii., published to men of letters, taste, and learning
in Florence and all Italy, is the strongest vindication
of their innocence against editors and scholars who
in various ways have attempted to disfigure or to
misconstrue them.

CHAPTER XIII.

angelo's design, except only in the cupola.—That is not finished in
all points as he wished it.—The rest of the church has been altered
wilfully.—Such vast undertakings in the art of building are fore-
doomed to incomplete accomplishment.

I.

THE correspondence which I used in the eleventh
chapter, while describing Michelangelo's difficulties
regarding the final contract with the Duke of
Urbino, proves that he had not begun to paint the
frescoes of the Cappella Paolina in October 1542.
They were carried on with interruptions during the
next seven years. These pictures, the last on which
his talents were employed, are two large subjects:
the Conversion of S. Paul, and the Martyrdom of
S. Peter. They have suffered from smoke and
other injuries of time even more than the frescoes
of the Sistine, and can now be scarcely appreciated
owing to discoloration. Nevertheless, at no period,
even when fresh from the master's hand, can they
have been typical of his style. It is true that
contemporaries were not of this opinion. Condivi
calls both of them "stupendous not only in the
general exposition of the histories but also in the
details of each figure."[1] It is also true that the
technical finish of these large compositions shows
a perfect mastery of painting, and that the great
designer has not lost his power of dealing at will

[1] Condivi, p. 64. *Cf.* Vasari, xii. p. 224.

with the human body. But the frigidity of old age
had fallen on his feeling and imagination. The
faces of his saints and angels here are more inex-
pressive than those of the Last Judgment. The
type of form has become still more rigidly schematic.
All those figures in violent attitudes have been
invented in the artist's brain without reference to
nature; and the activity of movement which he
means to suggest, is frozen, petrified, suspended.
The suppleness, the elasticity, the sympathy with
which Michelangelo handled the nude, when he
began to paint in the Sistine Chapel, have disappeared. We cannot refrain from regretting that
seven years of his energetic old age should have
been devoted to work so obviously indicative of
decaying faculties.

The Cappella Paolina ran a risk of destruction
by fire during the course of his operations there.
Michelangelo wrote to Del Riccio in 1545, reminding him that part of the roof had been consumed,
and that it would be necessary to cover it in roughly
at once, since the rain was damaging the frescoes
and weakening the walls.[1] When they were finished,
Paul III. appointed an official guardian with a fixed
salary, whose sole business it should be "to clean the
frescoes well and keep them in a state of cleanliness,
free from dust and other impurities, as also from
the smoke of candles lighted in both chapels during
divine service." This man had charge of the Sis-

[1] Lettere, No. cdliii.

tine as well as the Pauline Chapel; but his office does not seem to have been continued after the death of the Farnese. The first guardian nominated was Buonarroti's favourite servant Urbino.[1]

Vasari, after describing these frescoes in some detail, but without his customary enthusiasm, goes on to observe: "Michelangelo attended only, as I have elsewhere said, to the perfection of art. There are no landscapes, nor trees, nor houses; nor again do we find in his work that variety of movement and prettiness which may be noticed in the pictures of other men. He always neglected such decoration, being unwilling to lower his lofty genius to these details." That is indeed true of the arid desert of the Pauline frescoes. Then he adds: "They were his last productions in painting. He was seventy-five years old when he carried them to completion; and, as he informed me, he did so with great effort and fatigue—painting, after a certain age, and especially fresco-painting, not being in truth fit work for old men."[2]

The first of two acute illnesses, which showed that Michelangelo's constitution was beginning to give way, happened in the summer of 1544. On this occasion Luigi del Riccio took him into his own apartments at the Casa Strozzi; and here he nursed him with such personal devotion that the old man afterwards regarded Del Riccio as the

[1] Bottari, *Lett. Pitt.*, vol. vi. p. 37. No date.
[2] Vasari, xii. 225.

saviour of his life.   We learn this from the following pathetic sonnet : [1]—

> It happens that the sweet unfathomed sea
>   Of seeming courtesy sometimes doth hide
>   Offence to life and honour.   This descried,
>   I hold less dear the health restored to me.
> He who lends wings of hope, while secretly
>   He spreads a traitorous snare by the wayside,
>   Hath dulled the flame of love, and mortified
>   Friendship where friendship burns most fervently.
> Keep then, my dear Luigi, clear and pure,
>   That ancient love to which my life I owe,
>   That neither wind nor storm its calm may mar.
> For wrath and pain our gratitude obscure;
>   And if the truest truth of love I know,
>   One pang outweighs a thousand pleasures far.

Ruberto Strozzi, who was then in France, wrote
anxiously inquiring after his health.   In reply,
Michelangelo sent Strozzi a singular message by
Luigi del Riccio, to the effect that "if the king
of France restored Florence to liberty, he was
ready to make his statue on horseback out of
bronze at his own cost, and set it up in the
Piazza." [2]   This throws some light upon a passage
in a letter addressed subsequently to Lionardo

---

[1] No. vii. I feel inclined to refer this sonnet to a period of mis-
understanding between the two old friends, which will be duly noticed
in its proper place. It carries the tone of sought and accepted recon-
ciliation after the author's deepest feelings had been sharply wounded
by an apparent slight from his benefactor. See Lettere, No. cdlx., and
what I have said about the incident in this chapter, p. 192, below.

[2] Gaye, ii. 296. July 1544.

Buonarroti, when the tyrannous law, termed "La Polverina," enacted against malcontents by the Duke Cosimo de' Medici, was disturbing the minds of Florentine citizens.[1]   Michelangelo then wrote as follows : " I am glad that you gave me news of the edict ; because, if I have been careful up to this date in my conversation with exiles, I shall take more precautions for the future.   As to my having been laid up with an illness in the house of the Strozzi, I do not hold that I was in their house, but in the apartment of Messer Luigi del Riccio, who was my intimate friend ; and after the death of Bartolommeo Angelini, I found no one better able to transact my affairs, or more faithfully, than he did.   When he died, I ceased to frequent the house, as all Rome can bear me witness ; as they can also with regard to the general tenour of my life, inasmuch as I am always alone, go little around, and talk to no one, least of all to Florentines. When I am saluted on the open street, I cannot do less than respond with fair words and pass upon my way.   Had I knowledge of the exiles, who they are, I would not reply to them in any manner.   As I have said, I shall henceforward protect myself with diligence, the more that I have so much else to think about that I find it difficult to live."

This letter of 1548, taken in connection with the

---

[1] The law bore date March 11, 1548, and weighed heavily upon conspirators, rebels, and their heirs, who had sought to dislodge the Medici from power.   It owed its name to the man who drafted it, Jacopo Polverini of Prato.   The letter I refer to is No. cxcv.

circumstances of Michelangelo's illness in 1544, his exchange of messages with Ruberto degli Strozzi, his gift of the two Captives to that gentleman, and his presence in the house of the Strozzi during his recovery, shows the delicacy of the political situation at Florence under Cosimo's rule.[1]   Slight indications of a reactionary spirit in the aged artist exposed his family to peril.   Living in Rome, Michelangelo risked nothing with the Florentine government.   But " La Polverina " attacked the heirs of exiles in their property and persons.   It was therefore of importance to establish his non-complicity in revolutionary intrigues.   Luckily for himself and his nephew, he could make out a good case and defend his conduct. Though Buonarroti's sympathies and sentiments inclined him to prefer a republic in his native city, and though he threw his weight into that scale at the crisis of the siege, he did not forget his early obligations to the House of Medici.   Clement VII. accepted his allegiance when the siege was over, and set him immediately to work at the tasks he wished him to perform.   What is more, the Pope took pains and trouble to settle the differences between him and the Duke of Urbino.   The man had been no conspirator.   The architect and sculptor was coveted by every pope and prince in Italy. Still there remained a discord between his political

---

[1] The Strozzi, under their chieftain Filippo, whose plans failed at Montemurlo, and who died a prisoner at Florence, did all they could to upset the dukedom. There is no doubt, I think, that Michelangelo sympathised with their revolutionary ambition.

instincts, however prudently and privately indulged, and his sense of personal loyalty to the family at whose board he sat in youth, and to whom he owed his advancement in life.   Accordingly, we shall find that, though the Duke of Tuscany made advances to win him back to Florence, Michelangelo always preferred to live and die on neutral ground in Rome. Like the wise man that he was, he seems to have felt through these troublous times that his own duty, the service laid on him by God and nature, was to keep his force and mental faculties for art ; obliging old patrons in all kindly offices, suppressing republican aspirations—in one word, " sticking to his last," and steering clear of shoals on which the main raft of his life might founder.

From this digression, which was needful to explain his attitude toward Florence and part of his psychology, I return to the incidents of Michelangelo's illness at Rome in 1544.   Lionardo, having news of his uncle's danger, came post-haste to Rome.   This was his simple duty, as a loving relative.   But the old man, rendered suspicious by previous transactions with his family, did not take the action in its proper light.   We have a letter, indorsed by Lionardo in Rome as received upon the 11th of July, to this effect : [1] " Lionardo, I have been ill ; and you, at the instance of Ser Giovan Francesco (probably Fattucci), have come to make me dead, and to see what I have left.   Is there not enough of mine at Florence to

[1] Lettere, No. cxlix.

content you? You cannot deny that you are the
image of your father, who turned me out of my own
house in Florence. Know that I have made a will
of such tenour that you need not trouble your head
about what I possess at Rome. Go then with God,
and do not present yourself before me ; and do not
write to me again, and act like the priest in the fable.'

The correspondence between uncle and nephew
during the next months proves that this furious letter
wrought no diminution of mutual regard and affection. Before the end of the year he must have
recovered, for we find him writing to Del Riccio :[1]
"I am well again now, and hope to live yet some
years, seeing that God has placed my health under
the care of Maestro Baccio Rontini and the trebbian
wine of the Ulivieri." This letter is referred to
January 1545, and on the 9th of that month he
dictated a letter to his friend Del Riccio, in which
he tells Lionardo Buonarroti :[2] "I do not feel well,
and cannot write. Nevertheless I have recovered
from my illness, and suffer no pain now." We
have reason to think that Michelangelo fell gravely
ill again toward the close of 1545. News came
to Florence that he was dying; and Lionardo, not
intimidated by his experience on the last occasion,
set out to visit him. His *ricordo* of the journey
runs as follows :[3] "I note how on the 15th of

---

[1] Lettere, No. cdxlii.   [2] Ibid., No. clx.

[3] Lettere, p. 605. See Gotti, i. 299, for the second acute illness of
Michelangelo. Also compare the letter written to Lionardo on the 9th

January 1545 (Flor. style, *i.e.* 1546) I went to Rome by post to see Michelangelo, who was ill, and returned to-day, the 26th."

It is not quite easy to separate the records of these two acute illnesses of Michelangelo, falling between the summer of 1544 and the early spring of 1546. Still, there is no doubt that they signalised his passage from robust old age into a period of physical decline. Much of life survived in the hero yet; he had still to mould S. Peter's after his own mind, and to invent the cupola. Intellectually he suffered no diminution, but he became subject to a chronic disease of the bladder, and adopted habits suited to decaying faculty.

II.

We have seen that Michelangelo regarded Luigi del Riccio as his most trusty friend and adviser. The letters which he wrote to him during these years turn mainly upon business or poetical compositions. Some, however, throw light upon the private life of both men, and on the nature of their intimacy. I will select a few for special comment here. The following has no date; but it is interesting, because

of January 1545 (Flor. style?) by Michelangelo from Rome. Lettere, No. clx. The dates, owing to the differences of style used in Rome and Florence, make it difficult to know whether we are dealing with January 1546 or not. But it seems clear that Michelangelo had two illnesses between 1544 and 1546, on both of which occasions Lionardo came to Rome to visit him.

we may connect the feeling expressed in it with one
of Michelangelo's familiar sonnets.[1] "Dear Messer
Luigi, since I know you are as great a master of
ceremonies as I am unfit for that trade, I beg you
to help me in a little matter. Monsignor di Todi
(Federigo Cesi, afterwards Cardinal of S. Pancrazio)
has made me a present, which Urbino will describe
to you. I think you are a friend of his lordship:
will you then thank him in my name, when you find
a suitable occasion, and do so with those compliments which come easily to you, and to me are very
hard? Make me too your debtor for some tartlet."[2]

The sonnet is No. ix. of Signor Guasti's edition.
I have translated it thus:[3]—

> The sugar, candles, and the saddled mule,
>   Together with your cask of malvoisie,
>   So far exceed all my necessity
> That Michael and not I my debt must rule.
> In such a glassy calm the breezes fool
>   My sinking sails, so that amid the sea
>   My bark hath missed her way, and seems to be
> A wisp of straw whirled on a weltering pool.
> To yield thee gift for gift and grace for grace,
>   For food and drink and carriage to and fro,
>   For all my need in every time and place,
> O my dear lord, matched with the much I owe,
>   All that I am were no real recompense:
>   Paying a debt is not munificence.

---

[1] Lettere, No. cdxxxix. Milanesi assigns it to 1543. But he gives
no reason for this date. The sonnet belongs to about 1554.

[2] *Berlingozzo.* Michelangelo used to call his madrigals and sonnets
by this name. He is asking here for some verses by his friend.

[3] *Sonnets of Michelangelo and Campanella*, p. 39.

In the chapter upon Michelangelo's poetry I dwelt at length upon Luigi del Riccio's passionate affection for his cousin, Cecchino dei Bracci. This youth died at the age of sixteen, on January 8, 1545. Michelangelo undertook to design "the modest sepulchre of marble" erected to his memory by Del Riccio in the church of Araceli. He also began to write sonnets, madrigals, and epitaphs, which were sent from day to day. One of his letters gives an explanation of the eighth epitaph:[1] "Our dead friend speaks and says: if the heavens robbed all beauty from all other men on earth to make me only, as indeed they made me, beautiful; and if by the divine decree I must return at doomsday to the shape I bore in life, it follows that I cannot give back the beauty robbed from others and bestowed on me, but that I must remain for ever more beautiful than the rest, and they be ugly. This is just the opposite of the conceit you expressed to me yesterday; the one is a fable, the other is the truth."

Some time in 1545 Luigi went to Lyons on a visit to Ruberto Strozzi and Giuliano de' Medici.[2] This seems to have happened toward the end of the year; for we possess a letter indorsed by him, "sent to Lyons, and returned upon the 22nd of December."[3] This document contains several interesting details.

[1] Lettere, No. cdxlvii. The poem, *Rime*, p. 7, begins, *Non può per morte già.*

[2] Lettere, No. cdl. This de' Medici was a brother of Lorenzino, the murderer of Duke Alessandro.

[3] Lettere, No. cdlvii.

" All your friends are extremely grieved to hear about
your illness, the more so that we cannot help you;
especially Messer Donato (Giannotti) and myself.
However, we hope that it may turn out to be no
serious affair, God willing.   In another letter I told
you that, if you stayed away long, I meant to come
to see you.   This I repeat; for now that I have
lost the Piacenza ferry, and cannot live at Rome
without income, I would rather spend the little that
I have in hostelries, than crawl about here, cramped
up like a penniless cripple.   So, if nothing happens,
I have a mind to go to S. James of Compostella after
Easter;[1] and if you have not returned, I should like
to travel through any place where I shall hear that
you are staying.   Urbino has spoken to Messer
Aurelio, and will speak again.   From what he tells
me, I think that you will get the site you wanted
for the tomb of Cecchino.   It is nearly finished, and
will turn out handsome."

Michelangelo's project of going upon pilgrimage
to Galicia shows that his health was then good.
But we know that he soon afterwards had another
serious illness; and the scheme was abandoned.

This long and close friendship with Luigi comes
to a sudden termination in one of those stormy outbursts of petulant rage which form a special feature
of Michelangelo's psychology.   Some angry words
passed between them about an engraving, possibly
of the Last Judgment, which Buonarroti wanted to

[1] Pasqua d'Agnello.

destroy, while Del Riccio refused to obliterate the plate :[1]—

"Messer Luigi,—You seem to think I shall reply according to your wishes, when the case is quite the contrary. You give me what I have refused, and refuse me what I begged. And it is not ignorance which makes you send it me through Ercole, when you are ashamed to give it me yourself.

"One who saved my life has certainly the power to disgrace me; but I do not know which is the heavier to bear, disgrace or death. Therefore I beg and entreat you, by the true friendship which exists between us, to spoil that print (*stampa*), and to burn the copies that are already printed off. And if you choose to buy and sell me, do not so to others. If you hack me into a thousand pieces, I will do the same, not indeed to yourself, but to what belongs to you.

"MICHELANGELO BUONARROTI.

"Not painter, nor sculptor, nor architect, but what you will, but not a drunkard, as you said at your house."

Unfortunately, this is the last of the Del Riccio's letters. It is very probable that the irascible artist speedily recovered his usual tone, and returned to

---

[1] Lettere, No. cdlx. date 1546 (?) Von Scheffler is of opinion that the *stampa* in question was an imprint of certain poems by Michelangelo. See *op. cit.*, p. 178.

N

amity with his old friend.[1]   But Del Riccio departed
this life toward the close of this year, 1546.

Before resuming the narrative of Michelangelo's
art-work at this period, I must refer to the correspondence which passed between him and King
Francis I.   The King wrote an epistle in the spring
of 1546, requesting some fine monument from the
illustrious master's hand.[2]   Michelangelo replied
upon the 26th of April, in language of simple and
respectful dignity, fine, as coming from an aged
artist to a monarch on the eve of death:[3]—

"Sacred Majesty,—I know not which is greater,
the favour, or the astonishment it stirs in me, that
your Majesty should have deigned to write to a man
of my sort, and still more to ask him for things of
his which are all unworthy of the name of your
Majesty.   But be they what they may, I beg your
Majesty to know that for a long while since I have
desired to serve you ; but not having had an opportunity, owing to your not being in Italy, I have
been unable to do so.   Now I am old, and have
been occupied these many months with the affairs
of Pope Paul.   But if some space of time is still

[1] Michelangelo's last letter to his father, and Tommaso Cavalieri's
last letter to himself, show him in similar fits of temper.   Yet before
the final parting came, he loved and trusted and respected both again.

[2] Arch. Buon., Cod. viii. No. 341.   It is not autograph, but written
in good Italian by Del Aubespine, and signed by the King.   In
addition to some original work, he begs for copies of the Pietà della
Febbre and the Christ of the Minerva, to put up in one of his chapels.
The autograph is said to be at Lille.

[3] Lettere, No. cdlix.

granted to me after these engagements, I will do
my utmost to fulfil the desire which, as I have said
above, has long inspired me : that is, to make for
your Majesty one work in marble, one in bronze,
and one in painting.   And if death prevents my
carrying out this wish, should it be possible to
make statues or pictures in the other world, I shall
not fail to do so there, where there is no more growing old.   And I pray God that He grant your
Majesty a long and a happy life."

Francis died in 1547 ; and we do not know that
any of Michelangelo's works passed directly into his
hands, with the exception of the Leda, purchased
through the agency of Luigi Alamanni, and the two
Captives, presented by Ruberto Strozzi.

III.

The absorbing tasks imposed upon Buonarroti's
energies by Paul III., which are mentioned in this
epistle to the French king, were not merely the
frescoes of the Cappella Paolina, but also various
architectural and engineering schemes of some importance.   It is clear, I think, that at this period of
his hale old age, Michelangelo preferred to use what
still survived in him of vigour and creative genius
for things requiring calculation, or the exercise of

meditative fancy. The time had gone by when he could wield the brush and chisel with effective force. He was tired of expressing his sense of beauty and the deep thoughts of his brain in sculptured marble or on frescoed surfaces. He had exhausted the human form as a symbol of artistic utterance. But the extraordinary richness of his vein enabled him still to deal with abstract mathematical proportions in the art of building, and with rhythms in the art of writing. His best work, both as architect and poet, belongs to the period when he had lost power as sculptor and painter. This fact is psychologically interesting. Up to the age of seventy, he had been working in the plastic and the concrete. The language he had learned, and used with overwhelming mastery, was man : physical mankind, converted into spiritual vehicle by art. His grasp upon this region failed him now. Perhaps there was not the old sympathy with lovely shapes. Perhaps he knew that he had played on every gamut of that lyre. Emerging from the sphere of the sensuous, where ideas take plastic embodiment, he grappled in this final stage of his career with harmonical ratios and direct verbal expression, where ideas are disengaged from figurative form. The men and women, loved by him so long, so wonderfully wrought into imperishable shapes, " nurslings of immortality," recede. In their room arise, above the horizon of his intellect, the cupola of S. Peter's and a few imperishable poems, which will live as long as Italian claims a place among the languages. There is no comparison to be instituted between his actual achievements as a builder and a versifier. The whole tenor of his life made him more competent to deal with architecture than with literature. Nevertheless, it is significant that the versatile genius of the man was henceforth restricted to these two channels of expression, and that in both of them his last twenty years of existence produced bloom and fruit of unexpected rarity.

After writing this paragraph, and before I engage in the narrative of what is certainly the final manifestation of Michelangelo's genius as a creative artist, I ought perhaps to pause, and to give some account of those survivals from his plastic impulse, which occupied the old man's energies for several years. They were entirely the outcome of religious feeling; and it is curious to notice that he never approached so nearly to true Christian sentiment as in the fragmentary designs which we may still abundantly collect from this late autumn of his artist's life. There are countless drawings for some great picture of the Crucifixion, which was never finished : exquisite in delicacy of touch, sublime in conception, dignified in breadth and grand repose of style. Condivi tells us that some of these were made for the Marchioness of Pescara. But Michelangelo must have gone on producing them long after her death. With these phantoms of stupendous works to be, the Museums of Europe abound. We cannot bring them together, or condense them into a single centralised conception.[1] Their interest consists in their divergence and variety, showing the continuous poring of the master's mind upon a theme he could not definitely grasp. For those who love his work, and are in sympathy with his manner, these drawings, mostly in chalk, and very finely handled, have a supreme interest. They show him, in one sense, at his highest and his best, not only as a man of tender feeling, but also as a mighty draughtsman. Their incompleteness testifies to something pathetic —the humility of the imperious man before a theme he found to be beyond the reach of human faculty.

The tone, the *Stimmung*, of these designs corresponds so exactly to the sonnets of the same late period, that I feel impelled at this point to make his poetry take up the tale. But, as I cannot bring the cloud of witnesses of all those drawings into this small book, so am I unwilling to load its pages with poems which may be found elsewhere. Those who care to learn the heart of Michelangelo, when he felt near to God and face to face with death, will easily find access to the originals.[2]

Concerning the Deposition from the Cross, which now stands behind the high altar of the Florentine

---

[1] There is a complicated Crucifixion, or rather Deposition from the Cross, at the Bargello, Michelangelesque in style, which possesses considerable interest, as indicating an attempt, on the part of some follower, to carry out and combine a number of these scattered motives.

[2] *Rime*, Sonnets Nos. lxv., lxxvii. Translated by me under the same numbers in my *Sonnets of Michelangelo and Campanella*, *op. cit.*

Duomo, Condivi writes as follows :[1] " At the present time he has in hand a work in marble, which he carries on for his pleasure, as being one who, teeming with conceptions, must needs give birth each day to some of them. It is a group of four figures larger than life. A Christ taken from the cross, sustained in death by his Mother, who is represented in an attitude of marvellous pathos, leaning up against the corpse with breast, with arms, and lifted knee. Nicodemus from above assists her, standing erect and firmly planted, propping the dead Christ with a sturdy effort ; while one of the Maries, on the left side, though plunged in sorrow, does all she can to assist the afflicted Mother, failing under the attempt to raise her Son. It would be quite impossible to describe the beauty of style displayed in this group, or the sublime emotions expressed in those woe-stricken countenances. I am confident that the Pietà is one of his rarest and most difficult masterpieces ; particularly because the figures are kept apart distinctly, nor does the drapery of the one intermingle with that of the others." [2]

This panegyric is by no means pitched too high.

[1] Condivi, p. 65.

[2] Condivi speaks in the present tense, as though Michelangelo was still working on the Pietà when he wrote. Since he published his Life in 1553, it is probable that the group had not been abandoned much before that date. The fact that it was given to Antonio del Franzese, and not to Urbino, seems to indicate that Michelangelo tried to break it up after 1556, the date of Urbino's death. It may finally be mentioned that Vasari, in his first edition of 1550, describes it as a marvellous but incomplete piece of sculpture.

Justice has hardly been done in recent times to the noble conception, the intense feeling, and the broad manner of this Deposition. That may be due in part to the dull twilight in which the group is plunged, depriving all its lines of salience and relief. It is also true that in certain respects the composition is fairly open to adverse criticism. The torso of Christ overweighs the total scheme ; and his legs are unnaturally attenuated. The kneeling woman on the left side is slender, and appears too small in proportion to the other figures ; though, if she stood erect, it is probable that her height would be sufficient.

The best way to study Michelangelo's last work in marble is to take the admirable photograph produced under artificial illumination by Alinari. No sympathetic mind will fail to feel that we are in immediate contact with the sculptor's very soul, at the close of his life, when all his thoughts were weaned from earthly beauty, and he cried—

> Painting nor sculpture now can lull to rest
> My soul, that turns to his great love on high,
> Whose arms to clasp us on the cross were spread.

As a French critic has observed : " It is the most intimately personal and the most pathetic of his works. The idea of penitence exhales from it. The marble preaches the sufferings of the Passion ; it makes us listen to an act of bitter contrition and an act of sorrowing love."

Michelangelo is said to have designed the Pietà

for his own monument. In the person of Nicodemus, it is he who sustains his dead Lord in the gloom of the sombre Duomo. His old sad face, surrounded by the heavy cowl, looks down for ever with a tenderness beyond expression, repeating mutely through the years how much of anguish and of blood divine the redemption of man's soul hath cost.

The history of this great poem in marble, abandoned by its maker in some mood of deep dejection, is not without interest. We are told that the stone selected was a capital from one of the eight huge columns of the Temple of Peace.[1] Besides being hard and difficult to handle, the material betrayed flaws in working. This circumstance annoyed the master; also, as he informed Vasari, Urbino kept continually urging him to finish it.[2] One of his reasons for attacking the block had been to keep himself in health by exercise. Accordingly he hewed away with fury, and bit so deep into the marble that he injured one of the Madonna's elbows. When this happened, it was his invariable practice to abandon the piece he had begun upon, feeling that an incomplete performance was preferable to a lame conclusion. In his old age he suffered from sleeplessness; and it was his habit to rise from bed and work upon the Pietà, wearing a thick paper cap, in which he placed a lighted candle made of goat's tallow. This method of chiselling by the light of one candle must have complicated the technical difficulties of

[1] Gotti, i. 328.   [2] Vasari, xii. 248.

his labour. But what we may perhaps surmise to have been his final motive for the rejection of the work, was a sense of his inability, with diminished powers of execution, and a still more vivid sense of the importance of the motive, to accomplish what the brain conceived. The hand failed. The imagination of the subject grew more intimate and energetic. Losing patience then at last, he took a hammer and began to break the group up. Indeed, the right arm of the Mary shows a fracture. The left arm of the Christ is mutilated in several places. One of the nipples has been repaired, and the hand of the Madonna resting on the breast above it is cracked across. It would have been difficult to reduce the whole huge block to fragments; and when the work of destruction had advanced so far, Michelangelo's servant Antonio, the successor to Urbino, begged the remnants from his master. Tiberio Calcagni was a good friend of Buonarroti's at this time. He heard that Francesco Bandini, a Florentine settled in exile at Rome, earnestly desired some relic of the master's work. Accordingly, Calcagni, with Michelangelo's consent, bought the broken marble from Antonio for 200 crowns, pieced it together, and began to mend it. Fortunately, he does not seem to have elaborated the surface in any important particular ; for both the finished and unfinished parts bear indubitable marks of Michelangelo's own handling. After the death of Calcagni and Bandini, the Pietà remained for some time in the garden of Antonio,

Bandini's heir, at Montecavallo. It was transferred
to Florence, and placed among the marbles used in
erecting the new Medicean Chapel, until at last, in
1722, the Grand Duke Cosimo III. finally set it
up behind the altar of the Duomo.

Vasari adds that Michelangelo began another Pietà
in marble on a much smaller scale.[1] It is possible
that this may have been the unfinished group of two
figures (a dead Christ sustained by a bending man),
of which there is a cast in the Accademia at Florence.[2]
In some respects the composition of this fragment
bears a strong resemblance to the puzzling Deposition from the Cross in our National Gallery. The
trailing languor of the dead Christ's limbs is almost
identical in the marble and the painting.

While speaking of these several Pietàs, I must
not forget the medallion in high relief of the Madonna
clasping her dead Son, which adorns the Albergo dei
Poveri at Genoa. It is ascribed to Michelangelo,
was early believed to be his, and is still accepted
without hesitation by competent judges. In spite
of its strongly marked Michelangelesque mannerism,
both as regards feeling, facial type, and design, I
cannot regard the bas-relief, in its present condition
at least, as a genuine work, but rather as the production of some imitator, or the *rifacimento* of a
restorer. A similar impression may here be recorded

---

[1] Vasari, xii. 249.

[2] See Heath Wilson, p. 453. He says it is in the court of the Palazzo
Rondanini in the Corso at Rome.

regarding the noble portrait-bust in marble of Pope
Paul III. at Naples. This too has been attributed
to Michelangelo. But there is no external evidence
to support the tradition, while the internal evidence
from style and technical manipulation weighs strongly
against it. The medallions introduced upon the
heavily embroidered cope are not in his style. The
treatment of the adolescent female form in particular
indicates a different temperament. Were the ascrip-
tion made to Benvenuto Cellini, we might have more
easily accepted it. But Cellini would certainly have
enlarged upon so important a piece of sculpture in
his Memoirs. If then we are left to mere conjecture,
it would be convenient to suggest Guglielmo della
Porta, who executed the Farnese monument in S.
Peter's.

IV.

While still a Cardinal, Paul III. began to rebuild
the old palace of the Farnesi on the Tiber shore. It
closes one end of the great open space called the
Campo di Fiore, and stands opposite to the Villa
Farnesina, on the right bank of the river.[1] Antonio
da Sangallo was the architect employed upon this

---

[1] It is said that Michelangelo, acting under Pier Luigi Farnese's
orders, produced plans for connecting the palace and the villa by a
bridge.

work, which advanced slowly until Alessandro
Farnese's elevation to the Papacy. He then determined to push the building forward, and to complete it on a scale of magnificence befitting the
supreme Pontiff. Sangallo had carried the walls
up to the second story. The third remained to be
accomplished, and the cornice had to be constructed.
Paul was not satisfied with Sangallo's design, and
referred it to Michelangelo for criticism—possibly
in 1544. The result was a report, which we still
possess, in which Buonarroti, basing his opinion
on principles derived from Vitruvius, severely blames
Sangallo's plan under six separate heads.[1] He does
not leave a single merit, as regards either harmony
of proportion, or purity of style, or elegance of composition, or practical convenience, or decorative
beauty, or distribution of parts. He calls the
cornice barbarous, confused, bastard in style, discordant with the rest of the building, and so ill
suited to the palace as, if carried out, to threaten
the walls with destruction. This document has
considerable interest, partly as illustrating Michel-

[1] Lettere, No. cdxli. The document is in Michelangelo's well-known
handwriting; it also contains some details regarding the state of his
health and his inability to wait upon the Pope in person, which are
confirmed by Vasari's graphic account of his interview with Paul (x.
20). Still Milanesi doubts whether he composed it, on the ground that
the style differs from his own (with which opinion I agree), and also
that the language is not purely Tuscan. By adopting and transcribing
the report, Michelangelo made himself responsible for its contents.
Its chief interest lies in the acceptance of the Vitruvian tradition, as
magisterial and decisive.

angelo's views on architecture in general, and displaying a pedantry of which he was never elsewhere guilty, partly as explaining the bitter hostility aroused against him in Sangallo and the whole tribe of that great architect's adherents. We do not, unfortunately, possess the design upon which the report was made. But, even granting that it must have been defective, Michelangelo, who professed that architecture was not his art, might, one thinks, have spared his rival such extremity of adverse criticism. It exposed him to the taunts of rivals and ill-wishers; justified them in calling him presumptuous, and gave them a plausible excuse when they accused him of jealousy. What made it worse was, that his own large building, the Laurentian Library, glaringly exhibits all the defects he discovered in Sangallo's cornice.

I find it difficult to resist the impression that Michelangelo was responsible, to a large extent, for the ill-will of those artists whom Vasari calls " la setta Sangallesca." His life became embittered by their animosity, and his industry as Papal architect continued to be hampered for many years by their intrigues. But he alone was to blame at the beginning, not so much for expressing an honest opinion, as for doing so with insulting severity.

That Michelangelo may have been right in his condemnation of Sangallo's cornice is of course possible. Paul himself was dissatisfied, and eventually threw that portion of the building open to competition.   Perino del Vaga, Sebastiano del Piombo, and the young Giorgio Vasari are said to have furnished designs.[1]   Michelangelo did so also; and his plan was not only accepted, but eventually carried out.   Nevertheless Sangallo, one of the most illustrious professional architects then alive, could not but have felt deeply wounded by the treatment he received.   It was natural for his followers to exclaim that Buonarroti had contrived to oust their aged master, and to get a valuable commission into his own grasp, by the discourteous exercise of his commanding prestige in the world of art.

In order to be just to Michelangelo, we must remember that he was always singularly modest in regard to his own performances, and severe in self-criticism.   Neither in his letters nor in his poems does a single word of self-complacency escape his pen.   He sincerely felt himself to be an unprofitable servant: that was part of his constitutional depression.   We know, too, that he allowed strong temporary feelings to control his utterance.   The cruel criticism of Sangallo may therefore have been quite devoid of malice; and if it was as well founded as the criticism of that builder's plan for S. Peter's, then Michelangelo stands acquitted.   Sangallo's model exists; it is so large that you can walk inside

---

[1] See Vasari, x. 20, for an interesting account of his waiting with the other artists above-named upon Pope Paul III. with their designs. Michelangelo alone was prevented by ill-health from attending, and sent his drawing by the hand of Vasari.

it, and compare your own impressions with the following judgment:[1]—

" It cannot be denied that Bramante's talent as an architect was equal to that of any one from the times of the ancients until now. He laid the first plan of S. Peter, not confused, but clear and simple, full of light and detached from surrounding buildings, so that it interfered with no part of the palace. It was considered a very fine design, and indeed any one can see now that it is so. All the architects who departed from Bramante's scheme, as Sangallo has done, have departed from the truth ; and those who have unprejudiced eyes can observe this in his model. Sangallo's ring of chapels takes light from the interior as Bramante planned it ; and not only this, but he has provided no other means of lighting, and there are so many hiding-places, above and below, all dark, which lend themselves to innumerable knaveries, that the church would become a secret den for harbouring bandits, false coiners, for debauching nuns, and doing all sorts of rascality ; and when it was shut up at night, twenty-five men would be needed to search the building for rogues hidden there, and it would be difficult enough to find them. There is, besides, another inconvenience : the interior circle of buildings added to Bramante's plan would necessitate the destruction of the Paoline

---

[1] Lettere, No. cdlxxiv., written in 1555 to Bartolommeo Ferrantino (?) Inside the model left by Sangallo, any one is able to perceive that Michelangelo was justified, when he blamed its defective lighting and the superfluous room in the chapels round the building.

Chapel, the offices of the Piombo and the Ruota, and more besides. I do not think that even the Sistine would escape."

After this Michelangelo adds that to remove the outworks and foundations begun upon Sangallo's plan would not cost 100,000 crowns, as the sect alleged, but only 16,000. The material would be infinitely useful, the foundations important for the building, and the whole fabric would profit in something like 200,000 crowns and 300 years of time. "This is my dispassionate opinion; and I say this in truth, for to gain a victory here would be my own incalculable loss." Michelangelo means that, at the time when he wrote the letter in question, it was still in doubt whether Sangallo's design should be carried out or his own adopted; and, as usual, he looked forward with dread to undertaking a colossal architectural task.

Returning to the Palazzo Farnese, it only remains to be said that Michelangelo lived to complete the edifice. His genius was responsible for the inharmonious window above the main entrance. According to Vasari, he not only finished the exterior from the second story upwards, but designed the whole of the central courtyard above the first story, "making it the finest thing of its sort in Europe." [1] The interior, with the halls painted by Annibale Caracci, owed its disposition into chambers and galleries to his invention. The cornice has always been reckoned among

[1] Vasari, xii. 231.

his indubitable successes, combining as it does salience and audacity with a grand heroic air of grace. It has been criticised for disproportionate projection; and Michelangelo seems to have felt uneasy on this score, since he caused a wooden model of the right size to be made and placed upon the wall, in order to judge of its effect.

Taken as a whole, the Palazzo Farnese remains the most splendid of the noble Roman houses, surpassing all the rest in pomp and pride, though falling short of Peruzzi's Palazzo Massimo in beauty.

V.

The catastrophe of 1527, when Rome was taken by assault on the side of the Borgo without effective resistance being possible, rendered the fortification of the city absolutely necessary. Paul III. determined to secure a position of such vital importance to the Vatican by bastions. Accordingly he convened a diet of notables, including his architect-in-chief, Antonio da Sangallo. He also wished to profit by Michelangelo's experience, remembering the stout resistance offered to the Prince of Orange by his outworks at S. Miniato. Vasari tells an anecdote regarding this meeting which illustrates the mutual bad feeling of the two illustrious artists.[1] "After

[1] Va-ari, xii. 225.

much discussion, the opinion of Buonarroti was requested. He had conceived views widely differing
from those of Sangallo and several others, and these
he expressed frankly. Whereupon Sangallo told him
that sculpture and painting were his trade, not fortification. He replied that about them he knew but
little, whereas the anxious thought he had given to
city defences, the time he had spent, and the experience he had practically gained in constructing them,
made him superior in that art to Sangallo and all the
masters of his family. He proceeded to point out
before all present numerous errors in the works.
Heated words passed on both sides, and the Pope
had to reduce the men to silence. Before long he
brought a plan for the fortification of the whole
Borgo, which opened the eyes of those in power
to the scheme which was finally adopted. Owing to
changes he suggested, the great gate of Santo Spirito,
designed by Sangallo and nearly finished, was left
incomplete."

It is not clear what changes were introduced into
Sangallo's scheme. They certainly involved drawing the line of defence much closer to the city
than he intended. This approved itself to Pier
Luigi Farnese, then Duke of Castro, who presided
over the meetings of the military committee. It
was customary in carrying out works of fortification
to associate a practical engineer with the architect
who provided designs; and one of these men, Gian
Francesco Montemellino, a trusted servant of the

Farnesi, strongly supported the alteration. That Michelangelo agreed with Montemellino, and felt that they could work together, appears from a letter addressed to the Castellano of S. Angelo.[1] It seems to have been written soon after the dispute recorded by Vasari. In it he states, that although he differs in many respects from the persons who had hitherto controlled the works, yet he thinks it better not to abandon them altogether, but to correct them, alter the superintendence, and put Montemellino at the head of the direction. This would prevent the Pope from becoming disgusted with such frequent changes. "If affairs took the course he indicated, he was ready to offer his assistance, not in the capacity of colleague, but as a servant to command in all things." Nothing is here said openly about Sangallo, who remained architect-in-chief until his death. Still the covert wish expressed that the superintendence might be altered, shows a spirit of hostility against him; and a new plan for the lines must soon have been adopted. A despatch written to the Duke of Parma in September 1545 informs him that the old works were being abandoned, with the exception of the grand Doric gateway of S. Spirito. This is described at some length in another despatch of January 1546. Later on, in 1557, we find Michelangelo working as architect - in - chief with Jacopo Meleghino under his direction, but

[1] Lettere, No. cdxl. The date, as printed by Milanesi, is February 26, 1544. Gotti refers it to the same month in 1545.

the fortifications were eventually carried through by a more competent engineer, one Jacopo Fusto Castriotto of Urbino.[1]

VI.

Antonio da Sangallo died on October 3, 1546, at Terni, while engaged in engineering works intended to drain the Lake Velino. Michelangelo immediately succeeded to the offices and employments he had held at Rome. Of these, the most important was the post of architect-in-chief at S. Peter's. Paul III. conferred it upon him for life by a brief dated January 1, 1547.[2] He is there named "commissary, prefect, surveyor of the works, and architect, with full authority to change the model, form, and structure of the church at pleasure, and to dismiss and remove the working-men and foremen employed upon the same." The Pope intended to attach a special stipend to the onerous charge, but Michelangelo declined this honorarium, declaring that he meant to labour without recompense, for the love of God and the reverence he felt for the Prince of the Apostles. Although he might have had money for the asking, and sums were actually sent as presents by his Papal master, he persisted in this resolution, working steadily at S. Peter's without pay, until death gave him rest.

[1] See Gotti, i. 295–299, for the despatches.   [2] Vasari, xii. 393.

Michelangelo's career as servant to a Pope began with the design of that tomb which led Julius II. to destroy the old S. Peter's. He was now entering, after forty-two years, upon the last stage of his long life. Before the end came, he gave final form to the main features of the great basilica, raising the dome which dominates the Roman landscape like a stationary cloud upon the sky-line. What had happened to the edifice in the interval between 1505 and 1547 must be briefly narrated, although it is not within the scope of this work to give a complete history of the building.[1]

Bramante's original design had been to construct the church in the form of a Greek cross, with four large semicircular apses. The four angles made by the projecting arms of the cross were to be filled in with a complex but well-ordered scheme of shrines and chapels, so that externally the edifice would have presented the aspect of a square. The central piers, at the point of junction between the arms of the cross, supported a broad shallow dome, modelled upon that of the Pantheon. Similar domes of lesser dimensions crowned the out-buildings.[2] He began by erecting the piers which were intended to support the central dome; but working hastily and without

---

[1] The main source of information is Sebastiano Serlio's *Trattato d' Architettura*, Venezia, 1537-1547. But I may here refer my readers to the useful series of ground-plans and elevations published in Harford's *Illustrations of the Genius of Michelangelo*, and also to Burckhardt's *Geschichte der Renaissance in Italien*, pp. 106-111.

[2] See fig. 4 in Harford, and fig. 48 in Burckhardt.

due regard to solid strength, Bramante made these piers too weak to sustain the ponderous mass they had to carry. How he would have rectified this error cannot be conjectured. Death cut his labours short in 1514, and only a small portion of his work remains embedded at the present day within the mightier masses raised beneath Buonarroti's cupola.

Leo X. commissioned Raffaello da Urbino to continue his kinsman's work, and appointed Antonio da Sangallo to assist him in the month of January 1517.[1] Whether it was judged impossible to carry out Bramante's project of the central dome, or for some other reason unknown to us, Raffaello altered the plan so essentially as to design a basilica upon the conventional ground-plan of such churches. He abandoned the Greek cross, and adopted the Latin form by adding an elongated nave. The central piers were left in their places; the three terminal apses of the choir and transepts were strengthened, simplified, reduced to commonplace. Bramante's ground-plan is lucid, luminous, and exquisitely ordered in its intricacy. The true creation of a builder-poet's brain, it illustrates Leo Battista Alberti's definition of the charm of architecture, *tutta quella musica*, that melody and music of a graceful edifice. We are able to understand what Michelangelo meant when he remarked that all subsequent designers, by departing from it, had gone wrong.

---

[1] See Vasari, x. 9, note 1. It appears that Sangallo continued to act as one of the architects of S. Peter's till his death in 1546.

Raffaello's plan, if carried out, would have been monotonous and tame inside and out.

After the death of Raffaello in 1520, Baldassare Peruzzi was appointed to be Sangallo's colleague. This genial architect, in whose style all the graces were combined with dignity and strength, prepared a new design at Leo's request. Vasari, referring to this period of Peruzzi's life, says:[1] "The Pope, thinking Bramante's scheme too large and not likely to be in keeping, obtained a new model from Baldassare; magnificent and truly full of fine invention, also so wisely constructed that certain portions have been adopted by subsequent builders." He reverted to Bramante's main conception of the Greek cross, but altered the details in so many important points, both by thickening the piers and walls, and also by complicating the internal disposition of the chapels, that the effect would have been quite different. The ground-plan, which is all I know of Peruzzi's project, has always seemed to me by far the most beautiful and interesting of those laid down for S. Peter's. It is richer, more imaginative and suggestive, than Bramante's. The style of Bramante, in spite of its serene simplicity, had something which might be described as shallow clearness. In comparison with Peruzzi's style, it is what Gluck's melody is to Mozart's. The course of public events prevented this scheme from being carried out. First came the pontificate of Adrian VI., so sluggish in

[1] Vasari, viii. 227.

art-industry; then the pontificate of Clement VII.
so disastrous for Italy and Rome. Many years
elapsed before art and literature recovered from the
terror and the torpor of 1527. Peruzzi indeed returned to his office at S. Peter's in 1535, but his
death followed in 1537, when Antonio da Sangallo
remained master of the situation.

Sangallo had the good sense to preserve many
of Peruzzi's constructive features, especially in the
apses of the choir and transepts; but he added
a vast vestibule, which gave the church a length
equal to that of Raffaello's plan. Externally, he
designed a lofty central cupola and two flanking
spires, curiously combining the Gothic spirit with
Classical elements of style.[1] In order to fill in the
huge spaces of this edifice, he superimposed tiers of
orders one above the other. Church, cupola, and
spires are built up by a succession of Vitruvian
temples, ascending from the ground into the air.
The total impression produced by the mass, as we
behold it now in the great wooden model at S.
Peter's, is one of bewildering complexity.[2] Of architectural repose it possesses little, except what belongs
to a very original and vast conception on a colossal

---

[1] These spires in the model at S. Peter's strike an Englishman by
their singular resemblance to some of Wren's experiments in the same
hybrid style.

[2] In his *Life of Sangallo*, Vasari (x. 17) has given an account of his
model, which was made under the master's direction by Antonio
Labacco. The woodwork alone cost 4184 crowns. It is 28 feet long
by 18 feet wide, and about 15 feet high, so that any one can enter it
and move around freely.

scale. The extent of the structure is frittered by its multiplicity of parts.[1] Internally, as Michelangelo pointed out, the church would have been dark, inconvenient, and dangerous to public morals.

VII.

Whatever we may think of Michelangelo's failings as an architect, there is no doubt that at this period of his life he aimed at something broad and heroic in style. He sought to attain grandeur by greatness in the masses and by economy of the constituent parts. His method of securing amplitude was exactly opposite to that of Sangallo, who relied upon the multiplication rather than the simplification of details. A kind of organic unity was what Michelangelo desired. For this reason, he employed in the construction of S. Peter's those stupendous orders which out-soar the columns of Baalbec, and those grandiose curves which make the cupola majestic. A letter written to the Cardinal Ridolfo Pio of Carpi contains this explanation of his principles.[2] The last two sentences are highly significant :—

" Most Reverend Monsignor,—If a plan has divers parts, those which are of one type in respect to quality and quantity have to be decorated in the

---

[1] See Harford, *op. cit.*, plate 4.
[2] Lettere, No. cdxc., under date 1560.

same way and the same fashion. The like is true
of their counterparts. But when the plan changes
form entirely, it is not only allowable, but necessary,
to change the decorative appurtenances, as also with
their counterparts.   The intermediate parts are
always free, left to their own bent. The nose, which
stands in the middle of the forehead, is not bound
to correspond with either of the eyes ; but one hand
must balance the other, and one eye be like its
fellow. Therefore it may be assumed as certain
that the members of an architectural structure
follow the laws exemplified in the human body.
He who has not been or is not a good master of the
nude, and especially of anatomy, cannot understand
the principles of architecture."

It followed that Michelangelo's first object, when
he became Papal architect-in-chief, was to introduce
order into the anarchy of previous plans, and to
return, so far as this was now possible, to Bramante's
simpler scheme. He adopted the Greek cross, and
substituted a stately portico for the long vestibule
invented by Sangallo. It was not, however, in his
nature, nor did the changed taste of the times permit him to reproduce Bramante's manner. So far
as S. Peter's bears the mark of Michelangelo at all,
it represents his own peculiar genius. "The Pope,"
says Vasari, " approved his model, which reduced
the cathedral to smaller dimensions, but also to a
more essential greatness. He discovered that four
principal piers, erected by Bramante and left stand-

ing by Antonio da Sangallo, which had to bear the weight of the tribune, were feeble. These he fortified in part, constructing two winding staircases at the side, with gently sloping steps, up which beasts of burden ascend with building material, and one can ride on horseback to the level above the arches. He carried the first cornice, made of travertine, round the arches : a wonderful piece of work, full of grace, and very different from the others; nor could anything be better done in its kind. He began the two great apses of the transept; and whereas Bramante, Raffaello, and Peruzzi had designed eight tabernacles toward the Campo Santo, which arrangement Sangallo adhered to, he reduced them to three, with three chapels inside. Suffice it to say that he began at once to work with diligence and accuracy at all points where the edifice required alteration, to the end that its main features might be fixed, and that no one might be able to change what he had planned."[1] Vasari adds that this was the provision of a wise and prudent mind. So it was; but it did not prevent Michelangelo's successors from defeating his intentions in almost every detail, except the general effect of the cupola. This will appear in the sequel.

Antonio da Sangallo had controlled the building of S. Peter's for nearly thirty years before Michelangelo succeeded to his office. During that long space of time he formed a body of architects and

[1] Vasari, xii. 229.

workmen who were attached to his person and interested in the execution of his plans. There is good reason to believe that in Sangallo's days, as earlier in Bramante's, much money of the Church had been misappropriated by a gang of fraudulent and mutually indulgent craftsmen. It was not to be expected that these people should tamely submit to the intruder who put their master's cherished model on the shelf, and set about, in his high-handed way, to refashion the whole building from the bottom to the top. During Sangallo's lifetime no love had been lost between him and Buonarroti, and after his death it is probable that the latter dealt severely with the creatures of his predecessor. The Pope had given him unlimited powers of appointing and dismissing subordinates, controlling operations, and regulating expenditure. He was a man who abhorred jobs and corruption. A letter written near the close of his life, when he was dealing only with persons nominated by himself, proves this. He addressed the Superintendents of the Fabric of S. Peter's as follows :[1] " You know that I told Balduccio not to send his lime unless it were good. He has sent bad quality, and does not seem to think he will be forced to take it back ; which proves that he is in collusion with the person who accepted it. This gives great encouragement to the men I have dismissed for similar transactions. One who accepts bad goods needed for the fabric, when

[1] Lettere, No. cdxci., under date 1560.

I have forbidden them, is doing nothing else but making friends of people whom I have turned into enemies against myself. I believe there will be a new conspiracy. Promises, fees, presents corrupt justice. Therefore I beg you from this time forward, by the authority I hold from the Pope, not to accept anything which is not suitable, even though it comes to you from heaven. I must not be made to appear, what I am not, partial in my dealings." This fiery despatch, indicating not only Michelangelo's probity, but also his attention to minute details at the advanced age of eighty-six, makes it evident that he must have been a stern overseer in the first years of his office, terrible to the " sect of Sangallo," who were bent, on their part, to discredit him.

The sect began to plot and form conspiracies, feeling the violent old man's bit and bridle on their mouths, and seeing the firm seat he took upon the saddle. For some reason, which is not apparent, they had the Superintendents of the Fabric (a committee, including cardinals, appointed by the Pope) on their side. Probably these officials, accustomed to Sangallo and the previous course of things, disliked to be stirred up and sent about their business by the masterful new-comer. Michelangelo's support lay, as we shall see, in the four Popes who followed Paul III. They, with the doubtful exception of Marcello II., accepted him on trust as a thoroughly honest servant, and the only artist

capable of conducting the great work to its conclusion. In the last resort, when he was driven to
bay, he offered to resign, and was invariably coaxed
back by the final arbiter. The disinterested spirit
in which he fulfilled his duties, accepting no pay
while he gave his time and energy to their performance, stood him in good stead.[1] Nothing speaks
better for his perfect probity than that his enemies
were unable to bring the slightest charge of pecu-
lation or of partiality against him. Michelangelo's
conduct of affairs at S. Peter's reflects a splendid
light upon the tenor of his life, and confutes those
detractors who have accused him of avarice.

The duel between Michelangelo and the sect
opened in 1547. A letter written by a friend in
Florence on the 14th of May proves that his
antagonists had then good hopes of crushing him.[2]
Giovan Francesco Ughi begins by saying that he
has been silent because he had nothing special to
report. " But now Jacopo del Conte has come here
with the wife of Nanni di Baccio Bigio, alleging that
he has brought her because Nanni is so occupied at
S. Peter's. Among other things, he says that Nanni
means to make a model for the building which will
knock yours to nothing. He declares that what you
are about is mad and babyish. He means to fling
it all down, since he has quite as much credit with
the Pope as you have. You throw oceans of money
away and work by night, so that nobody may see

[1] See Vasari, xii. 228.   [2] Gotti, i. 309.

what you are doing. You follow in the footsteps of a Spaniard, having no knowledge of your own about the art of building, and he less than nothing. Nanni stays there in your despite: you did everything to get him removed; but the Pope keeps him, being convinced that nothing good can be done without him."[1] After this Ughi goes on to relate how Michelangelo's enemies are spreading all kinds of reports against his honour and good fame, criticising the cornice of the Palazzo Farnese, and hoping that its weight will drag the walls down. At the end he adds, that although he knows one ought not to write about such matters, yet the man's "insolence and blackguardly shamelessness of speech" compel him to put his friend on his guard against such calumnies.

After the receipt of this letter, Michelangelo sent it to one of the Superintendents of the Fabric, on whose sympathy he could reckon, with the following indorsement in his own handwriting: " Messer Bartolommeo (Ferrantino), please read this letter, and take thought who the two rascals are who, lying thus about what I did at the Palazzo Farnese, are now lying in the matter of the information they are laying before the deputies of S. Peter's. It comes upon me in return for the kindness I have shown them. But what else can one expect from a couple of the basest scoundrelly villains?"

---

[1] It is worth mentioning that this Nanni, who proved so hostile to Michelangelo, made a bronze copy of his Madonna della Febbre (for Luigi del Riccio, according to Vasari), which now adorns the Church of S. Spirito at Florence. It is an excellent piece of work.

Nanni di Baccio Bigio had, as it seems, good friends at court in Rome. He was an open enemy of Michelangelo, who, nevertheless, found it difficult to shake him off. In the history of S. Peter's the man's name will frequently occur.

Three years elapsed. Paul III. died, and Michelangelo wrote to his nephew Lionardo on the occasion :[1] "It is true that I have suffered great sorrow, and not less loss, by the Pope's death. I received benefits from his Holiness, and hoped for more and better. God willed it so, and we must have patience. His passage from this life was beautiful, in full possession of his faculties up to the last word. God have mercy on his soul." The Cardinal Giovan Maria Ciocchi, of Monte San Savino, was elected to succeed Paul, and took the title of Julius III. This change of masters was duly noted by Michelangelo in a letter to his " dearest friend," Giovan Francesco Fattucci at Florence.[2] It breathes so pleasant and comradely a spirit, that I will translate more than bears immediately on the present topic : "Dear friend, although we have not exchanged letters for many months past, still our long and excellent friendship has not been forgotten. I wish you well, as I have always done, and love you with all my heart, for your own sake, and for the numberless pleasant things in life you have afforded me. As regards old age, which weighs upon us both alike, I should be

---

[1] Lettere, No. ccxxxi., December 21, 1549.
[2] Ibid., No. cdlxvi., October 1549.

glad to know how yours affects you; mine, I must
say, does not make me very happy. I beg you,
then, to write me something about this. You know,
doubtless, that we have a new Pope, and who
he is. All Rome is delighted, God be thanked;
and everybody expects the greatest good from his
reign, especially for the poor, his generosity being
so notorious."

Michelangelo had good reason to rejoice over this
event, for Julius III. felt a real attachment to his
person, and thoroughly appreciated both his character
and his genius. Nevertheless, the enemies he had
in Rome now made a strong effort to dislodge
Buonarroti from his official position at S. Peter's.
It was probably about this time that the Superintendents of the Fabric drew up a memorial expressive
of their grievances against him. We possess a
document in Latin setting forth a statement of
accounts in rough.[1] "From the year 1540, when
expenditures began to be made regularly and in
order, from the very commencement as it were, up
to the year 1547, when Michelangelo, at his own
will and pleasure, undertook partly to build and
partly to destroy, 162,624 ducats were expended.
Since the latter date on to the present, during which
time the deputies have served like the pie at the
organ,[2] knowing nothing, nor what, nor how moneys
were spent, but only at the orders of the said Michel-

---

[1] Gotti, i. 311.
[2] "In quo deputati servierunt tanquam pica ad organum."

angelo, such being the will of Paul III. of blessed
memory, and also of the reigning Pontiff, 136,881
ducats have been paid out, as can be seen from our
books.   With regard to the edifice, what it is going
to be, the deputies can make no statement, all things
being hidden from them, as though they were out-
siders.   They have only been able to protest at
several times, and do now again protest, for the
easement of their conscience, that they do not like
the ways used by Michelangelo, especially in what
he keeps on pulling down.   The demolition has
been, and to-day is so great, that all who witness
it are moved to an extremity of pity.   Nevertheless,
if his Holiness be satisfied, we, his deputies, shall
have no reason to complain."   It is clear that
Michelangelo was carrying on with a high hand at
S. Peter's.

Although the date of this document is uncertain,
I think it may be taken in connection with a general
meeting called by Julius III., the incidents of which
are recorded by Vasari.   Michelangelo must have
demonstrated his integrity, for he came out of the
affair victorious, and obtained from the Pope a
brief confirming him in his office of architect-in-
chief, with even fuller powers than had been
granted by Paul III.[1]

[1] Gotti, ii. 133.   The brief is dated January 23, 1551.

VIII.

Vasari at this epoch becomes one of our most reliable authorities regarding the life of Michelangelo. He corresponded and conversed with him continuously, and enjoyed the master's confidence. We may therefore accept the following narrative as accurate :[1] " It was some little while before the beginning of 1551, when Vasari, on his return from Florence to Rome, found that the sect of Sangallo were plotting against Michelangelo; they induced the Pope to hold a meeting in S. Peter's, where all the overseers and workmen connected with the building should attend, and his Holiness should be persuaded by false insinuations that Michelangelo had spoiled the fabric. He had already walled in the apse of the King where the three chapels are, and carried out the three upper windows.[2] But it was not known what he meant to do with the vault. They then, misled by their shallow judgment, made Cardinal Salviati the elder, and Marcello Cervini, who was afterwards Pope, believe that S. Peter's would be badly lighted. When all were assembled, the Pope told Michelangelo that the deputies were of opinion the apse would have but little light. He answered : ' I should like to hear these deputies

---

[1] Vasari, xii. 238.

[2] See Lettere, Nos. cdlxxxiii., cdlxxxiv., to Vasari on the difficulties he had with the building of this apse.

speak.' The Cardinal Marcello rejoined : ' Here we
are.' Michelangelo then remarked : ' My lord,
above these three windows there will be other three
in the vault, which is to be built of travertine.'
' You never told us anything about this,' said the
Cardinal. Michelangelo responded : ' I am not,
nor do I mean to be obliged to tell your lordship
or anybody what I ought or wish to do. It is your
business to provide money, and to see that it is not
stolen. As regards the plans of the building, you
have to leave those to me.' Then he turned to the
Pope and said : ' Holy Father, behold what gains
are mine ! Unless the hardships I endure prove
beneficial to my soul, I am losing time and labour.'
The Pope, who loved him, laid his hands upon his
shoulders and exclaimed : ' You are gaining both
for soul and body, have no fear ! ' Michelangelo's
spirited self-defence increased the Pope's love, and
he ordered him to repair next day with Vasari to
the Vigna Giulia, where they held long discourses
upon art." It is here that Vasari relates how Julius
III. was in the habit of seating Michelangelo by
his side while they talked together.

Julius then maintained the cause of Michelangelo
against the deputies. It was during his pontificate
that a piece of engineering work committed to
Buonarroti's charge by Paul III. fell into the hands
of Nanni di Baccio Bigio.[1] The old bridge of Santa
Maria had long shown signs of giving way, and

----

[1] Vasari, xii. 240.

materials had been collected for rebuilding it. Nanni's friends managed to transfer the execution of this work to him from Michelangelo. The man laid bad foundations, and Buonarroti riding over the new bridge one day with Vasari, cried out: " George, the bridge is quivering beneath us; let us spur on, before it gives way with us upon it." Eventually, the bridge did fall to pieces, at the time of a great inundation. Its ruins have long been known as the Ponte Rotto.

On the death of Julius III. in 1555, Cardinal Cervini was made Pope, with the title of Marcellus II. This event revived the hopes of the sect, who once more began to machinate against Michelangelo. The Duke of Tuscany at this time was exceedingly anxious that he should take up his final abode at Florence; and Buonarroti, feeling he had now no strong support in Rome, seems to have entertained these proposals with alacrity. The death of Marcellus after a few weeks, and the election of Paul IV., who besought the great architect not to desert S. Peter's, made him change his mind. Several letters written to Vasari and the Grand Duke in this and the next two years show that his heart was set on finishing S. Peter's, however much he wished to please his friends and longed to end his days in peace at home.[1] " I was set to work upon S. Peter's against my will, and I have served now eight years gratis, and with the utmost injury and

[1] Lettere, Nos. cdlxxv.–vi., cdlxxxi.–ii.

discomfort to myself. Now that the fabric has been pushed forward and there is money to spend, and I am just upon the point of vaulting in the cupola, my departure from Rome would be the ruin of the edifice, and for me a great disgrace throughout all Christendom, and to my soul a grievous sin. Pray ask his lordship to give me leave of absence till S. Peter's has reached a point at which it cannot be altered in its main features. Should I leave Rome earlier, I should be the cause of a great ruin, a great disgrace, and a great sin." To the Duke he writes in 1557 that his special reasons for not wishing to abandon S. Peter's were, first, that the work would fall into the hands of thieves and rogues; secondly, that it might probably be suspended altogether; thirdly, that he owned property in Rome to the amount of several thousand crowns, which, if he left without permission, would be lost; fourthly, that he was suffering from several ailments. He also observed that the work had just reached its most critical stage (*i.e.*, the erection of the cupola), and that to desert it at the present moment would be a great disgrace.

The vaulting of the cupola had now indeed become the main preoccupation of Michelangelo's life. Early in 1557 a serious illness threatened his health, and several friends, including the Cardinal of Carpi, Donato Giannotti, Tommaso Cavalieri, Francesco Bandini, and Lottino, persuaded him that he ought to construct a large model, so that the execution of this most important feature of the edifice might not be impeded in the event of his death. It appears certain that up to this date no models of his on anything like a large intelligible scale had been provided for S. Peter's; and the only extant model attributable to Michelangelo's own period is that of the cupola. This may help to account for the fact that, while the cupola was finished much as he intended, the rest of his scheme suffered a thorough and injurious remodelling.

He wrote to his nephew Lionardo on the 13th of February 1557 about the impossibility of meeting the Grand Duke's wishes and leaving Rome:[1] "I told his Lordship that I was obliged to attend to S. Peter's until I could leave the work there at such a point that my plans would not be subsequently altered. This point has not been reached; and in addition, I am now obliged to construct a large wooden model for the cupola and lantern, in order that I may secure its being finished as it was meant to be. The whole of Rome, and especially the Cardinal of Carpi, puts great pressure on me to do this. Accordingly, I reckon that I shall have to remain here not less than a year; and so much time I beg the Duke to allow me for the love of Christ and S. Peter, so that I may not come home to Florence with a pricking conscience, but a mind easy about Rome." The model took about a year

[1] Lettere, No. cccii.

to make.   It was executed by a French master named Jean.[1]

All this while Michelangelo's enemies, headed by Nanni di Baccio Bigio, continued to calumniate and backbite.   In the end they poisoned the mind of his old friend the Cardinal of Carpi.   We gather this from a haughty letter written on the 13th of February 1560:[2] "Messer Francesco Bandini informed me yesterday that your most illustrious and reverend lordship told him that the building of S. Peter's could not possibly go on worse than it is doing.   This has grieved me deeply, partly because you have not been informed of the truth, and also because I, as my duty is, desire more than all men living that it should proceed well.   Unless I am much deceived, I think I can assure you that it could not possibly go on better than it now is doing. It may, however, happen that my own interests and old age expose me to self-deception, and consequently expose the fabric of S. Peter's to harm or injury against my will.   I therefore intend to ask permission on the first occasion from his Holiness to resign my office.   Or rather, to save time, I wish to request your most illustrious and reverend lordship by these present to relieve me of the annoyance to which I have been subject seventeen years, at the orders of the Popes, working without remuneration. It is easy enough to see what has been accomplished by my industry during this period.   I conclude by

---

[1] Vasari, xii. 252, 253.   [2] Lettere, No. cdxciii.

repeating my request that you will accept my resig- nation. You could not confer on me a more dis- tinguished favour."

Giovanni Angelo Medici, of an obscure Milanese family, had succeeded to Paul IV. in 1559. Pius IV. felt a true admiration for Michelangelo. He confirmed the aged artist in his office by a brief which granted him the fullest authority in life, and strictly forbade any departure from his designs for S. Peter's after death. Notwithstanding this powerful support, Nanni di Baccio Bigio kept trying to eject him from his post. He wrote to the Grand Duke in 1562, arguing that Buonarroti was in his dotage, and begging Cosimo to use his influence to obtain the place for himself. In reply the Grand Duke firmly told Nanni that he could not think of doing such a thing during Michelangelo's lifetime, but that after his death he would render what aid was in his power.[1] An incident happened in 1563 which enabled Nanni to give his enemy some real annoyance. Michelangelo was now so old that he felt obliged to leave the personal superintendence of the operations at S. Peter's to a clerk of the works. The man employed at this time was a certain Cesare da Castel Durante, who was murdered in August under the following circumstances, communicated by Tiberio Calcagni to Lionardo Buonarroti on the 14th of that month:[2] "I have only further to speak

[1] Gaye, iii. p. 66.
[2] Gotti, i. 321. Calcagni first mentions the murder in a letter of August 8. See Daelli, *Carte Mich. Ined.*, p. 39.

about the death of Cesare, clerk of the works, who was found by the cook of the Bishop of Forlì with his wife. The man gave Cesare thirteen stabs with his poignard, and four to his wife. The old man (*i.e.*, Michelangelo) is in much distress, seeing that he wished to give the post to that Pier Luigi, and has been unable to do so owing to the refusal of the deputies." This Pier Luigi, surnamed Gaeta, had been working since November 1561 as subordinate to Cesare; and we have a letter from Michelangelo to the deputies recommending him very warmly in that capacity.[1] He was also the house-servant and personal attendant of the old master, running errands for him and transacting ordinary business, like Pietro Urbano and Stefano in former years.[2] The deputies would not consent to nominate Pier Luigi as clerk of the works. They judged him to be too young, and were, moreover, persuaded that Michelangelo's men injured the work at S. Peter's. Accordingly they appointed Nanni di Baccio Bigio, and sent in a report, inspired by him, which severely blamed Buonarroti.[3] Pius IV., after the receipt of this report, had an interview with Michelangelo, which ended in his sending his own relative, Gabrio Serbelloni, to inspect the works at S. Peter's.[4] It

---

[1] Lettere, No. cdxciv. It is the last of the *Lettere a Diversi.*

[2] See a curious story about his being put into prison on a charge of robbery when Michelangelo sent him to change six old ducats. Daelli, *op. cit.*, p. 38.

[3] See Tiberio Calcagni's letter of September 2, 1563. Gotti, i. 321.

[4] Tib. Calcagni, in Daelli, *op. cit.*, p. 40.

was decided that Nanni had been calumniating the great old man. Accordingly he was dismissed with indignity.[1] Immediately after the death of Michelangelo, however, Nanni renewed his applications to the Grand Duke. He claimed nothing less than the post of architect-in-chief. His petition was sent to Florence under cover of a despatch from the Duke's envoy, Averardo Serristori. The ambassador related the events of Michelangelo's death, and supported Nanni as "a worthy man, your vassal and true servant."[2]

IX.

Down to the last days of his life, Michelangelo was thus worried with the jealousies excited by his superintendence of the building at S. Peter's ; and when he passed to the majority, he had not secured his heart's desire, to wit, that the fabric should be forced to retain the form he had designed for it. This was his own fault. Popes might issue briefs to the effect that his plans should be followed ; but when it was discovered that, during his lifetime, he kept the builders in ignorance of his intentions, and that he left no working models fit for use, except in the case of the cupola, a free course was opened for every kind of innovation. So it came to pass that subsequent architects changed the essential

[1] Vasari, xii. 267, 268.　　　　[2] Gaye, iii. 127-129.

features of his design by adding what might be called a nave, or, in other words, by substituting the Latin for the Greek cross in the ground-plan. He intended to front the mass of the edifice with a majestic colonnade, giving externally to one limb of the Greek cross a rectangular salience corresponding to its three semicircular apses. From this decastyle colonnade projected a tetrastyle portico, which introduced the people ascending from a flight of steps to a gigantic portal. The portal opened on the church, and all the glory of the dome was visible when they approached the sanctuary. Externally, according to his conception, the cupola dominated and crowned the edifice when viewed from a moderate or a greater distance. The cupola was the integral and vital feature of the structure. By producing one limb of the cross into a nave, destroying the colonnade and portico, and erecting a huge façade of *barocco* design, his followers threw the interior effect of the cupola into a subordinate position, and externally crushed it out of view, except at a great distance.[1] In like manner they dealt with every particular of his plan. As an old writer has remarked: "The cross which Michelangelo made Greek is now Latin; and if it be thus with the essential form, judge ye of the details!" It was not exactly their fault, but rather that of the master, who chose to work by drawings and small

---

[1] Harford's Illustrations, plate 7, supply a fair basis for the comparison of the original design and the existing church.

clay models, from which no accurate conception of his thought could be derived by lesser craftsmen.

We cannot, therefore, regard S. Peter's in its present state as the creation of Buonarroti's genius. As a building, it is open to criticism at every point. In spite of its richness and overwhelming size, no architect of merit gives it approbation. It is vast without being really great, magnificent without touching the heart, proudly but not harmoniously ordered. The one redeeming feature in the structure is the cupola; and that is the one thing which Michelangelo bequeathed to the intelligence of his successors. The curve which it describes finds no phrase of language to express its grace. It is neither ellipse nor parabola nor section of the circle, but an inspiration of creative fancy. It outsoars in vital force, in elegance of form, the dome of the Pantheon and the dome of Brunelleschi, upon which it was actually modelled. As a French architect, adverse to Michelangelo, has remarked:[1] "This portion is simple, noble, grand. It is an unparalleled idea, and the author of this marvellous cupola had the right to be proud of the thought which controlled his pencil when he traced it." An English critic, no less adverse to the Italian style, is forced to

---

[1] *L'Œuvre et la Vie*, p. 200. M. Garnier, however, calls attention to his belief that the curve of the cupola, as it now exists, is really due to Giacomo della Porta's divergence from the model. Ibid., p. 202. It will be seen by the sections published in Dr. Josef Durm's book, quoted below, that M. Garnier is in error.

admit that architecture "has seldom produced a more magnificent object" than the cupola, "if its bad connection with the building is overlooked."[1] He also adds that, internally, "the sublime concave" of this immense dome is the one redeeming feature of S. Peter's.

Michelangelo's reputation, not only as an imaginative builder, but also as a practical engineer in architecture, depends in a very large measure upon the cupola of S. Peter's. It is, therefore, of great importance to ascertain exactly how far the dome in its present form belongs to his conception. Fortunately for his reputation, we still possess the wooden model constructed under his inspection by a man called Giovanni Franzese. It shows that subsequent architects, especially Giacomo della Porta, upon whom the task fell of raising the vaults and lantern from the point where Michelangelo left the building, that is, from the summit of the drum, departed in no essential particular from his design. Della Porta omitted one feature, however, of Michelangelo's plan, which would have added greatly to the dignity and elegance of the exterior. The model shows that the entablature of the drum broke into projections above each of the buttresses. Upon these projections or consoles Buonarroti intended to place statues of saints. He also connected their pedestals with the spring of the vault by a series of inverted

[1] *Encyclopædia Britannica*, 9th edition : Art. "Architecture," vol. ii. p. 483.

curves sweeping upwards along the height of the shallow attic. The omission of these details not only weakened the support given to the arches of the dome, but it also lent a stilted effect to the cupola by abruptly separating the perpendicular lines of the drum and attic from the segment of the vaulting. This is an error which could even now be repaired, if any enterprising Pope undertook to complete the plan of the model. It may, indeed, be questioned whether the omission was not due to the difficulty of getting so many colossal statues adequately finished at a period when the fabric still remained imperfect in more essential parts.

Vasari, who lived in close intimacy with Michelangelo, and undoubtedly was familiar with the model, gives a confused but very minute description of the building. It is clear from this that the dome was designed with two shells, both of which were to be made of carefully selected bricks, the space between them being applied to the purpose of an interior staircase. The dormer windows in the outer sheath not only broke the surface of the vault, but also served to light this passage to the lantern. Vasari's description squares with the model, now preserved in a chamber of the Vatican basilica, and also with the present fabric.

It would not have been necessary to dwell at greater length upon the vaulting here but for difficulties which still surround the criticism of this salient feature of S. Peter's. Gotti published two plans of the cupola, which were made for him, he says, from accurate measurements of the model taken by Cavaliere Cesare Castelli, Lieut.-Col. of Engineers.[1] The section drawing shows three shells instead of two, the innermost or lowest being flattened out like the vault of the Pantheon. Professor Josef Durm, in his essay upon the Domes of Florence and S. Peter's, gives a minute description of the model for the latter, and prints a carefully executed copperplate engraving of its section.[2] It is clear from this work that at some time or other a third semi-spherical vault, corresponding to that of the Pantheon, had been contemplated. This would have been structurally of no value, and would have masked the two upper shells, which at present crown the edifice. The model shows that the dome itself was from the first intended to be composed of two solid vaults of masonry, in the space between which ran the staircase leading to the lantern. The lower and flatter shell, which appears also in the model, had no connection with the substantial portions of the edifice. It was an addition, perhaps an afterthought, designed possibly to serve as a ground for surface-decoration, or to provide an alternative scheme for the completion of the dome. Had Michelangelo really planned this innermost sheath, we could not credit him with the soaring sweep

[1] Gotti, ii. p. 136.
[2] *Die Dom Kuppel in Florenz und die Kuppel der Petruskirche in Rom.* Berlin : Ernst and Korn, 1887.

upwards of the mighty dome, its height and lightness, luminosity and space. The roof that met the eye internally would have been considerably lower and tamer, superfluous in the construction of the church, and bearing no right relation to the external curves of the vaulting. There would, moreover, have been a long dark funnel leading to the lantern. Heath Wilson would then have been justified in certain critical conclusions which may here be stated in his own words.[1] "According to Michelangelo's idea, the cupola was formed of three vaults over each other. Apparently the inner one was intended to repeat the curves of the Pantheon, whilst the outer one was destined to give height and majesty to the building externally. The central vault, more pyramidal in form, was constructed to bear the weight of the lantern, and approached in form the dome of the Cathedral at Florence by Brunelleschi. Judging by the model, he meant the outer dome to be of wood, thus anticipating the construction of Sir Christopher Wren."[2] Farther on, he adds that the architects who carried out the work "omitted entirely the inner lower vault, evidently to give height internally, and made the external cupola of brick as well as the internal; and, to prevent

---

[1] Heath Wilson, pp. 531–533.

[2] This is in abrupt collision with what Vasari says: "Alle *due volte* della cupola;" "dà ordine ch' ella si muri tutta di mattoni;" "Lascia accanto un vano, il quale ha a servire per la salita delle scale," Vasari, xii. 256, 257. It is clear throughout that Vasari only knew of two shells, both to be of brick.

it expanding, had recourse to encircling chains of iron, which bind it at the weakest parts of the curve." These chains, it may be mentioned parenthetically, were strengthened by Poleni, after the lapse of some years, when the second of the two shells showed some signs of cracking.[1]

From Dr. Durm's minute description of the cupola, there seems to be no doubt about the existence of this third vault in Michelangelo's wooden model. He says that the two outer shells are carved out of one piece of wood, while the third or innermost is made of another piece, which has been inserted. The sunk or hollow compartments, which form the laquear of this depressed vault, differ considerably in shape and arrangement from those which were adopted when it was finally rejected. The question now remains, whether the semi-spherical shell was abandoned during Michelangelo's lifetime and with his approval. There is good reason to believe that this may have been the case : first, because the tambour, which he executed, differs from the model in the arching of its windows ; secondly, because Fontana and other early writers on the cupola insist strongly on the fact that Michelangelo's own plans were strictly followed, although they never allude to the third or innermost vault. It is almost incredible that if Della Porta departed in so vital a point from Michelangelo's design, no notice should have been taken of the fact.

[1] *Memorie Istoriche della Gran Cupola del Tempio Vaticano, &c.* Giovanni Poleni. In Padova, 1747.

On the other hand, the tradition that Della Porta improved the curve of the cupola by making the spring upward from the attic more abrupt, is due probably to the discrepancy between the internal aspects of the model and the dome itself. The actual truth is that the cupola in its curve and its dimensions corresponds accurately to the proportions of the double outer vaulting of the model.

Taking, then, Vasari's statement in conjunction with the silence of Fontana, Poleni, and other early writers, and duly observing the care with which the proportions of the dome have been preserved, I think we may safely conclude that Michelanglo himself abandoned the third or semi-spherical vault, and that the cupola, as it exists, ought to be ascribed entirely to his conception. It is, in fact, the only portion of the basilica which remains as he designed it.

CHAPTER XIV.

1. To arrange Michelangelo's doings in the last twenty years of his life chronologically is almost impossible.—The reconstruction of the Capitol.—Michelangelo provides the general design.—Its partial execution.—Plans for the Church of S. Giovanni dei Fiorentini at Rome.—Tiberio Calcagni.—The help he gave to Michelangelo at this period, and the charm of his personality.—The bust of Brutus. —2. Correspondence with Vasari and Ammanati about the completion of the Laurentian Library. — Michelangelo's defective method of building without working plans prepared beforehand. —The Porta Pia, and designs for other gates in Rome. S. Maria degli Angeli, or the Baths of Diocletian, remodelled.—Catherine de' Medici, Queen-mother of France, requests the drawing for an equestrian statue to her late husband, Henri II.—Daniele da Volterra is to execute it in bronze.—History of its failure.—3. Leone Leoni's medal of Michelangelo.—The original wax model in Mr. Fortnum's collection.—Critique of Michelangelo's portraits in oils by Bugiardini, in fresco by Daniele da Volterra, in bronze by the same master, in painting by Venusti, in engraving by Bonasoni.—Details illustrating the existing copies of Volterra's bronze head.—4. Correspondence with Lionardo Buonarroti.— Projects for his marriage.—Advice upon the choice of a wife.— Purchase of a house in Florence and lands outside it.—Lionardo's abominable handwriting.—Death of Gian Simone.—5. Correspondence with Varchi about the rival claims of sculpture and painting, also concerning his discourse on Buonarroti's poems.— Cellini's portrait of Bindo Altoviti.—6. Lionardo's marriage to Cassandra Ridolfi. — Michelangelo's joy in the thought that his family will now be propagated.—Birth of a male heir, Buonarroto. —Michelangelo's reflections on the christening.—Intimate relations with Vasari. —The Duke of Florence sends Cellini as an envoy to Rome, in hopes of bringing Michelangelo back to his native city.—Michelangelo refuses to leave S. Peter's, and keeps the good grace of the Medicean princes.—Vasari, the Duke, and

I.

THERE is great difficulty in dealing chronologically
with the last twenty years of Michelangelo's life.
This is due in some measure to the multiplicity of
his engagements, but more to the tardy rate at
which his work, now almost wholly architectural,
advanced. I therefore judged it best to carry the
history of his doings at S. Peter's down to the
latest date ; and I shall take the same course now
with regard to the lesser schemes which occupied his
mind between 1545 and 1564, reserving for the last
the treatment of his private life during this period.

A society of gentlemen and artists, to which Buonarroti belonged, conceived the plan of erecting
buildings of suitable size and grandeur on the
Campidoglio. This hill had always been dear to
the Romans, as the central point of urban life since
the foundation of their city, through the days of the
Republic and the Empire, down to the latest Middle

Ages. But it was distinguished only by its ancient name and fame. No splendid edifices and majestic squares reminded the spectator that here once stood the shrine of Jupiter Capitolinus, to which conquering generals rode in triumph with the spoils and captives of the habitable world behind their laurelled chariots. Paul III. approved of the design, and Michelangelo, who had received the citizenship of Rome on March 20, 1546, undertook to provide a scheme for its accomplishment. We are justified in believing that the disposition of the parts which now compose the Capitol is due to his conception : the long steep flight of steps leading up from the Piazza Araceli; the irregular open square, flanked on the left hand by the Museum of Sculpture, on the right by the Palazzo dei Conservatori, and closed at its farther end by the Palazzo del Senatore. He also placed the equestrian statue of Marcus Aurelius Antoninus on its noble pedestal, and suggested the introduction of other antique specimens of sculpture into various portions of the architectural plan. The splendid double staircase leading to the entrance hall of the Palazzo del Senatore, and part of the Palazzo dei Conservatori, were completed during Michelangelo's lifetime. When Vasari wrote in 1568, the dead sculptor's friend, Tommaso dei Cavalieri, was proceeding with the work.[1] There is every reason, therefore, to assume that the latter building, at any rate, fairly corresponds to his intention.

[1] Vasari, xii. p. 230.

Vignola and Giacomo della Porta, both of them excellent architects, carried out the scheme, which must have been nearly finished in the pontificate of Innocent X. (1644–1655).[1]

Like the cupola of S. Peter's, the campidoglio has always been regarded as one of Michelangelo's most meritorious performances in architecture. His severe critic, M. Charles Garnier, says of the Capitol:[2] "The general composition of the edifice is certainly worthy of Buonarroti's powerful conception. The balustrade which crowns the façade is indeed bad and vulgar; the great pilasters are very poor in invention, and the windows of the first story are extremely mediocre in style. Nevertheless, there is a great simplicity of lines in these palaces; and the porticoes of the ground-floor might be selected for the beauty of their leading motive. The opposition of the great pilasters to the little columns is an idea at once felicitous and original. The whole has a fine effect; and though I hold the proportions of the ground-floor too low in relation to the first story, I consider this façade of the Capitol not only one of Michelangelo's best works, but also one of the best specimens of the building of that period. Deduction must, of course, be made for heaviness and improprieties of taste, which are not rare."

---

[1] The two side palaces correspond in their general design; but the façade of the Palazzo del Senatore has been wholly remodelled.

[2] *L'Œuvre et la Vie*, p. 198.

Next to these designs for the Capitol, the most important architectural work of Michelangelo's old age was the plan he made of a new church to be erected by the Florentines in Rome to the honour of their patron, S. Giovanni.   We find him writing to his nephew on the 15th of July 1559:[1]   "The Florentines are minded to erect a great edifice—that is to say, their church; and all of them with one accord put pressure on me to attend to this.   I have answered that I am living here by the Duke's permission for the fabric of S. Peter's, and that unless he gives me leave, they can get nothing from me." The consul and counsellors of the Florentine nation in Rome wrote upon this to the Duke, who entered with enthusiasm into their scheme, not only sending a favourable reply, but also communicating personally upon the subject with Buonarroti.[2]   Three of Michelangelo's letters on the subject to the Duke have been preserved.[3]   After giving a short history of the project, and alluding to the fact that Leo X. began the church, he says that the Florentines had appointed a building committee of five men, at whose request he made several designs.   One of these they selected, and according to his own opinion it was the best. "This I will have copied and drawn out more clearly

---

[1] Lettere, No. cccxiv.

[2] See the correspondence of October 19 to December 22, 1559, in Gaye, iii. 16–23.

[3] Lettere, No. cdlxxxvii.–ix., November 1, 1559; March 5, April 25, 1560.

than I have been able to do it, on account of old age, and will send it to your Most Illustrious Lordship." The drawings were executed and carried to Florence by the hand of Tiberio Calcagni.[1] Vasari, who has given a long account of this design, says that Calcagni not only drew the plans, but that he also completed a clay model of the whole church within the space of two days, from which the Florentines caused a larger wooden model to be constructed.[2] Michelangelo must have been satisfied with his conception, for he told the building-committee that "if they carried it out, neither the Romans nor the Greeks ever erected so fine an edifice in any of their temples. Words the like of which neither before nor afterwards issued from his lips ; for he was exceedingly modest." Vasari, who had good opportunities for studying the model, pronounced it to be "superior in beauty, richness and variety of invention to any temple which was ever seen." The building was begun, and 5000 crowns were spent upon it. Then money or will failed. The model and drawings perished.[3] Nothing remains for certain to show what Michelangelo's intentions were. The pre-

[1] The only letter of Calcagni's to Michelangelo preserved in the Arch. Buon. (Cod. vii. No. 130, date Pisa, April 8, 1560) refers to these drawings, which, he says, have given great satisfaction to the Duke. It is written in a beautiful clear hand, and breathes a charming spirit of affection and modesty.

[2] Vasari, xii. 263–265.

[3] Some designs for architecture have been connected with this church. But their critique is uncertain.

sent church of S. Giovanni dei Fiorentini in Strada Giulia is the work of Giacomo della Porta, with a façade by Alessandro Galilei.

Of Tiberio Calcagni, the young Florentine sculptor and architect, who acted like a kind of secretary or clerk to Michelangelo, something may here be said. The correspondence of this artist with Lionardo Buonarroti shows him to have been what Vasari calls him, " of gentle manners and discreet behaviour." [1]   He felt both veneration and attachment for the aged master, and was one of the small group of intimate friends who cheered his last years. We have seen that Michelangelo consigned the shattered Pietà to his care ; and Vasari tells us that he also wished him to complete the bust of Brutus, which had been begun, at Donato Giannotti's request, for the Cardinal Ridolfi.[2] This bust is said to have been modelled from an ancient cornelian in the possession of a certain Giuliano Ceserino. Michelangelo not only blocked the marble out, but brought it nearly to completion, working the surface with very fine-toothed chisels.   The sweetness of Tiberio Calcagni's nature is proved by the fact that he would not set his own hand to this masterpiece of sculpture.   As in the case of the Pietà, he left Buonarroti's work untouched, where mere repairs were not required.   Accordingly we still can trace

[1] Several of his letters are reproduced in Daelli's *Carte Mich. Inedite.* See above, p. 250, note, for a reference to the only letter written by him to his master.
[2] Vasari, xii. 264.

the fine-toothed marks of the chisel alluded to by Vasari, hatched and cross-hatched with right and left handed strokes in the style peculiar to Michelangelo. The Brutus remains one of the finest specimens of his creative genius. It must have been conceived and executed in the plenitude of his vigour, probably at the time when Florence fell beneath the yoke of Alessandro de' Medici, or rather when his murderer Lorenzino gained the name of Brutus from the exiles (1539). Though Vasari may be right in saying that a Roman intaglio suggested the stamp of face and feature, yet we must regard this Brutus as an ideal portrait, intended to express the artist's conception of resolution and uncompromising energy in a patriot eager to sacrifice personal feelings and to dare the utmost for his country's welfare. Nothing can exceed the spirit with which a violent temperament, habitually repressed, but capable of leaping forth like sudden lightning, has been rendered. We must be grateful to Calcagni for leaving it in its suggestively unfinished state.[1]

[1] The Brutus stands now in one of the halls of the Palazzo Bargello at Florence. On its pedestal is inscribed a distich, which has been erroneously attributed to Bembo :—

> Dum Bruto effigiem sculptor de marmore ducit,
> In mentem sceleris venit et abstinuit.

The Earl of Sandwich altered the sentiment thus :—

> Brutum effecisset sculptor ; sed mente recursat
> Tanta viri virtus : sistit et abstinuit.

PIETÀ, marble, about 1550. Museo dell'Opera del Duomo,
Florence. Collection of Creighton E. Gilbert.

II.

During these same years Michelangelo carried on a correspondence with Ammanati and Vasari about the completion of the Laurentian Library.[1] His letters illustrate what I have more than once observed regarding his unpractical method of commencing great works, without more than the roughest sketches, intelligible to himself alone, and useless to an ordinary craftsman. The Florentine artists employed upon the fabric wanted very much to know how he meant to introduce the grand staircase into the vestibule. Michelangelo had forgotten all about it. "With regard to the staircase of the library, about which so much has been said to me, you may believe that if I could remember how I had arranged it, I should not need to be begged and prayed for information. There comes into my mind, as in a dream, the image of a certain staircase; but I do not think this can be the one I then designed, for it seems so stupid. However, I will describe it." Later on he sends a little clay model of a staircase, just enough to indicate his general conception, but not to determine details. He suggests that the work would look better if carried out in walnut. We have every reason to suppose that the present stone flight of steps is far from being representative of his idea.

[1] Lettere, Nos. cdlxxxv., cdlxxxvi.

He was now too old to do more than furnish
drawings when asked to design some monument.
Accordingly, when Pius IV. resolved to erect a
tomb in Milan Cathedral to the memory of his
brother, Giangiacomo de' Medici, Marquis of Marignano, commonly called Il Medeghino, he requested
Michelangelo to supply the bronze-sculptor Leone
Leoni of Menaggio with a design.[1] This must have
been insufficient for the sculptor's purpose—a mere
hand-sketch not drawn to scale. The monument,
though imposing in general effect, is very defective
in its details and proportions. The architectural
scheme has not been comprehended by the sculptor,
who enriched it with a great variety of figures,
excellently wrought in bronze, and faintly suggesting Michelangelo's manner.

The grotesque *barocco* style of the Porta Pia,
strong in its total outline, but whimsical and weak
in decorative detail, may probably be ascribed to
the same cause.[2] It was sketched out by Michelangelo during the pontificate of Pius IV., and can
hardly have been erected under his personal supervision. Vasari says:[3] "He made three sketches,
extravagant in style and most beautiful, of which

[1] This man is always called "Il Cavaliere Aretino." But he was a
native of Menaggio on the Lake of Como, and for this reason was well
chosen to execute the great pirate's tomb.

[2] I allude to the design, an engraving of which will be found in
L'Œuvre et la Vie, p. 201. In its present state the only part of the
gate which can be referred to Michelangelo is the noble portal with the
bold architrave.

[3] Vasari, xii. 263.

the Pope selected the least costly; this was executed much to his credit, as may now be seen." To what extent he was responsible for the other sixteenth-century gates of Rome, including the Porta del Popolo, which is commonly ascribed to him, cannot be determined; though Vasari asserts that Michelangelo supplied the Pope with "many other models" for the restoration of the gates. Indeed it may be said of all his later work that we are dealing with uncertain material, the original idea emanating perhaps from Buonarroti's mind, but the execution having devolved upon journeymen.

Pius IV. charged Michelangelo with another great undertaking, which was the restoration of the Baths of Diocletian in the form of a Christian church. Criticism is reduced to silence upon his work in this place, because S. Maria degli Angeli underwent a complete remodelling by the architect Vanvitelli in 1749. This man altered the ground-plan from the Latin to the Greek type, and adopted the decorative style in vogue at the beginning of the eighteenth century. All that appears certain is that Michelangelo had very considerable remains of the Roman building to make use of. We may also perhaps credit tradition, when it tells us that the vast Carthusian cloister belongs to him, and that the three great cypress-trees were planted by his hand.

Henri the Second's death occurred in 1559; and his widow, Catherine de' Medici, resolved to erect an equestrian statue to his memory. She bethought her of the aged sculptor, who had been bred in the palace of her great-grandfather, who had served two Pontiffs of her family, and who had placed the mournful image of her father on the tomb at San Lorenzo. Accordingly she wrote a letter on the 14th of November in that year, informing Michelangelo of her intention, and begging him to supply at least a design upon which the best masters in the realm of France might work.[1] The statue was destined for the courtyard of the royal chateau at Blois, and was to be in bronze. Ruberto degli Strozzi, the Queen's cousin, happened about this time to visit Rome. Michelangelo having agreed to furnish a sketch, it was decided between them that the execution should be assigned to Daniele da Volterra. After nearly a year's interval, Catherine wrote again, informing Michelangelo that she had deposited a sum of 6000 golden crowns at the bank of Gianbattista Gondi for the work, adding:[2] "Consequently, since on my side nothing remains to be done, I entreat you by the affection you have always shown to my family, to our Florence, and lastly to art, that you will use all diligence and assiduity, so far as your years permit, in pushing forward this noble work, and making it a living likeness of my lord, as well as worthy of your own unrivalled genius. It is true that this will add nothing to the fame you now enjoy; yet

[1] Gotti, i. 349.　　　[2] Gotti, i. 351.

it will at least augment your reputation for most acceptable and affectionate devotion toward myself and my ancestors, and prolong through centuries the memory of my lawful and sole love ; for the which I shall be eager and liberal to reward you." It is probable that by this time (October 30, 1560) Michelangelo had forwarded his sketch to France, for the Queen criticised some details relating to the portrait of her husband. She may have remembered with what idealistic freedom the statues of the Dukes of Nemours and Urbino had been treated in the Medicean Sacristy. Anyhow, she sent a picture, and made her agent, Baccio del Bene, write a postscript to her letter, ordering Michelangelo to model the King's head without curls, and to adopt the rich modern style for his armour and the trappings of his charger. She particularly insisted upon the likeness being carefully brought out.[1]

Michelangelo died before the equestrian statue of Henri II. was finished. Cellini, in his Memoirs, relates that Daniele da Volterra worked slowly, and caused much annoyance to the Queen-mother of France. In 1562 her agent, Baccio del Bene, came to Florence on financial business with the Duke. He then proposed that Cellini should return to Paris and undertake the ornamental details of the tomb.

---

[1] See Gotti, ii. 145. The first of Catherine's letters is dated Blois, November 18, 1559. The second, Orleans, October 30, 1560. Both written by a secretary, and signed by the Queen-mother. Del Bene's letter bears the latter date. Arch. Buon., Cod. vii. Nos. 139, 140, 155.

The Duke would not consent, and Catherine de' Medici did not choose to quarrel with her cousin about an artist.[1] So this arrangement, which might have secured the completion of the statue on a splendid scale, fell through. When Daniele died in 1566, only the horse was cast;[2] and this part served finally for Biard's statue of Louis XIII.

III.

The sculptor Leone Leoni, who was employed upon the statue of Giangiacomo de' Medici in Milan, wrote frequently to Michelangelo, showing by his letters that a warm friendship subsisted between them, which was also shared by Tommaso Cavalieri. In the year 1560, according to Vasari, Leoni modelled a profile portrait of the great master, which he afterwards cast in medal form.[3] This is almost the most interesting, and it is probably the most genuine contemporary record which we possess regarding Michelangelo's appearance in the body. I may therefore take it as my basis for inquiring into the relative value of the many portraits said to have been modelled, painted, or sketched from

[1] *Memoirs*, lib. ii. cap. cxii.

[2] See Vasari's *Life of Daniele da Volterra*, xii. 100.

[3] This date is determined by Vasari's saying that the medal was made in the year of Giovanni de' Medici's visit to Rome to receive the Cardinal's hat. It is confirmed by a letter of Leoni's I shall quote below.

the hero in his lifetime.   So far as I am hitherto
aware, no claim has been put in for the authen-
ticity of any likeness, except Bonasoni's engraving,
anterior to the date we have arrived at.   While
making this statement, I pass over the prostrate
old man in the Victory, and the Nicodemus of the
Florentine Pietà, both of which, with more or less
reason, have been accepted as efforts after self-
portraiture.

After making due allowance for Vasari's too
notorious inaccuracies, deliberate misstatements, and
random jumpings at conclusions, we have the right
to accept him here as a first-rate authority.   He was
living at this time in close intimacy with Buonarroti,
enjoyed his confidence, plumed himself upon their
friendship, and had no reason to distort truth, which
must have been accessible to one in his position.
He says, then :[1] " At this time the Cavaliere Leoni
made a very lively portrait of Michelangelo upon a
medal, and to meet his wishes, modelled on the
reverse a blind man led by a dog, with this legend
round the rim : DOCEBO INIQUOS VIAS TUAS, ET IMPII
AD TE CONVERTENTUR.   It pleased Michelangelo so
much that he gave him a wax model of a Hercules
throttling Antæus, by his own hand, together with
some drawings.   Of Michelangelo there exist no
other portraits, except two in painting—one by
Bugiardini, the other by Jacopo del Conte ; and
one in bronze, in full relief, made by Daniele da

[1] Vasari, xii. 260.

Volterra : these, and Leoni's medal, from which (in the plural) many copies have been made, and a great number of them have been seen by me in several parts of Italy and abroad."

Leoni's medal, on the obverse, shows the old artist's head in profile, with strong lines of drapery rising to the neck and gathering around the shoulders. It carries this legend : MICHAELANGELUS BUONAR-ROTUS, FLO. R. A.E.T.S. ANN. 88, and is signed LEO. Leoni then assumed that Michelangelo was eighty-eight years of age when he cast the die. But if this was done in 1560, the age he had then attained was eighty-five. We possess a letter from Leoni in Milan to Buonarroti in Rome, dated March 14, 1561.[1] In it he says : "I am sending to your lordship, by the favour of Lord Carlo Visconti, a great man in this city, and beloved by his Holiness, four medals of your portrait : two in silver, and two in bronze. I should have done so earlier but for my occupation with the monument (of Medeghino), and for the certainty I feel that you will excuse my tardiness, if not a sin of ingratitude in me. The one enclosed within the little box has been worked up to the finest polish. I beg you to accept and keep this for the love of me. With the other three you will do as you think best. I say this because ambition has prompted me to send copies into Spain and Flanders, as I have also done to Rome and other places. I call it ambition, forasmuch as I have gained an over-

[1] Gotti, i. 346.

plus of benefits by acquiring the goodwill of your lordship, whom I esteem so highly.[1] Have I not received in little less than three months two letters written to me by you, divine man ; and couched not in terms fit for a servant of good heart and will, but for one beloved as a son ? I pray you to go on loving me, and when occasion serves, to favour me ; and to Signor Tomao dei Cavalieri say that I shall never be unmindful of him."

It is clear, then, I think, that Leoni's model was made at Rome in 1560, cast at Milan, and sent early in the spring of 1561 to Michelangelo. The wide distribution of the medals, two of which exist still in silver,[2] while several in bronze may be found in different collections, is accounted for by what Leoni says about his having given them away to various parts of Europe. We are bound to suppose that AET. 88 in the legend on the obverse is due to a misconception concerning Michelangelo's age. Old men are often ignorant or careless about the exact tale of years they have performed.

There is reason to believe that Leoni's original model of the profile, the likeness he shaped from life, and which he afterwards used for the medallion, is extant and in excellent preservation. Mr. C. Drury E. Fortnum (to whose monographs upon Michelangelo's portraits, kindly communicated by himself,

---

[1] Leoni means to intimate that he was acquiring fame by the diffusion of these portraits.

[2] One at Florence, the other at South Kensington.

I am deeply indebted at this portion of my work),
tells us how he came into possession of an exquisite
cameo, in flesh-coloured wax upon a black oval
ground.[1] This fragile work of art is framed in gilt
metal and glazed, carrying upon its back an Italian
inscription, which may be translated : " Portrait of
Michelangiolo Buonarroti, taken from the life, by
Leone Aretino, his friend." Comparing the relief
in wax with the medal, we cannot doubt that both
represent the same man ; and only cavillers will raise
the question whether both were fashioned by one
hand. Such discrepancies as occur between them
are just what we should expect in the work of a
craftsman who sought first to obtain an accurate
likeness of his subject, and then treated the same
subject on the lines of numismatic art.[2] The wax
shows a lean and subtly moulded face—the face of
a delicate old man, wiry and worn with years of deep
experience. The hair on head and beard is singularly natural ; one feels it to be characteristic of the
person. Transferring this portrait to bronze necessitated a general broadening of the masses, with a
coarsening of outline to obtain bold relief. Some-

[1] "On the Original Portrait of Michelangelo, by Leo Leone," a paper
published in the *Archæological Journal* (vol. xxxii.) ; "On the Bronze
Portrait Busts of Michelangelo, etc.," published later in the same
journal. I shall refer to these essays respectively as Fortnum 1 and
Fortnum 2.

[2] If we possessed the original model Cellini made for his medal of
Bembo, and were able to compare it with the bronze, I believe we
should observe the same qualities of realism in the former, and of
numismatic style in the latter.

thing of the purest truth has been sacrificed to plastic effect by thickening the shrunken throat; and this induced a corresponding enlargement of the occiput for balance.   Writing with photographs of these two models before me, I feel convinced that in the wax we have a portrait from the life of the aged Buonarroti as Leoni knew him, and in the bronze a handling of that portrait as the craftsman felt his art of metal-work required its execution.   There was a grand manner of medallion-portraiture in Italy, deriving from the times of Pisanello; and Leoni's bronze is worthy of that excellent tradition.   He preserved the salient features of Buonarroti in old age.   But having to send down to posterity a monumental record of the man, he added, insensibly or wilfully, both bulk and mass to the head he had so keenly studied.   What confirms me in the opinion that Mr. Fortnum's cameo is the most veracious portrait we possess of Michelangelo in old age, is that its fragility of structure, the tenuity of life vigorous but infinitely refined, reappears in the weak drawing made by Francesco d'Olanda of Buonarroti in hat and mantle.[1]   This is a comparatively poor and dreamy sketch.   Yet it has an air of veracity; and what the Flemish painter seized in the divine man he so much admired, was a certain slender grace and dignity of person—exactly the quality which Mr. Fortnum's cameo possesses.

[1] Reproduced in Yriarte's *Florence*, p. 295 (French edition; p. 280 English edition).

Before leaving this interesting subject, I ought to add that the blind man on the reverse of Leoni's medal is clearly a rough and ready sketch of Michelangelo, not treated like a portrait, but with indications sufficient to connect the figure with the highly wrought profile on the obverse.

Returning now to the passage cited from Vasari, we find that he reckons only two authentic portraits in painting of Michelangelo, one by Bugiardini, the other by Jacopo del Conte. He has neglected to mention two which are undoubtedly attempts to reproduce the features of the master by scholars he had formed. Probably Vasari overlooked them, because they did not exist as easel-pictures, but were introduced into great compositions as subordinate adjuncts. One of them is the head painted by Daniele da Volterra in his picture of the Assumption at the church of the Trinità de' Monti in Rome. It belongs to an apostle, draped in red, stretching arms aloft, close to a column, on the right hand of the painting as we look at it. This must be reckoned among the genuine likenesses of the great man by one who lived with him and knew him intimately. The other is a portrait placed by Marcello Venusti in the left-hand corner of his copy of the Last Judgment, executed, under Michelangelo's direction, for the Cardinal Farnese.[1] It has value for the same reasons as those which make us dwell upon Daniele da Volterra's picture. Moreover, it connects itself with

[1] Now in the Picture Gallery at Naples.

a series of easel-paintings. One of these, ascribed to Venusti, is preserved in the Museo Buonarroti at Florence ; another at the Capitol in Rome. Several repetitions of this type exist : they look like studies taken by the pupil from his master, and reproduced to order when death closed the scene, making friends wish for mementoes of the genius who had passed away. The critique of such works will always remain obscure.

What has become of the portrait of Del Conte mentioned by Vasari cannot now be ascertained. We have no external evidence to guide us.

On the other hand, certain peculiarities about the portrait in the Uffizi, especially the exaggeration of one eye, lend some colouring to the belief that we here possess the picture ascribed by Vasari to Bugiardini.[1]

Michelangelo's type of face was well accentuated, and all the more or less contemporary portraits of him reproduce it. Time is wasted in the effort to assign to little men their special part in the creation of a prevalent tradition. It seems to me, therefore, the function of sane criticism not to be particular about the easel-pictures ascribed to Venusti, Del Conte, and Bugiardini.

The case is different with a superb engraving by Giulio Bonasoni, a profile in a circle, dated 1546, and giving Buonarroti's age as seventy-two. This

---

[1] *Life of Bugiardini*, Vasari, x. 350. It is noticeable that this peculiarity about the right eye repeats itself in a large number of the doubtful portraits, pointing to a common origin.

shows the man in fuller vigour than the portraits we
have hitherto been dealing with. From other prints
which bear the signature of Bonasoni, we see that
he was interested in faithfully reproducing Michelangelo's work. What the relations between the
two men were remains uncertain, but Bonasoni
may have had opportunities of studying the master's
person. At any rate, as a product of the burin, this
profile is comparable for fidelity and veracity with
Leoni's model, and is executed in the same medallion
spirit.

So far, then, as I have yet pursued the analysis of
Michelangelo's portraits, I take Bonasoni's engraving
to be decisive for Michelangelo's appearance at the
age of seventy ; Leoni's model as of equal or of greater
value at the age of eighty ; Venusti's and Da Volterra's
paintings as of some importance for this later period ;
while I leave the attribution of minor easel-pictures
to Del Conte or to Bugiardini open.

It remains to speak of that " full relief in bronze
made by Daniele da Volterra," which Vasari mentions among the four genuine portraits of Buonarroti.
From the context we should gather that this head
was executed during the lifetime of Michelangelo,
and the conclusion is supported by the fact that
only a few pages later on Vasari mentions two other
busts modelled after his death. Describing the
catafalque erected to his honour in S. Lorenzo, he
says that the pyramid which crowned the structure
exhibited within two ovals (one turned toward the

chief door, and the other toward the high altar) "the head of Michelangelo in relief, taken from nature, and very excellently carried out by Santi Buglioni."[1] The words *ritratta dal naturale* do not, I think, necessarily imply that it was modelled from the life. Owing to the circumstances under which Michelangelo's obsequies were prepared, there was not time to finish it in bronze or stone; it may therefore have been one of those Florentine terra-cotta effigies which artists elaborated from a cast taken after death. That there existed such a cast is proved by what we know about the monument designed by Vasari in S. Croce.[2] "One of the statues was assigned to Battista Lorenzi, an able sculptor, together with the head of Michelangelo." We learn from another source that this bust in marble "was taken from the mask cast after his death."

The custom of taking plaster casts from the faces of the illustrious dead, in order to perpetuate their features, was so universal in Italy, that it could hardly have been omitted in the case of Michelangelo. The question now arises whether the bronze head ascribed by Vasari to Daniele da Volterra was executed during Michelangelo's lifetime or after his decease, and whether we possess it. There are eight heads of this species known to students of Michelangelo, which correspond so nicely in their measurements and general features as to force the

---

[1] Vasari, xii. 301.   [2] Ibid., 310, and Fortnum I, p. 4.

conclusion that they were all derived from an original moulded by one masterly hand.[1] Three of these heads are unmounted, namely, those at Milan, Oxford, and M. Piot's[2] house in Paris. One, that of the Capitoline Museum, is fixed upon a bust of *bigio morato* marble.[3] The remaining four examples are executed throughout in bronze as busts, agreeing in the main as to the head, but differing in minor details of drapery. They exist respectively in the Museo Buonarroti, the Accademia, and the Bargello at Florence, and in the private collection of M. Cottier of Paris. It is clear, then, that we are dealing with bronze heads cast from a common mould, worked up afterwards according to the fancy of the artist. That this original head was the portrait ascribed to Daniele da Volterra will be conceded by all who care to trace the history of the bust; but whether he modelled it after Michelangelo's death cannot be decided. Professional critics are of the opinion that a mask was followed by the master;[4] and this may have

[1] See Fortnum 2, pp. 7–10. Mr. Fortnum has given minute particulars concerning all the heads.

[2] Bequeathed by M. Piot to the Louvre, where it now is.

[3] A close inspection of this bronze shows that it was only carried down to the collar, which is that of a linen shirt, and quite realistic. This part of the portrait is joined very negligently to the marble. The skull is less massive behind the ears than in Leoni's medal, and has a peculiarly Florentine want of volume in the occiput. The workmanship of the bronze is rude, the surface smooth. The right eye looks a little away from the face. Have we here perhaps the parent mask of all the masks which issued from Daniele's workshop?

[4] Fortnum 2, p. 10.

been the case. Michelangelo died upon the 17th of February 1564. His face was probably cast in the usual course of things, and copies may have been distributed among his friends in Rome and Florence. Lionardo Buonarroti showed at once a great anxiety to obtain his uncle's bust from Daniele da Volterra. Possibly he ordered it while resident in Rome, engaged in winding up Michelangelo's affairs. At any rate, Daniele wrote on June 11 to this effect:[1] "As regards the portraits in metal, I have already completed a model in wax, and the work is going on as fast as circumstances permit: you may rely upon its being completed with due despatch and all the care I can bestow upon it." Nearly four months had elapsed since Michelangelo's decease, and this was quite enough time for the wax model to be made. The work of casting was begun, but Daniele's health at this time became so wretched that he found it impossible to work steadily at any of his undertakings. He sank slowly, and expired in the early spring of 1566.

What happened to the bronze heads in the interval between June 1564 and April 1566 may be partly understood from Diomede Leoni's correspondence. This man, a native of San Quirico, was Daniele's scholar, and an intimate friend of the Buonarroti family. On the 9th of September 1564 he wrote to Lionardo :[2] " Your two heads of that sainted man are coming to

---

[1] Daelli, *Cart. Mich. Ined.*, p. 58.   [2] Ibid., *op. cit.*, 60.

a good result, and I am sure you will be satisfied with them." It appears, then, that Lionardo had ordered two copies from Daniele. On the 21st of April 1565 Diomede writes again:[1] "I delivered your messages to Messer Daniele, who replies that you are always in his mind, as also the two heads of your lamented uncle. They will soon be cast, as also will my copy, which I mean to keep by me for my honour." The casting must have taken place in the summer of 1565, for Diomede writes upon the 6th of October:[2] "I will remind him (Daniele) of your two heads; and he will find mine well finished, which will make him wish to have yours chased without further delay." The three heads had then been cast; Diomede was polishing his up with the file; Daniele had not yet begun to do this for Lionardo's. We hear nothing more until the death of Daniele da Volterra. After this event occurred, Lionardo Buonarroti received a letter from Jacopo del Duca, a Sicilian bronze-caster of high merit, who had enjoyed Michelangelo's confidence and friendship.[3] He was at present employed upon the metal-work for Buonarroti's monument in the Church of the SS. Apostoli in Rome, and on the 18th of April he sent important information respecting the two heads left by Daniele.[4] "Messer Danielo had cast them, but they are in such a state as to require working over afresh with chisels and files.

---

[1] Daelli, *op. cit.*, p. 66.
[2] Gotti, i. 372.
[3] Vasari, xii. 263.
[4] Gotti, i. 373.

I am not sure, then, whether they will suit your purpose; but that is your affair. I, for my part, should have liked you to have the portrait from the hand of the lamented master himself, and not from any other. Your lordship must decide : appeal to some one who can inform you better than I do. I know that I am speaking from the love I bear you; and perhaps, if Danielo had been alive, he would have had them brought to proper finish. As for those men of his, I do not know what they will do." On the same day, a certain Michele Alberti wrote as follows :[1] "Messer Jacopo, your gossip, has told me that your lordship wished to know in what condition are the heads of the late lamented Michelangelo. I inform you that they are cast, and will be chased within the space of a month, or rather more. So your lordship will be able to have them; and you may rest assured that you will be well and quickly served." Alberti, we may conjecture, was one of Daniele's men alluded to by Jacopo del Duca. It is probable that just at this time they were making several *replicas* from their deceased master's model, in order to dispose of them at an advantage while Michelangelo's memory was still fresh. Lionardo grew more and more impatient. He appealed again to Diomede Leoni, who replied from San Quirico upon the 4th of June :[2] "The two heads were in existence when I left Rome, but not finished up. I imagine you have given orders to have them delivered

[1] Gotti, i. 373.   [2] Daelli, *op. cit.*, p. 72.

over to yourself. As for the work of chasing them, if you can wait till my return, we might intrust them to a man who succeeded very well with my own copy." Three years later, on September 17, 1569, Diomede wrote once again about his copy of Da Volterra's model:[1] "I enjoy the continual contemplation of his effigy in bronze, which is now perfectly finished and set up in my garden, where you will see it, if good fortune favours me with a visit from you."

The net result of this correspondence seems to be that certainly three bronze heads, and probably more, remained unfinished in Daniele da Volterra's workshop after his death, and that these were gradually cleaned and polished by different craftsmen, according to the pleasure of their purchasers. The strong resemblance of the eight bronze heads at present known to us, in combination with their different states of surface-finish, correspond entirely to this conclusion. Mr. Fortnum, in his classification, describes four as being not chased, one as "rudely and broadly chased," three as "more or less chased."[2]

Of these variants upon the model common to them all, we can only trace one with relative certainty. It is the bust at present in the Bargello Palace, whither it came from the Grand Ducal villa of Poggio Imperiale. By the marriage of the heiress of the ducal house of Della Rovere with

[1] Daelli, *op. cit.*, p. 79.   [2] Fortnum 2, p. 10.

a Duke of Tuscany, this work of art passed, with other art treasures, notably with a statuette of Michelangelo's Moses, into the possession of the Medici. A letter written in 1570 to the Duke of Urbino by Buonarroti's house-servant, Antonio del Franzese of Castel Durante, throws light upon the matter.[1] He begins by saying that he is glad to hear the Duke will accept the little Moses, though the object is too slight in value to deserve his notice. Then he adds: "The head of which your Excellency spoke in the very kind letter addressed to me at your command is the true likeness of Michelangelo Buonarroti, my old master; and it is of bronze, designed by himself. I keep it here in Rome, and now present it to your Excellency." Antonio then, in all probability, obtained one of the Daniele da Volterra bronzes; for it is wholly incredible that what he writes about its having been made by Michelangelo should be the truth.[2] Had Michelangelo really modelled his own portrait and cast it in bronze, we must have heard of this from other sources. Moreover, the Medicean bust of Michelangelo which is now placed in the Bargello, and which we believe to have come from Urbino, belongs indubitably to the series of portraits made from Daniele da Volterra's model.

To sum up this question of Michelangelo's authentic

---

[1] Gotti, i. 373.

[2] His words may perhaps only imply that Michelangelo meant it to be made. The original runs: "designato da lui proprio."

portraits : I repeat that Bonasoni's engraving represents him at the age of seventy ; Leoni's wax model
and medallions at eighty ; the eight bronze heads,
derived from Daniele's model, at the epoch of his
death.　In painting, Marco Venusti and Daniele da
Volterra helped to establish a traditional type by
two episodical likenesses, the one worked into
Venusti's copy of the Last Judgment (at Naples),
the other into Volterra's original picture of the
Assumption (at Trinità de' Monti, Rome).　For
the rest, the easel-pictures, which abound, can
hardly now be distributed, by any sane method of
criticism, between Bugiardini, Jacopo del Conte,
and Venusti.　They must be taken *en masse*, as
contributions to the study of his personality ; and,
as I have already said, the oil-painting of the Uffizi
may perhaps be ascribed with some show of probability to Bugiardini.[1]

---

[1] There is a puzzling easel-picture, formerly in the possession of the
Marchese Lottaringo della Stufa, which deserves mention here.　The
face is nearly full, turned to the spectator over the right shoulder ;
very pallid, with rugged features and a fatigued expression ; wrinkles
strongly marked.　The right eye is out of drawing with the left.　The
lower lip is dragged a little toward the right side, showing more beneath
moustache and beard than elsewhere.　The head is covered with a black
felt hat, not unlike that shown in Francesco d'Olanda's sketch.　The
key of colouring is black and ivory yellow, with reds worked into the
surface of the face.　A doubtful piece of work, yet interesting as diver-
gent from the types above named.

IV.

Michelangelo's correspondence with his nephew Lionardo gives us ample details concerning his private life and interests in old age.   It turns mainly upon the following topics : investment of money in land near Florence, the purchase of a mansion in the city, Lionardo's marriage, his own illnesses, the Duke's invitation, and the project of making a will, which was never carried out.   Much as Michelangelo loved his nephew, he took frequent occasions of snubbing him.   For instance, news reached Rome that the landed property of a certain Francesco Corboli was going to be sold.   Michelangelo sent to Lionardo requesting him to make inquiries ; and because the latter showed some alacrity in doing so, his uncle wrote him the following querulous epistle [1] : " You have been very hasty in sending me information regarding the estates of the Corboli.   I did not think you were yet in Florence. Are you afraid lest I should change my mind, as some one may perhaps have put it into your head ? I tell you that I want to go slowly in this affair, because the money I must pay has been gained here with toil and trouble unintelligible to one who was born clothed and shod as you were.   About your coming post-haste to Rome, I do not know that you

[1] Lettere, No. clxii, February 6, 1546.

came in such a hurry when I was a pauper and lacked bread. Enough for you to throw away the money that you did not earn. The fear of losing what you might inherit on my death impelled you. You say it was your duty to come, by reason of the love you bear me. The love of a woodworm! If you really loved me, you would have written now: 'Michelangelo, spend those 3000 ducats there upon yourself, for you have given us enough already: your life is dearer to us than your money.' You have all of you lived forty years upon me, and I have never had from you so much as one good word. 'Tis true that last year I scolded and rebuked you so that for very shame you sent me a load of trebbiano. I almost wish you hadn't! I do not write this because I am unwilling to buy. Indeed I have a mind to do so, in order to obtain an income for myself, now that I cannot work more. But I want to buy at leisure, so as not to purchase some annoyance. Therefore do not hurry."

Lionardo was careless about his handwriting, and this annoyed the old man terribly.[1]

"Do not write to me again. Each time I get one of your letters, a fever takes me with the trouble I have in reading it. I do not know where you learned to write. I think that if you were writing to the greatest donkey in the world you would do it with more care. Therefore do not add to the annoyances I have, for I have already quite enough of them."

[1] Lettere, No. cxlxviii., June 5, 1546.

He returns to the subject over and over again, and once declares that he has flung a letter of Lionardo's into the fire unread, and so is incapable of answering it.[1] This did not prevent a brisk interchange of friendly communications between the uncle and nephew.

Lionardo was now living in the Buonarroti house in Via Ghibellina. Michelangelo thought it advisable that he should remove into a more commodious mansion, and one not subject to inundations of the basement. He desired, however, not to go beyond the quarter of S. Croce, where the family had been for centuries established. The matter became urgent, for Lionardo wished to marry, and could not marry until he was provided with a residence. Eventually, after rejecting many plans and proffers of houses, they decided to enlarge and improve the original Buonarroti mansion in Via Ghibellina.[2] This house continued to be their town-mansion until the year 1852, when it passed by testamentary devise to the city of Florence. It is now the Museo Buonarroti.

Lionardo was at this time thirty, and was the sole hope of the family, since Michelangelo and his two surviving brothers had no expectation of offspring. His uncle kept reminding the young man that, if he did not marry and get children, the whole property of the Buonarroti would go to the Hospital or to S.

---

[1] Lettere, Nos. clxxxiv., cciv., ccxxiv.

[2] Ibid., Nos. clxxvi., ccxxviii., ccxxix. This decision was made in August 1549.

Martino.[1] This made his marriage imperative ; and Michelangelo's letters between March 5, 1547, and May 16, 1553, when the desired event took place, are full of the subject. He gives his nephew excellent advice as to the choice of a wife. She ought to be ten years younger than himself, of noble birth, but not of a very rich or powerful family ; Lionardo must not expect her to be too handsome, since he is no miracle of manly beauty ; the great thing is to obtain a good, useful, and obedient helpmate, who will not try to get the upper hand in the house, and who will be grateful for an honourable settlement in life.[2] The following passages may be selected, as specimens of Michelangelo's advice : "You ought not to look for a dower, but only to consider whether the girl is well brought up, healthy, of good character and noble blood. You are not yourself of such parts and person as to be worthy of the first beauty of Florence." "You have need of a wife who would stay with you, and whom you could command, and who would not want to live in grand style or to gad about every day to marriages and banquets. Where a court is, it is easy to become a woman of loose life ; especially for one who has no relatives."

Numerous young ladies were introduced by friends or matrimonial agents. Six years, however, elapsed before the suitable person presented herself in the

<hr />

[1] Two ways of saying that it would have to be expended in charities.

[2] See in particular Lettere, Nos. clxxv., clxxxii., cxciv., cciv., ccx., ccxx., ccxli., ccxlii., ccxlvi., cclv.

shape of Cassandra, daughter of Donato Ridolfi.
Meanwhile, in 1548, Michelangelo lost the elder
of his surviving brothers. Giovan Simone died
upon the 9th of January; and though he had given
but little satisfaction in his lifetime, his death was
felt acutely by the venerable artist.[1] " I received
news in your last of Giovan Simone's death. It
has caused me the greatest sorrow; for though
I am old, I had yet hoped to see him before he
died, and before I died. God has willed it so.
Patience! I should be glad to hear circumstantially
what kind of end he made, and whether he con-
fessed and communicated with all the sacraments
of the Church. If he did so, and I am informed
of it, I shall suffer less." A few days after the date
of this letter, Michelangelo writes again, blaming
Lionardo pretty severely for negligence in giving
particulars of his uncle's death and affairs. Later
on, it seems that he was satisfied regarding Giovan
Simone's manner of departure from this world. A
grudge remained against Lionardo because he had
omitted to inform him about the property. " I
heard the details from other persons before you
sent them, which angered me exceedingly."

[1] Lettere, Nos. cxci.–cxciii.

V.

The year 1549 is marked by an exchange of civilities between Michelangelo and Benedetto Varchi. The learned man of letters and minute historiographer of Florence probably enjoyed our great sculptor's society in former years : recently they had been brought into closer relations at Rome. Varchi, who was interested in critical and academical problems, started the question whether sculpture or painting could justly claim a priority in the plastic arts. He conceived the very modern idea of collecting opinions from practical craftsmen, instituting, in fact, what would now be called a " Symposium " upon the subject. A good number of the answers to his query have been preserved, and among them is a letter from Michelangelo. It contains the following passage, which proves in how deep a sense Buonarroti was by temperament and predilection a sculptor:[1] " My opinion is that all painting is the better the nearer it approaches to relief, and relief is the worse in proportion as it inclines to painting. And so I have been wont to think that sculpture is the lamp of painting, and that the difference between them might be likened to the difference between the sun and moon. Now that I have read your essay, in which you

[1] Lettere, No. cdlxii.

maintain that, philosophically speaking, things which fulfil the same purpose are essentially the same, I have altered my view. Therefore I say that, if greater judgment and difficulty, impediment and labour, in the handling of material do not constitute higher nobility, then painting and sculpture form one art. This being granted, it follows that no painter should underrate sculpture, and no sculptor should make light of painting. By sculpture I understand an art which operates by taking away superfluous material; by painting, one that attains its result by laying on. It is enough that both emanate from the same human intelligence, and consequently sculpture and painting ought to live in amity together, without these lengthy disputations. More time is wasted in talking about the problem than would go to the making of figures in both species. The man who wrote that painting was superior to sculpture, if he understood the other things he says no better, might be called a writer below the level of my maid-servant. There are infinite points not yet expressed which might be brought out regarding these arts; but, as I have said, they want too much time; and of time I have but little, being not only old, but almost numbered with the dead. Therefore, I pray you to have me excused. I recommend myself to you, and thank you to the best of my ability for the too great honour you have done me, which is more than I deserve."

Varchi printed this letter in a volume which he published at Florence in 1549, and reissued through another firm in 1590.[1] It contained the treatise alluded to above, and also a commentary upon one of Michelangelo's sonnets, "Non ha l'ottimo artista alcun concetto." [2] The book was duly sent to Michelangelo by the favour of a noble Florentine gentleman, Luca Martini. He responded to the present in a letter which deserves here to be recited. It is an eminent example of the urbanity observed by him in the interchange of these and similar courtesies :[3]—

" I have received your letter, together with a little book containing a commentary on a sonnet of mine. The sonnet does indeed proceed from me, but the commentary comes from heaven. In truth it is a marvellous production ; and I say this not on my own judgment only, but on that of able men, especially of Messer Donato Giannotti, who is never tired of reading it. He begs to be remembered to you. About the sonnet, I know very well what that is worth. Yet be it what it may, I cannot refrain from piquing myself a little on having been the cause of so beautiful and learned a commentary.

[1] *Due Lezioni di Messer Benedetto Varchi,* 1549. Firenze : Lorenzo Torrentino ; and again, 1590, Filippo Giunta.

[2] This discourse, conceived in a mixed spirit of scholasticism, Platonism, and æsthetical criticism, shows how highly Michelangelo's poems were esteemed by the rarest and most cultivated intellects of his age. It is reproduced in Guasti's edition of the *Rime*, pp. lxxxv.-cxii.

[3] Lettere, No. cdlxiii.

The author of it, by his words and praises, shows clearly that he thinks me to be other than I am; so I beg you to express me to him in terms corresponding to so much love, affection, and courtesy. I entreat you to do this, because I feel myself inadequate, and one who has gained golden opinions ought not to tempt fortune; it is better to keep silence than to fall from that height. I am old, and death has robbed me of the thoughts of my youth. He who knows not what old age is, let him wait till it arrives: he cannot know beforehand. Remember me, as I said, to Varchi, with deep affection for his fine qualities, and as his servant wherever I may be."

Three other letters belonging to the same year show how deeply Michelangelo was touched and gratified by the distinguished honour Varchi paid him.[1] In an earlier chapter of this book I have already pointed out how this correspondence bears upon the question of his friendship with Tommaso dei Cavalieri, and also upon an untenable hypothesis advanced by recent Florentine students of his biography.[2] The incident is notable in other ways, because Buonarroti was now adopted as a poet by the Florentine Academy. With a width of sympathy rare in such bodies, they condoned the ruggedness of his style and the uncouthness of his versification in their admiration for the high quality

[1] Lettere, Nos. cdlxiv.–vi.
[2] See above, Chapter XII.

of his meditative inspiration.[1]　To the triple crown of sculptor, painter, architect, he now added the laurels of the bard ; and this public recognition of his genius as a writer gave him well-merited pleasure in his declining years.

While gathering up these scattered fragments of Buonarroti's later life, I may here introduce a letter addressed to Benvenuto Cellini, which illustrates his glad acceptance of all good work in fellow-craftsmen :[2]—

" My Benvenuto,—I have known you all these years as the greatest goldsmith of whom the world ever heard, and now I am to know you for a sculptor of the same quality.　Messer Bindo Altoviti took me to see his portrait bust in bronze, and told me it was by your hand.　I admired it much, but was sorry to see that it has been placed in a bad light. If it had a proper illumination, it would show itself to be the fine work it is."

VI.

Lionardo Buonarroti was at last married to Cassandra, the daughter of Donato Ridolfi, upon

---

[1] When Michelangelo's poems were published, Mario Guidicci delivered two lectures on theses suggested by them before the Academy. They are printed by Guasti, *Rime*, cxiii.–cxxxv.

[2] Lettere, No. cdlxxi., date 1552.　Cellini's own account of this bust is worth reading.　See his *Memoirs*, lib. ii. caps. lxxix.–lxxxii.

the 16th of May 1553. One of the dearest wishes
which had occupied his uncle's mind so long, came
thus to its accomplishment. His letters are full
of kindly thoughts for the young couple, and of
prudent advice to the husband, who had not
arranged all matters connected with the settlements
to his own satisfaction.[1] Michelangelo congratu-
lated Lionardo heartily upon his happiness, and
told him that he was minded to send the bride a
handsome present, in token of his esteem.[2] " I
have not been able to do so yet, because Urbino
was away. Now that he has returned, I shall give
expression to my sentiments. They tell me that a
fine pearl necklace of some value would be very
proper. I have sent a goldsmith, Urbino's friend,
in search of such an ornament, and hope to find it;
but say nothing to her, and if you would like me to
choose another article, please let me know." This
letter winds up with a strange admonition: " Look
to living, reflect and weigh things well; for the
number of widows in the world is always larger
than that of the widowers." Ultimately he decided
upon two rings, one a diamond, the other a ruby.[3]
He tells Lionardo to have the stones valued in case
he has been cheated, because he does not understand such things; and is glad to hear in due course
that the jewels are genuine. After the proper
interval, Cassandra expected her confinement, and

[1] Lettere, Nos. cclix.–cclxiii.   [2] Ibid., No. cclxiii.
[3] Ibid., Nos. cclxxiv.–cclxxvi.

Michelangelo corresponded with his nephew as to the child's name in case it was a boy.[1] " I shall be very pleased if the name of Buonarroto does not die out of our family, it having lasted three hundred years with us." The child was born upon the 16th of May 1554, turned out a boy, and received the name of Buonarroto. Though Lionardo had seven other children, including Michelangelo the younger (born November 4, 1568), this Buonarroto alone continued the male line of the family. The old man in Rome remarked resignedly during his later years, when he heard the news of a baby born and dead,[2] that " I am not surprised ; there was never in our family more than one at a time to keep it going."

Buonarroto was christened with some pomp, and Vasari wrote to Michelangelo describing the festivities. In the year 1554, Cosimo de' Medici had thrown his net round Siena. The Marquis of Marignano reduced the city first to extremities by famine, and finally to enslavement by capitulation. These facts account for the tone of Michelangelo's answer to Vasari's letter :[3] " Yours has given me the greatest pleasure, because it assures me that you remember the poor old man ; and more perhaps because you were present at the triumph you narrate, of seeing another Buonarroto re-born. I thank you heartily for the information. But I must say that

---

[1] Lettere, Nos. cclxvii.-cclxx.
[2] See, for instance, Lettere, No. cccxii., December 2, 1558.
[3] Lettere, No. cdlxxii., April 1554, "what day I know not."

I am displeased with so much pomp and show. Man ought not to laugh when the whole world weeps. So I think that Lionardo has not displayed great judgment, particularly in celebrating a nativity with all that joy and gladness which ought to be reserved for the decease of one who has lived well." There is what may be called an Elizabethan note— something like the lyrical interbreathings of our dramatists—in this blending of jubilation and sorrow, discontent and satisfaction, birth and death thoughts.

We have seen that Vasari worked for a short time as pupil under Michelangelo, and that during the pontificate of Paul III. they were brought into frequent contact at Rome. With years their friendship deepened into intimacy, and after the date 1550 their correspondence forms one of our most important sources of information. Michelangelo's letters begin upon the 1st of August in that year. Vasari was then living and working for the Duke at Florence; but he had designed a chapel for S. Pietro a Montorio in Rome, where Julius III. wished to erect tombs to the memory of his ancestors; and the work had been allotted to Bartolommeo Ammanati under Michelangelo's direction. This business, otherwise of no importance in his biography, necessitated the writing of despatches, one of which is interesting, since it acknowledges the receipt of Vasari's celebrated book :[1]—

---

[1] Lettere, No. clxviii.

" Referring to your three letters which I have received, my pen refuses to reply to such high compliments. I should indeed be happy if I were in some degree what you make me out to be, but I should not care for this except that then you would have a servant worth something. However, I am not surprised that you, who resuscitate the dead, should prolong the life of the living, or that you should steal the half-dead from death for an endless period."

It seems that on this occasion he also sent Vasari the sonnet composed upon his Lives of the Painters. Though it cannot be called one of his poetical masterpieces, the personal interest attaching to the verses justifies their introduction here :[1]—

> With pencil and with palette hitherto
>   You made your art high Nature's paragon ;
>   Nay more, from Nature her own prize you won,
>   Making what she made fair more fair to view.
> Now that your learned hand with labour new
>   Of pen and ink a worthier work hath done,
>   What erst you lacked, what still remained her own,
>   The power of giving life, is gained for you.
> If men in any age with Nature vied
>   In beauteous workmanship, they had to yield
>   When to the fated end years brought their name.
> You, re-illuming memories that died,
>   In spite of Time and Nature have revealed
>   For them and for yourself eternal fame.

Vasari's official position at the ducal court of Florence brought him into frequent and personal

[1] *Rime*, Sonetti, No. xi. In my version, p. 41.

relations with Cosimo de' Medici. The Duke had long been anxious to lure the most gifted of his subjects back to Florence; but Michelangelo, though he remained a loyal servant to the Medicean family, could not approve of Cosimo's despotic rule. Moreover, he was now engaged by every tie of honour, interest, and artistic ambition to superintend the fabric of S. Peter's. He showed great tact, through delicate negotiations carried on for many years, in avoiding the Duke's overtures without sacrificing his friendship. Wishing to found his family in Florence and to fund the earnings of his life there, he naturally assumed a courteous attitude. A letter written by the Bishop Tornabuoni to Giovanni Francesco Lottini in Rome shows that these overtures began as early as 1546.[1] The prelate says the Duke is so anxious to regain "Michelangelo, the divine sculptor," that he promises "to make him a member of the forty-eight senators, and to give him any office he may ask for." The affair was dropped for some years, but in 1552 Cosimo renewed his attempts, and now began to employ Vasari and Cellini as ambassadors. Soon after finishing his Perseus, Benvenuto begged for leave to go to Rome; and before starting, he showed the Duke Michelangelo's friendly letter on the bust of Bindo Altoviti.[2] "He read it with much kindly interest, and said to me: 'Benvenuto, if you write to him, and can persuade him to return to Florence, I will

[1] Gaye, ii. 352. [2] *Memoirs,* Book ii. chap. lxxix.

T

make him a member of the Forty-eight.' Accordingly I wrote a letter full of warmth, and offered in
the Duke's name a hundred times more than my
commission carried; but not wanting to make any
mistake, I showed this to the Duke before I sealed
it, saying to his most illustrious excellency: 'Prince,
perhaps I have made him too many promises.' He
replied: 'Michel Agnolo deserves more than you
have promised, and I will bestow on him still greater
favours.' To this letter he sent no answer, and I
could see that the Duke was much offended with
him."

While in Rome, Cellini went to visit Michelangelo, and renewed his offers in the Duke's name.
What passed in that interview is so graphically told,
introducing the rustic personality of Urbino on the
stage, and giving a hint of Michelangelo's reasons
for not returning in person to Florence, that the
whole passage may be transcribed as opening a
little window on the details of our hero's domestic
life :[1]—

"Then I went to visit Michel Agnolo Buonarroti,
and repeated what I had written from Florence to
him in the Duke's name. He replied that he was
engaged upon the fabric of S. Peter's, and that this
would prevent him from leaving Rome. I rejoined
that, as he had decided on the model of that building, he could leave its execution to his man Urbino,
who would carry out his orders to the letter. I

[1] *Memoirs*, Book ii. chap. lxxxi.

added much about future favours, in the form of a
message from the Duke. Upon this he looked me
hard in the face, and said with a sarcastic smile:
'And you! to what extent are you satisfied with
him?' Although I replied that I was extremely
contented and was very well treated by his Excellency, he showed that he was acquainted with the
greater part of my annoyances, and gave as his final
answer that it would be difficult for him to leave
Rome. To this I added that he could not do better
than to return to his own land, which was governed
by a prince renowned for justice, and the greatest
lover of the arts and sciences who ever saw the light
of this world. As I have remarked above, he had
with him a servant of his who came from Urbino,
and had lived many years in his employment, rather
as valet and housekeeper than anything else; this
indeed was obvious, because he had acquired no
skill in the arts. Consequently, while I was pressing Michel Agnolo with arguments he could not
answer, he turned round sharply to Urbino, as
though to ask him his opinion. The fellow began
to bawl out in his rustic way: 'I will never leave
my master Michel Agnolo's side till I shall have
flayed him or he shall have flayed me.' These stupid
words forced me to laugh, and without saying farewell, I lowered my shoulders and retired."

This was in 1552. The Duke was loth to take a
refusal, and for the next eight years he continued
to ply Michelangelo with invitations, writing letters

by his own hand, employing his agents in Rome and Florence, and working through Vasari.[1] The letters to Vasari during this period are full of the subject. Michelangelo remains firm in his intention to remain at Rome and not abandon S. Peter's.[2] As years went on, infirmities increased, and the solicitations of the Duke became more and more irksome to the old man. His discomfort at last elicited what may be called a real cry of pain in a letter to his nephew : [3]—

" As regards my condition, I am ill with all the troubles which are wont to afflict old men. The stone prevents me passing water. My loins and back are so stiff that I often cannot climb upstairs. What makes matters worse is that my mind is much worried with anxieties. If I leave the conveniences I have here for my health, I can hardly live three days. Yet I do not want to lose the favour of the Duke, nor should I like to fail in my work at S. Peter's, nor in my duty to myself. I pray God to help and counsel me ; and if I were taken ill by some dangerous fever, I would send for you at once."

Meanwhile, in spite of his resistance to the Duke's wishes, Michelangelo did not lose the favour of the Medicean family. The delicacy of behaviour by means of which he contrived to preserve and strengthen it, is indeed one of the strongest evidences of his sincerity, sagacity, and prudence.

[1] See Gotti, i. 313–317.
[2] See above, Chap. XIII. See Lettere, Nos. cdlxxv., cdlxxvi., cdlxxxi.- iii. Compare the letters to Lionardo, Nos. cccii.–vi., year 1557.
[3] No. ccciv.

The Cardinal Giovanni, son of Cosimo, travelled to Rome in March 1560, in order to be invested with the purple by the Pope's hands. On this occasion Vasari, who rode in the young prince's train, wrote despatches to Florence which contain some interesting passages about Buonarroti.[1] In one of them (March 29) he says : "My friend Michelangelo is so old that I do not hope to obtain much from him." Beside the reiterated overtures regarding a return to Florence, the Church of the Florentines was now in progress, and Cosimo also required Buonarroti's advice upon the decoration of the Great Hall in the Palazzo della Signoria. In a second letter (April 8) Vasari tells the Duke: "I reached Rome, and immediately after the most reverend and illustrious Medici had made his entrance and received the hat from our lord's hands, a ceremony which I wished to see with a view to the frescoes in the Palace, I went to visit my friend, the mighty Michelangelo. He had not expected me, and the tenderness of his reception was such as old men show when lost sons unexpectedly return to them. He fell upon my neck with a thousand kisses, weeping for joy. He was so glad to see me, and I him, that I have had no greater pleasure since I entered the service of your Excellency, albeit I enjoy so many through your kindness. We talked about the greatness and the wonders which our God in heaven has wrought for you, and he lamented that he could not serve

[1] Gaye, iii. 27-32.

you with his body, as he is ready to do with his talents at the least sign of your will. He also expressed his sorrow at being unable to wait upon the Cardinal, because he now can move about but little, and is grown so old that he gets small rest, and is so low in health I fear he will not last long, unless the goodness of God preserves him for the building of S. Peter's." After some further particulars, Vasari adds that he hopes " to spend Monday and Tuesday discussing the model of the Great Hall with Michelangelo, as well as the composition of the several frescoes. I have all that is necessary with me, and will do my utmost, while remaining in his company, to extract useful information and suggestions." We know from Vasari's Life of Michelangelo that the plans for decorating the Palace were settled to his own and the Duke's satisfaction during these colloquies at Rome.[1]

Later on in the year, Cosimo came in person to Rome, attended by the Duchess Eleonora. Michelangelo immediately waited on their Highnesses, and was received with special marks of courtesy by the Duke, who bade him to be seated at his side, and discoursed at length about his own designs for Florence and certain discoveries he had made in the method of working porphyry. These interviews, says Vasari, were repeated several times

[1] Vasari, xii. 261. These despatches show why Cosimo wanted Michelangelo in Florence. He was engaged on many undertakings there (including the Sacristy of S. Lorenzo), to which Buonarroti alone held the clue.

during Cosimo's sojourn in Rome; and when the Crown-Prince of Florence, Don Francesco, arrived, this young nobleman showed his high respect for the great man by conversing with him cap in hand.[1]

The project of bringing Buonarroti back to Florence was finally abandoned; but he had the satisfaction of feeling that, after the lapse of more than seventy years, his long connection with the House of Medici remained as firm and cordial as it had ever been. It was also consolatory to know that the relations established between himself and the reigning dynasty in Florence would prove of service to Lionardo, upon whom he now had concentrated the whole of his strong family affection.

In estimating Michelangelo as man, independent of his eminence as artist, the most singular point which strikes us is this persistent preoccupation with the ancient house he desired so earnestly to rehabilitate. He treated Lionardo with the greatest brutality. Nothing that this nephew did, or did not do, was right. Yet Lionardo was the sole hope of the Buonarroti-Simoni stock. When he married and got children, the old man purred with satisfaction over him, but only as a breeder of the race; and he did all in his power to establish Lionardo in a secure position.[2]

[1] Vasari, xii. 262.
[2] Unfortunately, we do not know what Lionardo felt about his uncle. The Arch. Buon. contains no drafts of his letters. He must have suffered much, and borne in patience.

VII.

Returning to the history of Michelangelo's domestic life, we have to relate two sad events which happened to him at the end of 1555. On the 28th of September he wrote to Lionardo:[1] "The bad news about Gismondo afflicts me deeply. I am not without my own troubles of health, and have many annoyances besides. In addition to all this, Urbino has been ill in bed with me three months, and is so still, which causes me much trouble and anxiety." Gismondo, who had been declining all the summer, died upon the 13th of November. His brother in Rome was too much taken up with the mortal sickness of his old friend and servant Urbino to express great sorrow. "Your letter informs me of my brother Gismondo's death, which is the cause to me of serious grief. We must have patience; and inasmuch as he died sound of mind and with all the sacraments of the Church, let God be praised. I am in great affliction here. Urbino is still in bed, and very seriously ill. I do not know what will come of it. I feel this trouble as though he were my own son, because he has lived in my service twenty-five years, and has been very faithful. Being old, I have no time to form another servant to my purpose; and so I am sad exceedingly. If

[1] The letters to Lionardo about Gismondo and Urbino are Nos. cclxxxi.–lxxxiv.

then, you know of some devout person, I beg you to have prayers offered up to God for his recovery."

The next letter gives a short account of his death :—

"I inform you that yesterday, the 3rd of December, at four o'clock, Francesco called Urbino passed from this life, to my very great sorrow. He has left me sorely stricken and afflicted ; nay, it would have been sweeter to have died with him, such is the love I bore him. Less than this love he did not deserve ; for he had grown to be a worthy man, full of faith and loyalty. So, then, I feel as though his death had left me without life, and I cannot find heart's ease. I should be glad to see you, therefore ; only I cannot think how you can leave Florence because of your wife."

To Vasari he wrote still more passionately upon this occasion : [1]—

"I cannot write well ; yet, in answer to your letter, I will say a few words. You know that Urbino is dead. I owe the greatest thanks to God, at the same time that my own loss is heavy and my sorrow infinite. The grace He gave me is that, while Urbino kept me alive in life, his death taught me to die without displeasure, rather with a deep and real desire. I had him with me twenty-six years, and found him above measure faithful and sincere. Now that I had made him rich, and thought to keep him as the staff and rest of my

[1] Lettere, No. cdlxxvii.

old age, he has vanished from my sight; nor have I hope left but that of seeing him again in Paradise. God has given us good foundation for this hope in the exceedingly happy ending of his life. Even more than dying, it grieved him to leave me alive in this treacherous world, with so many troubles; and yet the better part of me is gone with him, nor is there left to me aught but infinite distress. I recommend myself to you, and beg you, if it be not irksome, to make my excuses to Messer Benvenuto (Cellini) for omitting to answer his letter. The trouble of soul I suffer in thought about these things prevents me from writing. Remember me to him, and take my best respects to yourself."

How tenderly Michelangelo's thought dwelt upon Urbino appears from this sonnet, addressed in 1556 to Monsignor Lodovico Beccadelli: [1]—

God's grace, the cross, our troubles multiplied,
    Will make us meet in heaven, full well I know:
    Yet ere we yield our breath on earth below,
    Why need a little solace be denied?
Though seas and mountains and rough ways divide
    Our feet asunder, neither frost nor snow
    Can make the soul her ancient love forego;
    Nor chains nor bonds the wings of thought have tied.
Borne by these wings, with thee I dwell for aye,
    And weep, and of my dead Urbino talk,
    Who, were he living, now perchance would be—
For so 'twas planned—thy guest as well as I.
    Warned by his death, another way I walk
    To meet him where he waits to live with me.

---

[1] Guasti, *Rime*, Sonnet lxvii. My version, p. 105.

By his will, dated November 24, 1555, Urbino, whose real name was Francesco degli Amadori of Castel Durante, appointed his old friend and master one of his executors and the chief guardian of his widow and children.[1] A certain Roso de Rosis and Pietro Filippo Vandini, both of Castel Durante, are named in the trust; and they managed the estate. Yet Michelangelo was evidently the principal authority. A voluminous correspondence preserved in the Buonarroti Archives proves this; for it consists of numerous letters addressed by Urbino's executors and family from Castel Durante and elsewhere to the old sculptor in Rome. Urbino had married a woman of fine character and high intelligence, named Cornelia Colonnelli. Two of her letters are printed by Gotti, and deserve to be studied for the power of their style and the elevation of their sentiments.[2] He has not made use, however, of the other documents, all of which have some interest as giving a pretty complete view of a private family and its vexations, while they illustrate the conscientious fidelity with which Michelangelo discharged his duties as trustee. Urbino had a brother, also resident at Castel Durante, Raffaello's celebrated pupil in fresco-painting, Il Fattorino. This man and Vandini, together with Cornelia and her parents and her second husband, Giulio Brunelli, all wrote letters to Rome about the welfare of the children and the financial

---

[1] The document is printed by Gotti, vol. ii. pp. 137-141.
[2] Vol. i. pp. 334-338.

affairs of the estate.[1] The coexecutor Roso de Rosis did not write ; it appears from one of Cornelia's despatches that he took no active interest in the trust, while Brunelli even complains that he withheld moneys which were legally due to the heirs. One of Michelangelo's first duties was to take care that Cornelia got a proper man for her second husband. Her parents were eager to see her married, being themselves old, and not liking to leave a comparatively young widow alone in the world with so many children to look after. Their choice fell first upon a very undesirable person called Santagnolo, a young man of dissolute habits, ruined constitution, bad character, and no estate.[2] She refused, with spirit, to sign the marriage contract ; and a few months later wrote again to inform her guardian that a suitable match had been found in the person of Giulio Brunelli of Gubbio, a young doctor of laws, then resident at Castel Durante in the quality of podestà.[3] Michelangelo's suspicions must have been aroused by the unworthy conduct of her parents in the matter of Santagnolo ; for we infer that he at first refused to sanction this second match. Cornelia and the parents wrote once more, assuring him that Brunelli was an excellent man, and entreat-

[1] Il Fattorino's letters are to be found in the Arch. Buon., Cod. vi. Nos. 5–9. Brunelli's, ibid., Cod. vi. Nos. 120-129. Cornelia's, ibid., Cod. vii. Nos. 156–184. The parents, Guido and Antonia del Colonello, ibid., Cod. vii. No. 163. Vandini, ibid., Cod. xi. Nos. 730–738.

[2] Cornelia's letter of October 4, 1558.

[3] Letter of January 10, 1559. Cod. vii.

ing him not to open his ears to malignant gossip.[1]
On the 15th of June Brunelli himself appears upon
the scene, announcing his marriage with Cornelia,
introducing himself in terms of becoming modesty
to Michelangelo, and assuring him that Urbino's
children have found a second father.[2] He writes
again upon the 29th of July, this time to announce
the fact that Il Fattorino has spread about false
rumours to the effect that Cornelia and himself intend to leave Castel Durante and desert the children.
Their guardian must not credit such idle gossip,
for they are both, sincerely attached to the children,
and intend to do the best they can for them.
Family dissensions began to trouble their peace.
In the course of the next few months Brunelli
discovers that he cannot act with the Fattorino
or with Vandini; Cornelia's dowry is not paid;
Roso refuses to refund money due to the heirs;
Michelangelo alone can decide what ought to be
done for the estate and his wards. The Fattorino
writes that Vandini has renounced the trust, and
that all Brunelli's and his own entreaties cannot
make him resume it. For himself, he is resolved
not to bear the burden alone. He has his own shop
to look after, and will not let himself be bothered.[3]
Unluckily, none of Michelangelo's answers have

---

[1] Letters of April 18 and 20, 1559. Ibid.
[2] June 15, 1559, Cod. vi. No. 220. "E stia sicura che li putti di
francesco hanno raquistato un altro patre."
[3] Cod. vi. No. 6, June 6, 1561.

been preserved. We possess only one of his letters
to Cornelia, which shows that she wished to place
her son and his godson, Michelangelo, under his
care at Rome. He replied that he did not feel
himself in a position to accept the responsibility.[1]
"It would not do to send Michelangelo, seeing
that I have nobody to manage the house and no
female servants; the boy is still of tender age, and
things might happen which would cause me the
utmost annoyance. Moreover, the Duke of Florence
has during the last month been making me the
greatest offers, and putting strong pressure upon
me to return home. I have begged for time to
arrange my affairs here and leave S. Peter's in
good order. So I expect to remain in Rome all
the summer; and when I have settled my business,
and yours with the Monte della Fede, I shall
probably remove to Florence this winter and take
up my abode there for good. I am old now, and
have not the time to return to Rome. I will travel
by way of Urbino; and if you like to give me Michelangelo, I will bring him to Florence, with more love
than the sons of my nephew Lionardo, and will
teach him all the things which I know that his father
desired that he should learn."

[1] *Lett. Pitt.*, vol. i. p. 13. It bears date March 28. Milanesi reprint-
ing it (Lettere, No. cdlxxx.) assigns it to the year 1557. The autograph
is in the Codex Vaticanus, p. 100. On the back there is a faint brown
sketch for a Christ upon the cross in some soft chalk.

VIII.

The year 1556 was marked by an excursion which took Michelangelo into the mountain district of Spoleto. Paul IV.'s anti-Spanish policy had forced the Viceroy of Naples to make a formidable military demonstration. According to the Duke of Alva, at the head of a powerful force, left Naples on the 1st of September and invaded the Campagna. The Romans dreaded a second siege and sack; not without reason, although the real intention of the expedition was to cow the fiery Pope into submission. It is impossible, when we remember Michelangelo's liability to panics, not to connect his autumn journey with a wish to escape from trouble in Rome. On the 31st of October he wrote to Lionardo that he had undertaken a pilgrimage to Loreto, but feeling tired, had stopped to rest at Spoleto. While he was there, a messenger arrived post-haste from Rome, commanding his immediate return. He is now once more at home there, and as well as the troublous circumstances of the times permit.[1] Later on he told Vasari:[2] "I have recently enjoyed a great pleasure, though purchased at the cost of great discomfort and expense, among the mountains of Spoleto, on a visit to those hermits.

[1] Lettere, No. ccxcix.
[2] Ibid., No. cdlxxix., December 28, 1556.

Consequently, I have come back less than half myself to Rome ; for of a truth there is no peace to be found except among the woods." This is the only passage in the whole of Michelangelo's correspondence which betrays the least feeling for wild nature. We cannot pretend, even here, to detect an interest in landscape or a true appreciation of country life. Compared with Rome and the Duke of Alva, those hermitages of the hills among their chestnut-groves seemed to him haunts of ancient peace. That is all; but when dealing with a man so sternly insensible to the charm of the external world, we have to be contented with a little.[1]

In connection with this brief sojourn at Spoleto I will introduce two letters written to Michelangelo by the Archbishop of Ragusa from his See. The first is dated March 28, 1557, and was sent to Spoleto, probably under the impression that Buonarroti had not yet returned to Rome. After lamenting the unsettled state of public affairs, the Archbishop adds : " Keep well in your bodily health; as for that of your soul, I am sure you cannot be ill, knowing what prudence and piety keep you in perpetual companionship." The second

[1] It ought to be mentioned in this connection that among Michelangelo's unfinished poems is a series of octave stanzas in praise of rural life. But whatever merit the piece may have belongs to its abstruse allegories of the passions and vices which perplex the souls of men in cities. The country is disposed of in a few conventional stanzas, which any student of Dante, Poliziano, and Lorenzo de' Medici could have written. See Rime, pp. 317-324.

followed at the interval of a year, April 6, 1558, and gave a pathetic picture of the meek old prelate's discomfort in his Dalmatian bishopric. He calls Ragusa "this exceedingly ill-cultivated vineyard of mine. Oftentimes does the carnal man in me revolt and yearn for Italy, for relatives and friends ; but the spirit keeps desire in check, and compels it to be satisfied with that which is the pleasure of our Lord." Though the biographical importance of these extracts is but slight, I am glad, while recording the outlines of Buonarroti's character, to cast a side-light on his amiable qualities, and to show how highly valued he was by persons of the purest life.[1]

IX.

There was nothing peculiarly severe about the infirmities of Michelangelo's old age. We first hear of the dysuria from which he suffered, in 1548. He writes to Lionardo thanking him for pears :[2] "I duly received the little barrel of pears you sent me. There were eighty-six. Thirty-three of them I sent to the Pope, who praised them as fine, and who

---

[1] Arch. Buon., Cod. x. Nos. 640, 641. "Stia bene del corpo, che dell' animo son certo non può star male, sapendo quanta prudenza e pietà li tengano di continuo compagnia." "Questa mia vigna assai inculta ; il senso spesse volte se risente et desidera italia et parenti et amici. Ma lo spirito lo fa star quieto e contentarse di quello che piace al signore."

[2] Lettere, No. cxcix., May 2.

enjoyed them. I have lately been in great difficulty
from dysuria. However, I am better now. And
thus I write to you, chiefly lest some chatterbox
should scribble a thousand lies to make you jump."
In the spring of 1549 he says that the doctors
believe he is suffering from calculus:[1] "The pain
is great, and prevents me from sleeping. They
propose that I should try the mineral waters of
Viterbo; but I cannot go before the beginning of
May. For the rest, as concerns my bodily condition, I am much the same as I was at thirty. This
mischief has crept upon me through the great
hardships of my life and heedlessness." A few
days later he writes that a certain water he is
taking, whether mineral or medicine, has been
making a beneficial change.[2] The following letters
are very cheerful, and at length he is able to
write:[3] "With regard to my disease, I am greatly
improved in health, and have hope, much to the
surprise of many; for people thought me a lost
man, and so I believed. I have had a good doctor,
but I put more faith in prayers than I do in
medicines." His physician was a very famous man,
Realdo Colombo. In the summer of the same year

[1] Lettere, No. ccxiv., March 15.
[2] Ibid., No. ccxv., March 23. It was probably a prescription; for in
1560 a friend of his wrote for the recipe, referring to the years in Rome
subsequent to 1546. See Gotti, ii. 140. In the Buonarroti Archives
I saw a doctor's prescription for the stone, but omitted to copy it.
Codex, xii. 53.
[3] Ibid., No. ccxix., April 25, 1549.

he tells Lionardo that he has been drinking for the last two months water from a fountain forty miles distant from Rome.[1] "I have to lay in a stock of it, and to drink nothing else, and also to use it in cooking, and to observe rules of living to which I am not used."

Although the immediate danger from the calculus passed away, Michelangelo grew feebler yearly. We have already seen how he wrote to Lionardo while Cosimo de' Medici was urging him to come to Florence in 1557. Passages in his correspondence with Lionardo like the following are frequent :[2] "Writing is the greatest annoyance to my hand, my sight, my brains. So works old age!" "I go on enduring old age as well as I am able, with all the evils and discomforts it brings in its train; and I recommend myself to Him who can assist me." It was natural, after he had passed the ordinary term of life and was attacked with a disease so serious as the stone, that his thoughts should take a serious tone. Thus he writes to Lionardo :[3] "This illness has made me think of setting the affairs of my soul and body more in order than I should have done. Accordingly, I have drawn up a rough sketch of a will, which I will send you by the next courier if I am able, and you can tell me what you think." The will provided that Gismondo

---

[1] Lettere, No. ccxxiv., June 8. Probably the water of Viterbo.
[2] Ibid., Nos. ccciv., cccxiv., cccxxii.
[3] Ibid., No. ccxv. and No. ccxvii. Compare No. ccl.

and Lionardo Buonarroti should be his joint-heirs, without the power of dividing the property. This practically left Lionardo his sole heir after Gismondo's life-tenancy of a moiety. It does not, however, seem to have been executed, for Michelangelo died intestate. Probably, he judged it simplest to allow Lionardo to become his heir-general by the mere course of events. At the same time, he now displayed more than his usual munificence in charity. Lionardo was frequently instructed to seek out a poor and gentle family, who were living in decent distress, *poveri vergognosi*, as the Italians called such persons. Money was to be bestowed upon them with the utmost secrecy; and the way which Michelangelo proposed, was to dower a daughter or to pay for her entrance into a convent. It has been suggested that this method of seeking to benefit the deserving poor denoted a morbid tendency in Michelangelo's nature;[1] but any one who is acquainted with Italian customs in the Middle Ages and the Renaissance must be aware that nothing was commoner than to dower poor girls or to establish them in nunneries by way of charity. Urbino, for example, by his will bound his executors to provide for the marriage of two honest girls with a dowry of twenty florins apiece within the space of four years from his death.[2]

The religious sonnets, which are certainly among

[1] Parlagreco, *op. cit.*, p. 86.
[2] See the original will in Gotti, ii. 138.

the finest of Michelangelo's compositions, belong to
this period. Writing to Vasari on the 10th of September 1554, he begins :[1] " You will probably say that
I am old and mad to think of writing sonnets ; yet
since many persons pretend that I am in my second
childhood, I have thought it well to act accordingly." Then follows this magnificent piece of
verse, in which the sincerest feelings of the pious
heart are expressed with a sublime dignity :[2]—

> Now hath my life across a stormy sea,
>   Like a frail bark, reached that wide port where all
>   Are bidden, ere the final reckoning fall
>   Of good and evil for eternity.
> Now know I well how that fond phantasy
>   Which made my soul the worshipper and thrall
>   Of earthly art is vain ; how criminal
>   Is that which all men seek unwillingly.
> Those amorous thoughts which were so lightly dressed,
>   What are they when the double death is nigh ?
>   The one I know for sure, the other dread.
> Painting nor sculpture now can lull to rest
>   My soul, that turns to His great love on high,
>   Whose arms to clasp us on the cross were spread.

A second sonnet, enclosed in a letter to Vasari,
runs as follows :[3]—

> The fables of the world have filched away
>   The time I had for thinking upon God ;
>   His grace lies buried 'neath oblivion's sod,
>   Whence springs an evil crop of sins alway.

---

[1] Lettere, No. cdlxxiii.
[2] *Rime*, Sonnet lxvi. In my version, p. 102.   [3] Ibid., p. 103.

What makes another wise, leads me astray,
    Slow to discern the bad path I have trod :
    Hope fades, but still desire ascends that God
    May free me from self-love, my sure decay.
Shorten half-way my road to heaven from earth !
    Dear Lord, I cannot even half-way rise
    Unless Thou help me on this pilgrimage.
Teach me to hate the world so little worth,
    And all the lovely things I clasp and prize,
    That endless life, ere death, may be my wage.

While still in his seventieth year, Michelangelo
had educated himself to meditate upon the thought
of death as a prophylactic against vain distractions
and the passion of love.[1] "I may remind you that
a man who would fain return unto and enjoy his
own self ought not to indulge so much in merry-
makings and festivities, but to think on death.
This thought is the only one which makes us know
our proper selves, which holds us together in the
bond of our own nature, which prevents us from
being stolen away by kinsmen, friends, great men
of genius, ambition, avarice, and those other sins
and vices which filch the man from himself, keep
him distraught and dispersed, without ever per-
mitting him to return unto himself and reunite his
scattered parts.   Marvellous is the operation of
this thought of death, which, albeit death, by his
nature, destroys all things, preserves and supports
those who think on death, and defends them from
all human passions."   He supports this position

[1] Donato Giannotti's Dialogue.   See Guasti, *Rime*, p. xxxi.

by reciting a madrigal he had composed, to show how the thought of death is the greatest foe to love :[1]—

> Not death indeed, but the dread thought of death
>   Saveth and severeth
>   Me from the heartless fair who doth me slay :
>   And should, perchance, some day
>   The fire consuming blaze o'er measure bright,
>   I find for my sad plight
> No help but from death's form fixed in my heart;
> Since, where death reigneth, love must dwell apart.

In some way or another, then, Michelangelo used the thought of death as the mystagogue of his spirit into the temple of eternal things—τὰ αἴδια, *die bleibenden Verhältnisse*—and as the means of maintaining self-control and self-coherence amid the ever-shifting illusions of human life.[2] This explains why in his love-sonnets he rarely speaks of carnal beauty except as the manifestation of the divine idea, which will be clearer to the soul after death than in the body.

When his life was drawing toward its close, Michelangelo's friends were not unnaturally anxious about his condition. Though he had a fairly good servant in Antonio del Franzese,[3] and was surrounded

---

[1] *Rime,* Madrigali, No. xvi.

[2] Vasari (xii. 249, 250) says : "Toward the close of his life there arose in him no thought which was not graven with the idea of death, whence one could easily perceive that he was making his retreat toward God."

[3] Was this man the son of Giovanni Franzese, whom Michelangelo employed to make the model of the cupola ? (Vasari, xii. 253).

by well-wishers like Tommaso Cavalieri, Daniele da Volterra, and Tiberio Calcagni, yet he led a very solitary life, and they felt he ought to be protected. Vasari tells us that he communicated privately with Averardo Serristori, the Duke's ambassador in Rome, recommending that some proper housekeeper should be appointed, and that due control should be instituted over the persons who frequented his house. It was very desirable, in case of a sudden accident, that his drawings and works of art should not be dispersed, but that what belonged to S. Peter's, to the Laurentian Library, and to the Sacristy should be duly assigned.[1] Lionardo Buonarroti must have received similar advice from Rome, for a furious letter is extant, in which Michelangelo, impatient to the last of interference, literally rages at him :[2]—

"I gather from your letter that you lend credence to certain envious and scoundrelly persons, who, since they cannot manage me or rob me, write you a lot of lies. They are a set of sharpers, and you are so silly as to believe what they say about my affairs, as though I were a baby. Get rid of them, the scandalous, envious, ill-lived rascals. As for my suffering the mismanagement you write about, I tell you that I could not be better off, or more faithfully served and attended to in all things. As for my being robbed, to which I think you allude, I assure you that I have people in my house whom I can trust and repose on. Therefore, look to your

[1] Vasari, xii. 269.   [2] Lettere, No. cccxl., August 21, 1563.

own life, and do not think about my affairs, because I know how to take care of myself if it is needful, and am not a baby. Keep well."

This is the last letter to Lionardo. It is singular that Michelangelo's correspondence with his father, with Luigi del Riccio, with Tommaso dei Cavalieri, and with his nephew, all of whom he sincerely loved, should close upon a note of petulance and wrath. The fact is no doubt accidental. But it is strange.

X.

We have frequently had occasion to notice the extreme pain caused to Michelangelo's friends by his unreasonable irritability and readiness to credit injurious reports about them. These defects of temper justified to some extent his reputation for savagery, and they must be reckoned among the most salient features of his personality. I shall therefore add three other instances of the same kind which fell under my observation while studying the inedited documents of the Buonarroti Archives. Giovanni Francesco Fattucci was, as we well know, his most intimate friend and trusted counsellor during long and difficult years, when the negotiations with the heirs of Pope Julius were being carried on ; yet there exists one letter of unaffected sorrow from this excellent man, under date October 14,

1545, which shows that for some unaccountable reason Michelangelo had suddenly chosen to mistrust him.[1] Fattucci begins by declaring that he is wholly guiltless of things which his friend too credulously believed upon the strength of gossip. He expresses the deepest grief at this unjust and suspicious treatment. The letter shows him to have been more hurt than resentful. Another document signed by Francesco Sangallo (the son of his old friend Giuliano), bearing no date, but obviously written when they were both in Florence, and therefore before the year 1535, carries the same burden of complaint.[2] The details are sufficiently picturesque to warrant the translation of a passage. After expressing astonishment at Michelangelo's habit of avoiding his society, he proceeds : "And now, this morning, not thinking that I should annoy you, I came up and spoke to you, and you received me with a very surly countenance. That evening, too, when I met you on the threshold with Granacci, and you left me by the shop of Pietro Osaio, and the other forenoon at S. Spirito, and to-day, it struck

[1] Arch. Buon., Cod. viii. No. 279.

[2] Arch. Buon., Cod. xi. No. 681. "Perora istammattina io non pensando darvi noia macostavi et voi mi facesti molto cattiva cera, et riscontrato quella sera ch' io vi trovai in sul ucio col Granaccio e poi mi lasasti a bottega di Pietro Osaio (?), et laltra mattina a Santo Spirito, ed istamattina mie parso istrano massimo presente il Piloto ed altri tanti, ch' io penso che voi abiate mecho qualche cosa, ma mi maraviglio voi non mi chiariate lanimo vostro, perchè potresti avere qualche cosa che saria falsa." This language singularly resembles that of Fattucci, and of Cavalieri in the noble letter published in the 12th chapter, p. 148, above.

me as extremely strange, especially in the presence
of Piloto and so many others.   I cannot help thinking that you must have some grudge against me;
but I marvel that you do not open out your mind
to me, because it may be something which is wholly
false." The letter winds up with an earnest protest
that he has always been a true and faithful friend.
He begs to be allowed to come and clear the matter
up in conversation, adding that he would rather
lose the good-will of the whole world than Michelangelo's.

The third letter is somewhat different in tone,
and not so personally interesting. Still it illustrates
the nervousness and apprehension under which
Michelangelo's acquaintances continually lived. The
painter commonly known as Rosso Fiorentino was
on a visit to Rome, where he studied the Sistine
frescoes. They do not appear to have altogether
pleased him, and he uttered his opinion somewhat
too freely in public. Now he pens a long elaborate
epistle, full of adulation, to purge himself of having
depreciated Michelangelo's works. People said that
"when I reached Rome, and entered the chapel
painted by your hand, I exclaimed that I was not
going to adopt that manner." One of Buonarroti's
pupils had been particularly offended. Rosso pro-
tests that he rather likes the man for his loyalty;
but he wishes to remove any impression which
Michelangelo may have received of his own irre-
verence or want of admiration. The one thing he

is most solicitous about is not to lose the great man's good-will.[1]

It must be added, at the close of this investigation, that however hot and hasty Michelangelo may have been, and however readily he lent his ear to rumours, he contrived to renew the broken threads of friendship with the persons he had hurt by his irritability.

[1] Arch. Buon., Cod. x. No. 659. "Ch' io qua giugniendo e in la cappella da voi dipinta entrando dicevi che non volevo pigliare quella maniera."

CHAPTER XV.

I.

DURING the winter of 1563–64 Michelangelo's friends in Rome became extremely anxious about his health,

and kept Lionardo Buonarroti from time to time informed of his proceedings. After New Year it was
clear that he could not long maintain his former
ways of life. Though within a few months of ninety,
he persisted in going abroad in all weathers, and
refused to surround himself with the comforts befitting a man of his eminence and venerable age. On
the 14th of February he seems to have had a kind
of seizure. Tiberio Calcagni, writing that day to
Lionardo, gives expression to his grave anxiety:[1]
" Walking through Rome to-day, I heard from many
persons that Messer Michelangelo was ill. Accordingly I went at once to visit him, and although it
was raining I found him out of doors on foot. When
I saw him, I said that I did not think it right
and seemly for him to be going about in such
weather. 'What do you want?' he answered; 'I
am ill, and cannot find rest anywhere.' The uncertainty of his speech, together with the look and
colour of his face, made me feel extremely uneasy
about his life. The end may not be just now, but
I fear greatly that it cannot be far off." Michelangelo did not leave the house again, but spent the
next four days partly reclining in an arm-chair,
partly in bed. Upon the 15th following, Diomede
Leoni wrote to Lionardo, enclosing a letter by the
hand of Daniele da Volterra, which Michelangelo had
signed.[2] The old man felt his end approaching, and
wished to see his nephew. " You will learn from

---

[1] Daelli, *Carte Mich. Ined.*, p. 41.   [2] Gotti, i. 353.

the enclosure how ill he is, and that he wants you to come to Rome. He was taken ill yesterday. I therefore exhort you to come at once, but do so with sufficient prudence. The roads are bad now, and you are not used to travel by post. This being so, you would run some risk if you came post-haste. Taking your own time upon the way, you may feel at ease when you remember that Messer Tommaso dei Cavalieri, Messer Daniele, and I are here to render every possible assistance in your absence. Beside us, Antonio, the old and faithful servant of your uncle, will be helpful in any service that may be expected from him." Diomede reiterates his advice that Lionardo should run no risks by travelling too fast. "If the illness portends mischief, which God forbid, you could not with the utmost haste arrive in time. . . . I left him just now, a little after 8 P.M., in full possession of his faculties and quiet in his mind, but oppressed with a continued sleepiness. This has annoyed him so much that, between three and four this afternoon, he tried to go out riding, as his wont is every evening in good weather. The coldness of the weather and the weakness of his head and legs prevented him ; so he returned to the fireside, and settled down into an easy chair, which he greatly prefers to the bed." No improvement gave a ray of hope to Michelangelo's friends, and two days later, on the 17th, Tiberio Calcagni took up the correspondence with Lionardo :[1] "This is

[1] Gotti, i. 354.

to beg you to hasten your coming as much as possible, even though the weather be unfavourable. It is certain now that our dear Messer Michelangelo must leave us for good and all, and he ought to have the consolation of seeing you." Next day, on the 18th, Diomede Leoni wrote again : " He died without making a will, but in the attitude of a perfect Christian, this evening, about the Ave Maria. I was present, together with Messer Tommaso dei Cavalieri and Messer Daniele da Volterra, and we put everything in such order that you may rest with a tranquil mind. Yesterday Michelangelo sent for our friend Messer Daniele, and besought him to take up his abode in the house until such time as you arrive, and this he will do."

It was at a little before five o'clock on the afternoon of February 18, 1564, that Michelangelo breathed his last. The physicians who attended him to the end were Federigo Donati, and Gherardo Fidelissimi, of Pistoja. It is reported by Vasari that, during his last moments, " he made his will in three sentences, committing his soul into the hands of God, his body to the earth, and his substance to his nearest relatives; enjoining upon these last, when their hour came, to think upon the sufferings of Jesus Christ." [1]

On the following day, February 19, Averardo Serristori, the Florentine envoy in Rome, sent a despatch to the Duke, informing him of Michel-

---

[1] Vasari, xii. 269.

angelo's decease :[1] "This morning, according to an arrangement I had made, the Governor sent to take an inventory of all the articles found in his house. These were few, and very few drawings. However, what was there they duly registered. The most important object was a box sealed with several seals, which the Governor ordered to be opened in the presence of Messer Tommaso dei Cavalieri and Maestro Daniele da Volterra, who had been sent for by Michelangelo before his death. Some seven or eight thousand crowns were found in it, which have now been deposited with the Ubaldini bankers. This was the command issued by the Governor, and those whom it concerns will have to go there to get the money. The people of the house will be examined as to whether anything has been carried away from it. This is not supposed to have been the case. As far as drawings are concerned, they say that he burned what he had by him before he died. What there is shall be handed over to his nephew when he comes, and this your Excellency can inform him."

The objects of art discovered in Michelangelo's house were a blocked-out statue of S. Peter, an unfinished Christ with another figure,[2] and a statuette of Christ with the cross, resembling the Cristo Risorto of S. Maria Sopra Minerva. Ten original

[1] *Legazioni di Averardo Serristori*, Firenze : Le Monnier, 1853, p. 414.

[2] Possibly the fragment of a Pietà which stands in the Palazzo Rondanini, Corso, Rome. D. da Volterra calls this group a Pietà in the letter cited below.

drawings were also catalogued, one of which (a Pietà) belonged to Tommaso dei Cavalieri ; another (an Epiphany) was given to the notary, while the rest came into the possession of Lionardo Buonarroti. The cash-box, which had been sealed by Tommaso dei Cavalieri and Diomede Leoni, was handed over to the Ubaldini, and from them it passed to Lionardo Buonarroti at the end of February.[1]

II.

Lionardo travelled by post to Rome, but did not arrive until three days after his uncle's death. He began at once to take measures for the transport of Michelangelo's remains to Florence, according to the wish of the old man, frequently expressed and solemnly repeated two days before his death.[2] The corpse had been deposited in the Church of the SS. Apostoli, where the funeral was celebrated with becoming pomp by all the Florentines in Rome, and by artists of every degree. The Romans had come to regard Buonarroti as one of themselves, and, when the report went abroad that he had expressed a wish to be buried in Florence, they refused to believe it, and began to project a decent monument to his

[1] The original documents concerning this administration of Michel-angelo's effects will be found in Gotti, ii. 148–156.

[2] See a long letter by Daniele da Volterra to Vasari (Gotti, i. 357), date March 17. It confirms the particulars I have brought together above.

memory in the Church of the SS. Apostoli. In order to secure his object, Lionardo was obliged to steal the body away, and to despatch it under the guise of mercantile goods to the custom-house of Florence. Vasari wrote to him from that city upon the 10th of March, informing him that the packing-case had duly arrived, and had been left under seals until his, Lionardo's, arrival at the custom-house.[1]

About this time two plans were set on foot for erecting monuments to Michelangelo's memory. The scheme started by the Romans immediately after his death took its course, and the result is that tomb at the SS. Apostoli, which undoubtedly was meant to be a statue-portrait of the man.[2] Vasari received from Lionardo Buonarroti commission to erect the tomb in S. Croce. The correspondence of the latter, both with Vasari and with Jacopo del Duca, who superintended the Roman monument, turns for some time upon these tombs.[3] It is much to Vasari's credit that he wanted to place the Pietà which Michelangelo had broken, above the S. Croce sepulchre. He

---

[1] Gotti, i. 361.

[2] The correspondence published by Gotti, i. 360–372, about it makes this clear. In one of the letters from Diomede Leoni, lithographed by Daelli (Carte Mich., Ined., p. 82), mention is made of an epitaph by Paulus Manutius, beginning *Unus ex omni memoria*. The present inscription is by another scholar. The monument in the SS. Apostoli at Rome aims at portraiture. Michelangelo is lying with his head raised and resting on the left hand. He wears the doublet and apron used by him when working. On a table are ranged the implements of his art. A little genius leans against it, weeping ; another offers a book to Michelangelo.

[3] See Daelli, *op. cit.*, pp. 64 *et seq.*

writes upon the subject in these words :[1] " When
I reflect that Michelangelo asserted, as is well known
also to Daniele, Messer Tommaso dei Cavalieri, and
many other of his friends, that he was making the
Pietà of five figures, which he broke, to serve for his
own tomb, I think that his heir ought to inquire
how it came into the possession of Bandini. Besides,
there is an old man in the group who represents the
person of the sculptor. I entreat you, therefore, to
take measures for regaining this Pietà, and I will
make use of it in my design. Pierantonio Bandini
is very courteous, and will probably consent. In this
way you will gain several points. You will assign to
your uncle's sepulchre the group he planned to place
there, and you will be able to hand over the statues
in Via Mozza to his Excellency, receiving in return
enough money to complete the monument." Of the
marbles in the Via Mozza at Florence, where Michelangelo's workshop stood, I have seen no catalogue,
but they certainly comprised the Victory, probably
also the Adonis and the Apollino. There had been
some thought of adapting the Victory to the tomb
in S: Croce. Vasari, however, doubted whether
this group could be applied in any forcible sense
allegorically to Buonarroti as man or as artist.

Eventually, as we know, the very mediocre monument designed by Vasari, which still exists at S. Croce,
was erected at Lionardo Buonarroti's expense, the
Duke supplying a sufficiency of marble.

[1] See Daelli, *op. cit.*, p. 55, March 18, 1564.

III.

It ought here to be mentioned that, in the spring of 1563, Cosimo founded an Academy of Fine Arts, under the title of " Arte del Disegno." It embraced all the painters, architects, and sculptors of Florence in a kind of guild, with privileges, grades, honours, and officers.[1] The Duke condescended to be the first president of this academy. Next to him, Michelangelo was elected unanimously by all the members as their uncontested principal and leader, " inasmuch as this city, and peradventure the whole world, hath not a master more excellent in the three arts." The first great work upon which the Duke hoped to employ the guild was the completion of the sacristy at S. Lorenzo. Vasari's letter to Michelangelo shows that up to this date none of the statues had been erected in their proper places, and that it was intended to add a great number of figures, as well as to adorn blank spaces in the walls with frescoes. All the best artists of the time, including Gian Bologna, Cellini, Bronzino, Tribolo, Montelupo, Ammanati, offered their willing assistance, " forasmuch as there is not one of us but hath learned in this sacristy, or rather in this our school, whatever

---

[1] A full description of the new corporation is given in a letter written by Vasari to Michelangelo. Bottari, *Lett. Pitt.*, iii. 78. I have translated the part of it which concerns the sacristy in Chap. X. above.

excellence he possesses in the arts of design." We know already only too well that the scheme was never carried out, probably in part because Michelangelo's rapidly declining strength prevented him from furnishing these eager artists with the necessary working drawings. Cosimo's anxiety to gain possession of any sketches left in Rome after Buonarroti's death may be ascribed to this project for completing the works begun at S. Lorenzo.

Well then, upon the news of Michelangelo's death, the academicians were summoned by their lieutenant, Don Vincenzo Borghini, to deliberate upon the best way of paying him honour, and celebrating his obsequies with befitting pomp.[1] It was decided that all the leading artists should contribute something, each in his own line, to the erection of a splendid catafalque, and a sub-committee of four men was elected to superintend its execution. These were Angelo Bronzino and Vasari, Benvenuto Cellini and Ammanati, friends of the deceased, and men of highest mark in the two fields of painting and sculpture. The church selected for the ceremony was S. Lorenzo ; the orator appointed was Benedetto Varchi. Borghini, in his capacity of lieutenant or official representative, obtained the Duke's assent to the plan, which was subsequently carried out, as we shall see in due course.

Notwithstanding what Vasari wrote to Lionardo about his uncle's coffin having been left at the

[1] Vasari, xii. 285.

Dogana, it seems that it was removed upon the very day of its arrival, March 11, to the Oratory of the Assunta, underneath the church of S. Pietro Maggiore.[1] On the following day the painters, sculptors, and architects of the newly founded academy met together at this place, intending to transfer the body secretly to S. Croce. They only brought a single pall of velvet, embroidered with gold, and a crucifix, to place upon the bier. When night fell, the elder men lighted torches, while the younger crowded together, vying one with another for the privilege of carrying the coffin. Meantime the Florentines, suspecting that something unusual was going forward at S. Pietro, gathered round, and soon the news spread through the city that Michelangelo was being borne to S. Croce. A vast concourse of people in this way came unexpectedly together, following the artists through the streets, and doing pathetic honour to the memory of the illustrious dead. The spacious church of S. Croce was crowded in all its length and breadth, so that the pall-bearers had considerable difficulty in reaching the sacristy with their precious burden. In that place Don Vincenzo Borghini, who was lieutenant of the academy, ordered that the coffin should be opened. "He thought he should be doing what was pleasing to many of those present; and, as he afterwards admitted, he was personally anxious to behold in death one whom he had never seen in life, or at any rate so long ago as to have quite for-

[1] Vasari, xii. 290.

gotten the occasion. All of us who stood by expected
to find the corpse already defaced by the outrage of
the sepulchre, inasmuch as twenty-five days had
elapsed since Michelangelo's death, and twenty-one
since his consignment to the coffin; but, to our great
surprise, the dead man lay before us perfect in all his
parts, and without the evil odours of the grave;
indeed, one might have thought that he was resting
in a sweet and very tranquil slumber. Not only did
the features of his countenance bear exactly the same
aspect as in life, except for some inevitable pallor,
but none of his limbs were injured, or repulsive to the
sight. The head and cheeks, to the touch, felt just
as though he had breathed his last but a few hours
since." As soon as the eagerness of the multitude
calmed down a little, the bier was carried into the
church again, and the coffin was deposited in a
proper place behind the altar of the Cavalcanti.

When the academicians decreed a catafalque for
Michelangelo's solemn obsequies in S. Lorenzo, they
did not aim so much at worldly splendour or gorgeous
trappings as at an impressive monument, combining
the several arts which he had practised in his lifetime. Being made of stucco, woodwork, plaster,
and such perishable materials, it was unfortunately
destined to decay. But Florence had always been
liberal, nay, lavish, of her genius in triumphs,
masques, magnificent street architecture, evoked to
celebrate some ephemeral event. A worthier occasion would not occur again; and we have every

reason to believe that the superb structure, which
was finally exposed to view upon the 14th of July,
displayed all that was left at Florence of the grand
style in the arts of modelling and painting. They
were decadent indeed ; during the eighty-nine years
of Buonarroti's life upon earth they had expanded,
flourished, and flowered with infinite variety in rapid
evolution. He lived to watch their decline ; yet the
sunset of that long day was still splendid to the eyes
and senses.

The four deputies appointed by the academy held
frequent sittings before the plan was fixed, and the
several parts had been assigned to individual craftsmen. Ill health prevented Cellini from attending,
but he sent a letter to the lieutenant, which throws
some interesting light upon the project in its earlier
stages. A minute description of the monument
was published soon after the event.[2] Another may
be read in the pages of Vasari. Varchi committed
his oration to the press, and two other panegyrical
discourses were issued, under the names of Leonardo
Salviati and Giovan Maria Tarsia.[3] Poems composed
on the occasion were collected into one volume, and
distributed by the Florentine firm of Sermatelli.[4]
To load these pages with the details of allegorical

---

[1] Gotti, i. 365.

[2] *Esequie del Divino Michelangelo Buonarroti, celebrate in Firenze
dall' Academia, &c.* Firenze : Giunti, 1564.

[3] Varchi's *Orazione Funerale, &c.,* was printed by the Giunti in 1564.

[4] *Poesie di diversi autori latini e volgari, &c.* Firenze : Sermatelli,
1564. It is said to be a very rare book. See Vasari, xii. 310, note 1.

statues and pictures which have long passed out
of existence, and to cite passages from funeral
speeches, seems to me useless.[1] It is enough to
have directed the inquisitive to sources where their
curiosity may be gratified.

IV.

It would be impossible to take leave of Michelangelo without some general survey of his character
and qualities. With this object in view I do not
think I can do better than to follow what Condivi
says at the close of his biography, omitting those
passages which have been already used in the body
of this book, and supplementing his summary with
illustrative anecdotes from Vasari. Both of these
men knew him intimately during the last years of
his life; and if it is desirable to learn how a man
strikes his contemporaries, we obtain from them a
lively and veracious, though perhaps a slightly flat-
tered, picture of the great master whom they studied
with love and admiration from somewhat different
points of view. This will introduce a critical examination of the analysis to which the psychology of
Michelangelo has recently been subjected.

---

[1] See Vasari, xii. 309, note 2, for an account of the gradual dispersion
of the models and canvasses which adorned the catafalque.

Condivi opens his peroration with the following paragraphs :—

"Now, to conclude this gossiping discourse of mine, I say that it is my opinion that in painting and sculpture nature bestowed all her riches with a full hand upon Michelangelo. I do not fear reproach or contradiction when I repeat that his statues are, as it were, inimitable. Nor do I think that I have suffered myself to exceed the bounds of truth while making this assertion. In the first place, he is the only artist who has handled both brush and mallet with equal excellence. Then we have no relics left of antique paintings to compare with his ; and though many classical works in statuary survive, to whom among the ancients does he yield the palm in sculpture ? In the judgment of experts and practical artists, he certainly yields to none ; and were we to consult the vulgar, who admire antiquity without criticism, through a kind of jealousy toward the talents and the industry of their own times, even here we shall find none who say the contrary ; to such a height has this great man soared above the scope of envy. Raffaello of Urbino, though he chose to strive in rivalry with Michelangelo, was wont to say that he thanked God for having been born in his days, since he learned from him a manner very different from that which his father, who was a painter, and his master, Perugino, taught him. Then, too, what proof of his singular excellence could be wished for, more convincing and more valid, than

the eagerness with which the sovereigns of the world
contended for him? Beside four pontiffs, Julius,
Leo, Clement, and Paul, the Grand Turk, father of
the present Sultan, sent certain Franciscans with
letters begging him to come and reside at his court.
By orders on the bank of the Gondi at Florence, he
provided that whatever sums were asked for should
be disbursed to pay the expenses of his journey; and
when he should have reached Cossa, a town near
Ragusa, one of the greatest nobles of the realm was
told off to conduct him in most honourable fashion
to Constantinople. Francis of Valois, King of
France, tried to get him by many devices, giving
instructions that, whenever he chose to travel, 3000
crowns should be told out to him in Rome. The
Signory of Venice sent Bruciolo to Rome with an
invitation to their city, offering a pension of 600
crowns if he would settle there. They attached no
conditions to this offer, only desiring that he should
honour the republic with his presence, and stipulat-
ing that whatever he might do in their service should
be paid as though he were not in receipt of a fixed
income. These are not ordinary occurrences, or such
as happen every day, but strange and out of common
usage; nor are they wont to befall any but men of
singular and transcendent ability, as was Homer, for
whom many cities strove in rivalry, each desirous of
acquiring him and making him its own.

"The reigning pope, Julius III., holds him in no
less esteem than the princes I have mentioned. This

sovereign, distinguished for rare taste and judgment, loves and promotes all arts and sciences, but is most particularly devoted to painting, sculpture, and architecture, as may be clearly seen in the buildings which his Holiness has erected in the Vatican and the Belvedere, and is now raising at his Villa Giulia (a monument worthy of a lofty and generous nature, as indeed his own is), where he has gathered together so many ancient and modern statues, such a variety of the finest pictures, precious columns, works in stucco, wall-painting, and every kind of decoration, of the which I must reserve a more extended account for some future occasion, since it deserves a particular study, and has not yet reached completion. This Pope has not used the services of Michelangelo for any active work, out of regard for his advanced age. He is fully alive to his greatness, and appreciates it, but refrains from adding burdens beyond those which Michelangelo himself desires ; and this regard, in my opinion, confers more honour on him than any of the great undertakings which former pontiffs exacted from his genius. It is true that his Holiness almost always consults him on works of painting or of architecture he may have in progress, and very often sends the artists to confer with him at his own house. I regret, and his Holiness also regrets, that a certain natural shyness, or shall I say respect or reverence, which some folk call pride, prevents him from having recourse to the benevolence, goodness, and liberality of such a pontiff, and one so much his friend. For the Pope, as I first heard from the Most Rev. Monsignor of Forlì, his Master of the Chamber, has often observed that, were this possible, he would gladly give some of his own years and his own blood to add to Michelangelo's life, to the end that the world should not so soon be robbed of such a man. And this, when I had access to his Holiness, I heard with my own ears from his mouth. Moreover, if he happens to survive him, as seems reasonable in the course of nature, he has a mind to embalm him and keep him ever near to his own person, so that his body in death shall be as everlasting as his works. This he said to Michelangelo himself at the commencement of his reign, in the presence of many persons. I know not what could be more honourable to Michelangelo that such words, or a greater proof of the high account in which he is held by his Holiness.

"So then Michelangelo, while he was yet a youth, devoted himself not only to sculpture and painting, but also to all those other arts which to them are allied or subservient, and this he did with such absorbing energy that for a time he almost entirely cut himself off from human society, conversing with but very few intimate friends. On this account some folk thought him proud, others eccentric and capricious, although he was tainted with none of these defects; but, as hath happened to many men of great abilities, the love of study and the perpetual practice of his art rendered him solitary, being so

taken up with the pleasure and delight of these
things that society not only afforded him no solace,
but even caused him annoyance by diverting him
from meditation, being (as the great Scipio used to
say) never less alone than when he was alone.
Nevertheless, he very willingly embraced the friendship of those whose learned and cultivated conversation could be of profit to his mind, and in whom
oomo boamo of genius shone forth : as, for example,
the most reverend and illustrious Monsignor Pole,
for his rare virtues and singular goodness; and like-
wise the most reverend, my patron, Cardinal Crispo,
in whom he discovered, beside his many excellent
qualities, a distinguished gift of acute judgment; he
was also warmly attached to the Cardinal of S. Croce,
a man of the utmost gravity and wisdom, whom I
have often heard him name in the highest terms;
and to the most reverend Maffei, whose goodness
and learning he has always praised : indeed, he loves
and honours all the dependants of the house of
Farnese, owing to the lively memory he cherishes of
Pope Paul, whom he invariably mentions with the
deepest reverence as a good and holy old man;
and in like manner the most reverend Patriarch of
Jerusalem, sometime Bishop of Cesena, has lived for
some time in close intimacy with him, finding peculiar
pleasure in so open and generous a nature. He was
also on most friendly terms with my very reverend
patron the Cardinal Ridolfi, of blessed memory, that
refuge of all men of parts and talent. There are

several others whom I omit for fear of being prolix, as Monsignor Claudio Tolomei, Messer Lorenzo Ridolfi, Messer Donato Giannotti, Messer Lionardo Malespini, Lottino, Messer Tommaso dei Cavalieri, and other honoured gentlemen. Of late years he has become deeply attached to Annibal Caro, of whom he told me that it grieves him not to have come to know him earlier, seeing that he finds him much to his taste."[1]

"In like manner as he enjoyed the converse of learned men, so also did he take pleasure in the study of eminent writers, whether of prose or verse. Among these he particularly admired Dante, whose marvellous poems he hath almost all by heart. Nevertheless, the same might perhaps be said about his love for Petrarch. These poets he not only delighted in studying, but he also was wont to compose from time to time upon his own account. There are certain sonnets among those he wrote which give a very good notion of his great inventive power and judgment. Some of them have furnished Varchi with the subject of Discourses. It must be remembered, however, that he practised poetry for his amusement, and not as a profession, always depreciating his own talent and appealing to his ignorance in these matters. Just in the same way he has perused the Holy Scriptures with great care and industry, studying not merely the Old Testament,

---

[1] At this point Condivi introduces the passage upon Vittoria which I have already used in Chapter XII.

but also the New, together with their commentators, as, for example, the writings of Savonarola, for whom he always retained a deep affection, since the accents of the preacher's living voice rang in his memory.[1]

"He has given away many of his works, the which, if he had chosen to sell them, would have brought him vast sums of money. A single instance of this generosity will suffice—namely, the two statues which he presented to his dearest friend, Messer Ruberto Strozzi.[2] Nor was it only of his handiwork that he has been liberal. He opened his purse readily to poor men of talent in literature or art, as I can testify, having myself been the recipient of his bounty. He never showed an envious spirit toward the labours of other masters in the crafts he practised, and this was due rather to the goodness of his nature than to any sense of his own superiority. Indeed, he always praised all men of excellence without exception, even Raffaello of Urbino, between whom and himself there was of old time some rivalry in painting.[3] I have only heard him say that Raffaello did not derive his mastery in that art so much from nature as from prolonged study. Nor is it true, as many persons assert to his discredit, that he has been unwilling to impart instruction. On the con-

---

[1] Here comes the passage about Michelangelo's sense of beauty and theories of love, which I have used in Chapter XII., followed by the description of his sober manner of life, used in Chapter II.

[2] The two Captives of the Louvre.

[3] See Michelangelo's own letters about Bramante, Sebastiano del Piombo, and Cellini in confirmation of this.

trary, he did so readily, as I know by personal experience, for to me he unlocked all the secrets of the arts he had acquired. Ill-luck, however, willed that he should meet either with subjects ill adapted to such studies, or else with men of little perseverance, who, when they had been working a few months under his direction, began to think themselves pastmasters. Moreover, although he was willing to teach, he did not like it to be known that he did so, caring more to do good than to seem to do it. I may add that he always attempted to communicate the arts to men of gentle birth, as did the ancients, and not to plebeians."[1]

V.

To this passage about Michelangelo's pupils we may add the following observations by Vasari :[2]

[1] Vasari (xii. 277) has developed what Condivi says about the generosity of Michelangelo. He reckons up the number of models and drawings lavished upon Tommaso dei Cavalieri, Bindo Altoviti, Fra Sebastiano, Antonio Mini, Gherardo Perini ; describes the cartoon of Cupid kissing Venus, which he made for Baccio Bettini, and the *Noli me tangere* designed for the Marchese del Vasto, both of which were painted by Pontormo ; and after mentioning the donation of the Captives to Ruberto Strozzi, alludes to the Pietà bestowed upon his servan Antonio del Franzese. "Who can accuse that man of avarice who gives away for nothing things which might have brought him thousands of crowns ?" Then he reckons up the sums of money spent in alms, the largesse of 2000 crowns to Urbino, the frequent donations made to Lionardo Buonarroti, and the bequest to him of all his property. "Such bounty we are wont to think the special virtue of Cæsars and mighty Pontiffs."

[2] Vasari, xii. 274.

" He loved his workmen, and conversed with them on friendly terms. Among these I will mention Jacopo Sansovino, Rosso, Pontormo, Daniele da Volterra, and Giorgio Vasari. To the last of these men he showed unbounded kindness, and caused him to study architecture, with the view of employing his services in that art. He exchanged thoughts readily with him, and discoursed upon artistic topics. Those are in the wrong who assert that he refused to communicate his stores of knowledge. He always did so to his personal friends, and to all who sought his advice. It ought, however, to be mentioned that he was not lucky in the craftsmen who lived with him, since chance brought him into contact with people unfitted to profit by his example. Pietro Urbano of Pistoja was a man of talent but no industry. Antonio Mini had the will but not the brains, and hard wax takes a bad impression. Ascanio dalla Ripa Transone (*i.e.*, Condivi) took great pains, but brought nothing to perfection either in finished work or in designs. He laboured many years upon a picture for which Michelangelo supplied the drawing. At last the expectations based upon this effort vanished into smoke. I remember that Michelangelo felt pity for his trouble, and helped him with his own hand. Nothing, however, came of it. He often told me that if he had found a proper subject he should have liked, old as he was, to have recommenced anatomy, and to have written on it for the use of his workmen.

*

However, he distrusted his own powers of expressing what he wanted in writing, albeit his letters
show that he could easily put forth his thoughts
in a few brief words."

About Michelangelo's kindness to his pupils and
servants there is no doubt. We have only to remember his treatment of Pietro Urbano and Antonio Mini, Urbino and Condivi, Tiberio Calcagni
and Antonio del Franzese. A curious letter from
Michelangelo to Andrea Quarantesi, which I have
quoted in another connection, shows that people
were eager to get their sons placed under his
charge. The inedited correspondence in the Buonarroti Archives abounds in instances illustrating the
reputation he had gained for goodness. We have
two grateful letters from a certain Pietro Bettino
in Castle Durante speaking very warmly of Michelangelo's attention to his son Cesare.[1] Two to the
same effect from Amilcare Anguissola in Cremona
acknowledge services rendered to his daughter
Sofonisba, who was studying design in Rome.[2]
Pietro Urbano wrote twenty letters between the
years 1517 and 1525, addressing him in terms like
"carissimo quanto padre."[3] After recovering from
his illness at Pistoja, he expresses the hope that he
will soon be back again at Florence (September 18,
1519): "Dearest to me like the most revered of

[1] Cod. vi. Nos. 90, 91, dates October 24, 1561, and August 12, 1563.
[2] Ibid., vi. Nos. 35, 36, dates May 7, 1557, and May 17, 1558.
[3] Ibid., x. Nos. 614–633.

fathers, I send you salutations, announcing that I am a little better, but not yet wholly cured of that flux ; still I hope before many days are over to find myself at Florence."[1] A certain Silvio Falcone, who had been in his service, and who had probably been sent away because of some misconduct, addressed a letter from Rome to him in Florence, which shows both penitence and warm affection.[2] " I am and shall always be a good servant to you in every place where I may be. Do not remember my stupidity in those past concerns, which I know that, being a prudent man, you will not impute to malice. If you were to do so, this would cause me the greatest sorrow ; for I desire nothing but to remain in your good grace, and if I had only this in the world, it would suffice me." He begs to be remembered to Pietro Urbano, and requests his pardon if he has offended him. Another set of letters, composed in the same tone by a man who signs himself Silvio di Giovanni da Cepparello, was written by a sculptor honourably

---

[1] " Carisimo quanto maggior padre, salute, etc. Avisovi, come io sono un poco migliorato, ma pure anchora no sono ristagniato del flusso, pure i spero fra pochi dì essere sano e verromme a firenze."

[2] Cod. viii., December 6, 1517. "Io ve sono e serro sempre buono servitore in tutti li lochi dove io serro, e non vogliate ricordare dela mia ignioranza dele cose passate lequale so che voi considerarete como homo prudente non esser facte con malitia : e quando voi pensassero altrimente me serria grandissimo dolore : perchè io non desidero altro che di stare in gratia vostra e se io non avessi altro che questo al mondo me basteria." There is a letter from him dated August 17, 1514. This Silvio was in Michelangelo's service on the occasion of the incident with Signorelli, described in Lettere, No. cccliv. Michelangelo alludes to him as a competent witness.

mentioned in Vasari's Life of Andrea da Fiesole for his work at S. Lorenzo, in Genoa, and elsewhere. They show how highly the fame of having been in Michelangelo's employ was valued. He says that he is now working for Andrea Doria, Prince of Melfi, at Genoa.[1] Still he should like to return, if this were possible, to his old master's service : " For if I lost all I had in the world, and found myself with you, I should think myself the first of men." A year later Silvio was still at work for Prince Doria and the Fieschi, but he again begs earnestly to be taken back by Michelangelo. " I feel what obligations I am under for all the kindness received from you in past times. When I remember the love you bore me while I was in your service, I do not know how I could repay it; and I tell you that only through having been in your service, wherever I may happen now to be, honour and courtesy are paid me ; and that is wholly due to your excellent renown, and not to any merit of my own."[2]

The only letter from Ascanio Condivi extant in the Buonarroti Archives may here be translated in

---

[1] Cod. vii. No. 146, April 6, 1532. "Quando io perdesse cio che ho al mondo et fussi apreso di voi mi pareria esser il primo homo del mondo."

[2] "Imperochè mi par havere grandissimo obligo per il beneficio da voi ricevuto neli passati tempi, che quando io me ricordo delo amore quale mi portasti immentre io fui al vostro servitio non mi par possibile poterò mai restorarvi, et dicovi solamente per essere io stato al servitio vostro in tuti quelli lochi dove io mi ritrovo m' è fato honore e cortesia e questo è solo per la bona fama che è di voi e non già per merito di mia virtú." Date April 13, 1532.

full, since its tone does honour both to master
and servant :[1]—

"Unique lord and my most to be observed patron,
—I have already written you two letters, but almost
think you cannot have received them, since I have
heard no news of you. This I write merely to beg
that you will remember to command me, and to
make use not of me alone, but of all my household,
since we are all your servants. Indeed, my most
honoured and revered master, I entreat you deign
to dispose of me and do with me as one is wont
to do with the least of servants. You have the
right to do so, since I owe more to you than to
my own father, and I will prove my desire to
repay your kindness by my deeds. I will now end
this letter, in order not to be irksome, recommending myself humbly, and praying you to let me have
the comfort of knowing that you are well: for a
greater I could not receive. Farewell."

It cannot be denied that Michelangelo sometimes
treated his pupils and servants with the same irritability, suspicion, and waywardness of temper as
he showed to his relatives and friends. It is only
necessary to recall his indignation against Lapo and
Lodovico at Bologna, Stefano at Florence, Sandro
at Serravalle, all his female drudges, and the anony-
mous boy whom his father sent from Rome. That
he was a man " gey ill to live with" seems indis-

---

[1] Cod. vii. No. 149, date May 24, 1555 (?). I shall print the original
in the Appendix.

putable. This may in part account for the fact that, unlike other great Italian masters, he formed no school. The *frescanti* who came from Florence to assist him in the Sistine Chapel were dismissed with abruptness, perhaps even with brutality. Montelupo and Montorsoli, among sculptors, Marcello Venusti and Pontormo, Daniele da Volterra and Sebastiano del Piombo, among painters, felt his direct influence. But they did not stand in the same relation to him as Raffaello's pupils to their master. The work of Giulio Romano, Giovanni da Udine, Francesco Penni, Perino del Vaga, Primaticcio, at Rome, at Mantua, and elsewhere, is a genial continuation of Raffaello's spirit and manner after his decease. Nothing of the sort can be maintained about the statues and the paintings which display a study of the style of Michelangelo. And this holds good in like manner of his imitators in architecture. For worse rather than for better, he powerfully and permanently affected Italian art; but he did not create a body of intelligent craftsmen, capable of carrying on his inspiration, as Giulio Romano expanded the Loggie of the Vatican into the Palazzo del Te. I have already expressed my opinions regarding the specific quality of the Michelangelesque tradition in a passage which I may perhaps be here permitted to resume :[1]—

"Michelangelo formed no school in the strict sense of the word ; yet his influence was not the less felt

[1] *Renaissance in Italy*, vol. iii. pp. 493–495.

on that account, nor less powerful than Raffaello's. During his manhood a few painters endeavoured to add the charm of oil-colouring to his designs, and long before his death the seduction of his mighty mannerism began to exercise a fatal charm for all the schools of Italy. Painters incapable of fathoming his intention, unsympathetic to his rare type of intellect, and gifted with less than a tithe of his native force, set themselves to reproduce whatever may be justly censured in his works. To heighten and enlarge their style was reckoned a chief duty of aspiring craftsmen, and it was thought that recipes for attaining to this final perfection of the modern arts might be extracted without trouble from Michelangelo's masterpieces. Unluckily, in proportion as his fame increased, his peculiarities became with the advance of age more manneristic and defined, so that his imitators fixed precisely upon that which sober critics now regard as a deduction from his greatness. They failed to perceive that he owed his grandeur to his personality, and that the audacities which fascinated them became mere whimsical extravagances when severed from his *terribilità*, and sombre simplicity of impassioned thought. His power and his spirit were alike unique and incommunicable, while the admiration of his youthful worshippers betrayed them into imitating the externals of a style that was rapidly losing spontaneity. Therefore they fancied they were treading in his footsteps and using the grand manner when they covered church-roofs and canvases with sprawling figures in distorted attitudes. Instead of studying nature, they studied Michelangelo's cartoons, exaggerating by their unintelligent discipleship his wilfulness and arbitrary choice of form.

"Vasari's and Cellini's criticisms of a master they both honestly revered may suffice to illustrate the false method adopted by these mimics of Michelangelo's ideal. To charge him with faults proceeding from the weakness and blindness of the Decadence—the faults of men too blind to read his , art aright, too weak to stand on their own feet without him—would be either stupid or malicious. If at the close of the sixteenth century the mannerists sought to startle and entrance the world by empty exhibitions of muscular anatomy misunderstood, and by a braggadocio display of meaningless effects—crowding their compositions with studies from the nude, and painting agitated groups without a discernible cause for agitation—the crime surely lay with the patrons who liked such decoration, and with the journeymen who provided it. Michelangelo himself always made his manner serve his thought. We may fail to appreciate his manner and may be incapable of comprehending his thought, but only insincere or conceited critics will venture to gauge the latter by what they feel to be displeasing in the former. What seems lawless in him follows the law of a profound and peculiar genius, with which, whether we like it or not, we must reckon. His imitators were devoid of thought, and too indifferent to question whether there was any law to be obeyed. Like the jackass in the fable, they assumed the dead lion's skin, and brayed beneath it, thinking they could roar."

VI.

Continuing these scattered observations upon Michelangelo's character and habits, we may collect what Vasari records about his social intercourse with brother-artists. Being himself of a saturnine humour, he took great delight in the society of persons little better than buffoons. Writing the Life of Jacopo surnamed L'Indaco, a Florentine painter of some merit, Vasari observes :[1] " He lived on very familiar terms of intimacy with Michelangelo ; for that great artist, great above all who ever were, when he wished to refresh his mind, fatigued by studies and incessant labours of the body and the intellect, found no one more to his liking and more congenial to his humour than was Indaco." Nothing is recorded concerning their friendship, except that Buonarroti frequently invited Indaco to meals ; and one day, growing tired of the man's incessant chatter, sent him out to buy figs,

[1] Vasari, vi. 133. It will be remembered that this Indaco was one of the painters brought from Florence by Michelangelo to help him in the Sistine.

and then locked the house-door, so that he could not enter when he had discharged his errand. A boon-companion of the same type was Menighella, whom Vasari describes as "a mediocre and stupid painter of Valdarno, but extremely amusing."[1] He used to frequent Michelangelo's house, "and he, who could with difficulty be induced to work for kings, would lay aside all other occupations in order to make drawings for this fellow." What Menighella wanted was some simple design or other of S. Rocco, S. Antonio, or S. Francesco, to be coloured for one of his peasant patrons. Vasari says that Michelangelo modelled a very beautiful Christ for this humble friend, from which Menighella made a cast, and repeated it in papier-maché, selling these crucifixes through the country-side. What would not the world give for one of them, even though Michelangelo is said to have burst his sides with laughing at the man's stupidity![2] Another familiar of the same sort was a certain stone-cutter called Domenico Fancelli, and nicknamed Topolino. From a letter addressed to him by Buonarroti in 1523 it appears that he was regarded as a "very dear friend."[3] According to Vasari, Topolino thought himself an able sculptor, but was in reality extremely feeble. He blocked out a marble Mercury, and

[1] Vasari, xii. 281.

[2] Springer, in his *Raffael und Michelangelo*, remarks that the crucifixes current among the Italian people still bear a close resemblance to his style. I have not observed this.

[3] Lettere, No. ccclxxx.

begged the great master to pronounce a candid opinion on its merits. "You are a madman, Topolino," replied Michelangelo, "to attempt this art of statuary. Do you not see that your Mercury is too short by more than a third of a cubit from the knees to the feet? You have made him a dwarf, and spoiled the whole figure." "Oh, that is nothing! If there is no other fault, I can easily put that to rights. Leave the matter to me." Michelangelo laughed at the man's simplicity, and went upon his way. Then Topolino took a piece of marble, and cut off the legs of his Mercury below the knees. Next he fashioned a pair of buskins of the right height, and joined these on to the truncated limbs in such wise that the tops of the boots concealed the lines of juncture. When Buonarroti saw the finished statue, he remarked that fools were gifted with the instinct for rectifying errors by expedients which a wise man would not have hit upon.

Another of Michelangelo's buffoon friends was a Florentine celebrity, Piloto, the goldsmith. We know that he took this man with him when he went to Venice in 1530; but Vasari tells no characteristic stories concerning their friendship. It may be remarked that Il Lasca describes Piloto as a "most entertaining and facetious fellow," assigning him the principal part in one of his indecent novels.[1] The painter Giuliano Bugiardini ought to

[1] *Le Cene*, i. 2.

be added to the same list. Messer Ottaviano de'
Medici begged him to make a portrait of Michelangelo, who gave him a sitting without hesitation,
being extremely partial to the man's company.[1]   At
the end of two hours Giuliano exclaimed: "Michelangelo, if you want to see yourself, stand up; I
have caught the likeness." Michelangelo did as
he was bidden, and when he had examined the
portrait, he laughed and said: "What the devil
have you been about? You have painted me with
one of my eyes up in the temple." Giuliano stood
some time comparing the drawing with his model's
face, and then remarked: "I do not think so; but
take your seat again, and I shall be able to judge
better when I have you in the proper pose." Michelangelo, who knew well where the fault lay, and how
little judgment belonged to his friend Bugiardini,
resumed his seat, grinning. After some time of
careful contemplation, Giuliano rose to his feet and
cried: "It seems to me that I have drawn it right,
and that the life compels me to do so." "So then,"
replied Buonarroti, "the defect is nature's, and see
you spare neither the brush nor art."

Both Sebastiano del Piombo and Giorgio Vasari
were appreciated by Michelangelo for their lively
parts and genial humour. The latter has told an
anecdote which illustrates the old man's eccentricity.[2]   He was wont to wear a cardboard hat at
night, into which he stuck a candle, and then

[1] Vasari, x. 350.   [2] Ibid., xii. 276.

worked by its light upon his statue of the Pietà. Vasari observing this habit, wished to do him a kindness by sending him 40 lbs. of candles made of goat's fat, knowing that they gutter less than ordinary dips of tallow. His servant carried them politely to the house two hours after nightfall, and presented them to Michelangelo. He refused, and said he did not want them. The man answered: " Sir, they have almost broken my arms carrying them all this long way from the bridge, nor will I take them home again. There is a heap of mud opposite your door, thick and firm enough to hold them upright. Here then I will set them all up, and light them." When Michelangelo heard this, he gave way : " Lay them down ; I do not mean you to play pranks at my house-door." Vasari tells another anecdote about the Pietà.[1] Pope Julius III. sent him late one evening to Michelangelo's house for some drawing. The old man came down with a lantern, and hearing what was wanted, told Urbino to look for the cartoon. Meanwhile, Vasari turned his attention to one of the legs of Christ, which Michelangelo had been trying to alter. In order to prevent his seeing, Michelangelo let the lamp fall, and they remained in darkness. He then called for a light, and stepped forth from the enclosure of planks behind which he worked. As he did so, he remarked, " I am so old that oftentimes Death plucks me by the cape to go with him, and one day

[1] Vasari, p. 281.

this body of mine will fall like the lantern, and the light of life will be put out." Of death he used to say, that "if life gives us pleasure, we ought not to expect displeasure from death, seeing it is made by the hand of the same master."[1]

Among stories relating to craftsmen, these are perhaps worth gleaning.[2] While he was working on the termini for the tomb of Julius, he gave directions to a certain stone-cutter: "Remove such and such parts here to-day, smooth out in this place, and polish up in that." In course of time, without being aware of it, the man found that he had produced a statue, and stared astonished at his own performance. Michelangelo asked, "What do you think of it?" "I think it very good," he answered, "and I owe you a deep debt of gratitude." "Why do you say that?" "Because you have caused me to discover in myself a talent which I did not know that I possessed."—A certain citizen, who wanted a mortar, went to a sculptor and asked him to make one. The fellow, suspecting some practical joke, pointed out Buonarroti's house, and said that if he wanted mortars, a man lived there whose trade it was to make them. The customer accordingly addressed himself to Michelangelo, who, in his turn suspecting a trick, asked who had sent him. When he knew the sculptor's name, he promised to carve the mortar, on the condition that it should be

---

[1] Vasari, p. 278.
[2] Ibid., xii. pp. 278–283, and notes.

paid for at the sculptor's valuation. This was settled, and the mortar turned out a miracle of arabesques and masks and grotesque inventions, wonderfully wrought and polished. In due course of time the mortar was taken to the envious and suspicious sculptor, who stood dumbfounded before it, and told the customer that there was nothing left but to carry this masterpiece of carving back to him who fashioned it, and order a plain article for himself.—At Modena he inspected the terra-cotta groups by Antonio Begarelli, enthusiastically crying out, "If this clay could become marble, woe to antique statuary."—A Florentine citizen once saw him gazing at Donatello's statue of S. Mark upon the outer wall of Orsammichele. On being asked what he thought of it, Michelangelo replied, "I never saw a figure which so thoroughly represents a man of probity ; if S. Mark was really like that, we have every reason to believe everything which he has said." To the S. George in the same place he is reported to have given the word of command, "March !"—Some one showed him a set of medals by Alessandro Cesari, upon which he exclaimed, "The death hour of art has struck ; nothing more perfect can be seen than these." — Before Titian's portrait of Duke Alfonso di Ferrara he observed that he had not thought art could perform so much, adding that Titian alone deserved the name of painter.—He was wont to call Cronaca's church of S. Francesco al Monte "his lovely peasant girl," and Ghiberti's doors

in the Florentine Baptistery " the Gates of Paradise."
—Somebody showed him a boy's drawings, and excused their imperfection by pleading that he had
only just begun to study: "That is obvious," he
answered. A similar reply is said to have been
made to Vasari, when he excused his own frescoes
in the Cancelleria at Rome by saying they had been
painted in a few days.—An artist showed him a
Pietà which he had finished: "Yes, it is indeed a
pietà (pitiful object) to see."—Ugo da Carpi signed
one of his pictures with a legend declaring he had
not used a brush on it: "It would have been better
had he done so."—Sebastian del Piombo was ordered
to paint a friar in a chapel at S. Pietro a Montorio.
Michelangelo observed, "He will spoil the chapel."
Asked why, he answered, "When the friars have
spoiled the world, which is so large, it surely is an
easy thing for them to spoil such a tiny chapel."—
A sculptor put together a number of figures imitated
from the antique, and thought he had surpassed
his models. Michelangelo remarked, "One who
walks after another man, never goes in front of
him ; and one who is not able to do well by his
own wit, will not be able to profit by the works of
others." [1]—A painter produced some notably poor
picture, in which only an ox was vigorously drawn :
"Every artist draws his own portrait best," said
Michelangelo.—He went to see a statue which was in
the sculptor's studio, waiting to be exposed before the

[1] This was said probably apropos of Bandinelli's copy of the Laocoon.

public. The man bustled about altering the lights, in order to show his work off to the best advantage : "Do not take this trouble; what really matters will be the light of the piazza;" meaning that the people in the long-run decide what is good or bad in art.—Accused of want of spirit in his rivalry with Nanni di Baccio Bigio, he retorted, "Men who fight with folk of little worth win nothing."— A priest who was a friend of his said, "It is a pity that you never married, for you might have had many children, and would have left them all the profit and honour of your labours." Michelangelo answered, "I have only too much of a wife in this art of mine. She has always kept me struggling on. My children will be the works I leave behind me. Even though they are worth naught, yet I shall live awhile in them. Woe to Lorenzo Ghiberti if he had not made the gates of S. Giovanni! His children and grandchildren have sold and squandered the substance that he left. The gates are still in their places."

VII.

This would be an appropriate place to estimate Michelangelo's professional gains in detail, to describe the properties he acquired in lands and houses, and to give an account of his total fortune.

We are, however, not in the position to do this accurately. We only know the prices paid for a few of his minor works. He received, for instance, thirty ducats for the Sleeping Cupid, and 450 ducats for the Pietà of S. Peter's. He contracted with Cardinal Piccolomini to furnish fifteen statues for 500 ducats. In all of these cases the costs of marble, workmen, workshop, fell on him. He contracted with Florence to execute the David in two years, at a salary of six golden florins per month, together with a further sum when the work was finished. It appears that 400 florins in all (including salary) were finally adjudged to him. In these cases all incidental expenses had been paid by his employers. He contracted with the Operai del Duomo to make twelve statues in as many years, receiving two florins a month, and as much as the Operai thought fit to pay him when the whole was done. Here too he was relieved from incidental expenses. For the statue of Christ at S. Maria sopra Minerva he was paid 200 crowns.

These are a few of the most trustworthy items we possess, and they are rendered very worthless by the impossibility of reducing ducats, florins, and crowns to current values. With regard to the bronze statue of Julius II. at Bologna, Michelangelo tells us that he received in advance 1000 ducats, and when he ended his work there remained only 4½ ducats to the good. In this case, as in most of his great operations, he entered at the commencement into a contract with his patron, sending in an estimate of what he thought it would be worth his while to do the work for. The Italian is "pigliare a cottimo;" and in all of his dealings with successive Popes Michelangelo evidently preferred this method. It must have sometimes enabled the artist to make large profits; but the nature of the contract prevents his biographer from forming even a vague estimate of their amount. According to Condivi, he received 3000 ducats for the Sistine vault, working at his own costs. According to his own statement, several hundred ducats were owing at the end of the affair. It seems certain that Julius II. died in Michelangelo's debt, and that the various contracts for his tomb were a source of loss rather than of gain.

Such large undertakings as the sacristy and library of S. Lorenzo were probably agreed for on the contract system. But although there exist plenty of memoranda recording Michelangelo's disbursements at various times for various portions of these works, we can strike no balance showing an approximate calculation of his profits. What renders the matter still more perplexing is, that very few of Michelangelo's contracts were fulfilled according to the original intention of the parties. For one reason or another they had to be altered and accommodated to circumstances.

It is clear that, later on in life, he received money for drawings, for architectural work, and for models, the execution of which he bound himself to super-intend.   Cardinal Grimani wrote saying he would pay the artist's own price for a design he had re-quested.   Vasari observes that the sketches he gave away were worth thousands of crowns.   We know that he was offered a handsome salary for the super-intendence of S. Peter's, which he magnanimously and piously declined to touch.   But what we cannot arrive at is even a rough valuation of the sums he earned in these branches of employment.

Again, we know that he was promised a yearly salary from Clement VII., and one more handsome from Paul III.   But the former was paid irregu-larly, and half of the latter depended on the profits of a ferry, which eventually failed him altogether. In each of these cases, then, the same circumstances of vagueness and uncertainty throw doubt on all investigation, and render a conjectural estimate impossible.   Moreover, there remain no documents to prove what he may have gained, directly or in-directly, from succeeding Pontiffs.   That he felt the loss of Paul III., as a generous patron, is proved by a letter written on the occasion of his death; and Vasari hints that the Pope had been munificent in largesses bestowed upon him.   But of these occa-sional presents and emoluments we have no accurate information; and we are unable to state what he derived from Pius IV., who was certainly one of his best friends and greatest admirers.

At his death in Rome he left cash amounting to

something under 9000 crowns. But, since he died intestate, we have no will to guide us as to the extent and nature of his whole estate. Nor, so far as I am aware, has the return of his property, which Lionardo Buonarroti may possibly have furnished to the state of Florence, been yet brought to light.[1]

That he inherited some landed property at Settignano from his father is certain; and he added several plots of ground to the paternal acres. He also is said to have bought a farm in Valdichiana (doubtful), and other pieces of land in Tuscany. He owned a house at Rome, a house and workshop in the Via Mozza at Florence, and he purchased the Casa Buonarroti in Via Ghibellina. But we have no means of determining the total value of these real assets.

In these circumstances I feel unable to offer any probable opinion regarding the amount of Michelangelo's professional earnings, or the exact way in which they were acquired. That he died possessed of a considerable fortune, and that he was able during his lifetime to assist his family with large donations, cannot be disputed. But how he came to command so much money does not appear. His frugality, bordering upon penuriousness, impressed contemporaries. This, considering the length of his life, may account for not contemptible accumulations.

---

[1] On application to the Archivio di Stato, in the Uffizi at Florence, I discovered that Michelangelo died during a period when the former *Catasto* was suspended.

VIII.

We have seen that Michelangelo's contemporaries found fault with several supposed frailties of his nature. These may be briefly catalogued under the following heads: A passionate violence of temper (*terribilità*), expressing itself in hasty acts and words; extreme suspiciousness and irritability; solitary habits, amounting to misanthropy or churlishness; eccentricity and melancholy bordering on madness; personal timidity and avarice; a want of generosity in imparting knowledge, and an undue partiality for handsome persons of his own sex. His biographers, Condivi and Vasari, thought these charges worthy of serious refutation, which proves that they were current. They had no difficulty in showing that his alleged misanthropy, melancholy, and madness were only signs of a studious nature absorbed in profound meditations. They easily refuted the charges of avarice and want of generosity in helping on young artists. But there remained a great deal in the popular conception which could not be dismissed, and which has recently been corroborated by the publication of his correspondence. The opinion that Michelangelo was a man of peculiar, and in some respects not altogether healthy nervous temperament, will force itself upon all those who have fairly weighed the evidence of the letters in

connection with the events of his life.   It has been
developed in a somewhat exaggerated form, of late
years, by several psychologists of the new school
(Parlagreco and Lombroso in Italy, Nisbet in
England), who attempt to prove that Michelangelo
was the subject of neurotic disorder.   The most
important and serious essay in this direction is a
little book of great interest and almost hypercritical
acumen published recently at Naples.[1]   Signor
Parlagreco lays great stress upon Michelangelo's
insensibility to women, his " strange and contra-
dictory feeling about feminine beauty."   He seeks
to show, what is indeed, I think, capable of demonstration, that the man's intense devotion to art
and study, his solitary habits and constitutional
melancholy, caused him to absorb the ordinary
instincts and passions of a young man into his
æsthetic temperament ; and that when, in later
life, he began to devote his attention to poetry,
he treated love from the point of view of mystical
philosophy.   In support of this argument Parlagreco
naturally insists upon the famous friendship with
Vittoria Colonna, and quotes the Platonising poems
commonly attributed to this emotion.   He has
omitted to mention, what certainly bears upon the
point of Michelangelo's frigidity, that only one out
of the five Buonarroti brothers, sons of Lodovico,
married.   Nor does he take into account the fact

---

[1] *Michelangelo Buonarroti (Il Vecchio): Studio di Carlo Parlagreco.*
Napoli : Fratelli Orfeo, 1888.

that Raffaello da Urbino, who was no less devoted
and industrious in art and study, retained the
liveliest sensibility to female charms.   In other
words, the critic appears to neglect that common-
sense solution of the problem, which is found in a
cold and physically sterile constitution as opposed
to one of greater warmth and sensuous activity.

Parlagreco attributes much value to what he
calls the religious terrors and remorse of Michelangelo's old age ; says that "his fancy became
haunted with doubts and fears ; every day discover-
ing fresh sins in the past, inveighing against the
very art which made him famous among men, and
seeking to propitiate Paradise for his soul by acts
of charity to dowerless maidens." The sonnets to
Vasari and some others are quoted in support of
this view.   But the question remains, whether it is
not exaggerated to regard pious aspirations, and a
sense of human life's inadequacy at its close, as the
signs of nervous malady.   The following passage
sums up Parlagreco's theory in a succession of
pregnant sentences.[1]   "An accurate study, based
upon his correspondence in connection with the
events of the artist's life and the history of his
works, has enabled me to detect in his character
a persistent oscillation.   Continual contradictions
between great and generous ideas upon the one side,
and puerile ideas upon the other ; between the will
and the word, thought and action ; an excessive

[1] *Op. cit.*, p. 93.

irritability and the highest degree of susceptibility ; constant love for others, great activity in doing good, sudden sympathies, great outbursts of enthusiasm, great fears ; at times an unconsciousness with respect to his own actions; a marvellous modesty in the field of art, an unréasonable vanity regarding external appearances : [1]—these are the diverse manifestations of psychical energy in Buonarroti's life ; all which makes me believe that the mighty artist was affected by a degree of neuropathy bordering closely upon hysterical disease." He proceeds to support this general view by several considerations, among which the most remarkable are Michelangelo's asseverations to friends : [2] " You will say that I am old and mad to make sonnets, but if people assert that I am on the verge of dotage, I have wished to act up to my character:" "You will say that I am old and mad ; but I answer that there is no better way of keeping sane and free from anxiety, than by being mad:" "As regards the madness they ascribe to me, it does harm to nobody but myself:" "I enjoyed last evening, because it drew me out of my melancholy and mad humour."

Reviewing Parlagreco's argument in general, I think it may be justly remarked that if the qualities rehearsed above constitute hysterical neuro-

---

[1] This refers to Michelangelo's pride in his pedigree. But it neglects the notorious simplicity of his personal life.

[2] *Op. cit.*, p. 101.

pathy, then every testy, sensitive, impulsive, and benevolent person is neuropathically hysterical. In particular we may demur to the terms "puerile ideas," "unreasonable vanity regarding external appearances." It would be difficult to discover puerility in any of Buonarroti's utterances; and his only vanity was a certain pride in the supposed descent of his house from that of Canossa. The frequent allusions to melancholy and madness do not constitute a confession of these qualities. They express Michelangelo's irritation at being always twitted with unsociability and eccentricity. In the conversations recorded by Francesco d'Olanda he quietly and philosophically exculpates men of the artistic temperament from such charges, which were undoubtedly brought against him, and which the recluse manner of his life to some extent accounted for.

It may be well here to resume the main points of the indictment brought against Michelangelo's sanity by the neo-psychologists. In the first place, he admired male more than female beauty, and preferred the society of men to that of women. But this peculiarity, in an age and climate which gave large licence to immoderate passions, exposed him to no serious malignancy of rumour. Such predilections were not uncommon in Italy. They caused scandal when they degenerated into vice, and rarely failed in that case to obscure the good fame of persons subject to them. Yet Michelangelo, surrounded by jealous rivals, was only very lightly touched by the breath of calumny in his lifetime. Aretino's malicious insinuation and Condivi's cautious vindication do not suffice to sully his memory with any dark suspicion. He lived with an almost culpable penuriousness in what concerned his personal expenditure. But he was generous towards his family, bountiful to his dependants, and liberal in charity. He suffered from constitutional depression, preferred solitude to crowds, and could not brook the interference of fashionable idlers with his studious leisure. But, as he sensibly urged in self-defence, these eccentricities, so frequent with men of genius, ought to have been ascribed to the severe demands made upon an artist's faculties by the problems with which he was continually engaged ; the planning of a Pope's mausoleum, the distribution of a score of histories and several hundreds of human figures on a chapel-vaulting, the raising of S. Peter's cupola in air : none of which tasks can be either lightly undertaken or carried out with ease. At worst, Michelangelo's melancholy might be ascribed to that *morbus eruditorum* of which Burton speaks. It never assumed the form of hypochondria, hallucination, misogyny, or misanthropy. He was irritable, suspicious, and frequently unjust both to his friends and relatives on slight occasions. But his relatives gave him good reason to be fretful by their greediness, ingratitude, and stupidity ; and when he lost his temper he recovered it with singular ease. It is also noticeable

that these paroxysms of crossness on which so much
stress has been laid, came upon him mostly when
he was old, worn out with perpetual mental and
physical fatigue, and troubled by a painful disease
of the bladder. There is nothing in their nature,
frequency, or violence to justify the hypothesis of
more than a hyper-sensitive nervous temperament;
and without a temperament of this sort how could
an artist of Michelangelo's calibre and intensity perform his life-work? In old age he dwelt upon the
thought of death, meditated in a repentant spirit on
the errors of his younger years, indulged a pious
spirit, and clung to the cross of Christ. But when
a man has passed the period allotted for the average
of his race, ought not these preoccupations to be
reckoned to him rather as appropriate and meritorious? We must not forget that he was born and
lived as a believing Christian, in an age of immorality
indeed, but one which had not yet been penetrated
with scientific conceptions and materialism. There
is nothing hysterical or unduly ascetic in the religion
of his closing years. It did not prevent him from
taking the keenest interest in his family, devoting
his mind to business and the purchase of property,
carrying on the Herculean labour of building the
mother-church of Latin Christendom. He was subject, all through his career, to sudden panics, and
suffered from a constitutional dread of assassination.
We can only explain his flight from Rome, his
escape from Florence, the anxiety he expressed

about his own and his family's relations to the
Medici, by supposing that his nerves were sensitive
upon this point. But, considering the times in
which he lived, the nature of the men around him,
the despotic temper of the Medicean princes, was
there anything morbid in this timidity? A student
of Cellini's Memoirs, of Florentine history, and of
the dark stories in which the private annals of the
age abound, will be forced to admit that imaginative
men of acute nervous susceptibility, who loved a
quiet life and wished to keep their mental forces
unimpaired for art and thought, were justified in
feeling an habitual sense of uneasiness in Italy of
the Renaissance period. Michelangelo's timidity, real
as it was, did not prevent him from being bold upon
occasion, speaking the truth to popes and princes,
and making his personality respected. He was even
accused of being too "terrible," too little of a
courtier and time-server.

When the whole subject of Michelangelo's temperament has been calmly investigated, the truth
seems to be that he did not possess a nervous temperament so evenly balanced as some phlegmatic
men of average ability can boast of. But who
could expect the creator of the Sistine, the sculptor
of the Medicean tombs, the architect of the cupola,
the writer of the sonnets, to be an absolutely normal
individual? To identify genius with insanity is a
pernicious paradox. To recognise that it cannot
exist without some inequalities of nervous energy,

some perturbations of nervous function, is reasonable. In other words, it is an axiom of physiology that the abnormal development of any organ or any faculty is balanced by some deficiency or abnormality elsewhere in the individual. This is only another way of saying that the man of genius is not a mediocre and ordinary personality: in other words, it is a truism, the statement of which appears superfluous. Rather ought we, in Michelangelo's case, to dwell upon the remarkable sobriety of his life, his sustained industry under very trying circumstances, his prolonged intellectual activity into extreme old age, the toughness of his constitution, and the elasticity of that nerve-fibre which continued to be sound and sane under the enormous and varied pressure put upon it over a period of seventy-five laborious years.

If we dared attempt a synthesis or reconstitution of this unique man's personality, upon the data furnished by his poems, letters, and occasional utterances, all of which have been set forth in their proper places in this work, I think we must construct him as a being gifted, above all his other qualities and talents, with a burning sense of abstract beauty and an eager desire to express this through several forms of art—design, sculpture, fresco-painting, architecture, poetry. The second point forced in upon our mind is that the same man vibrated acutely to the political agitation of his troubled age, to mental influences of various kinds, and finally to a persistent nervous susceptibility, which made him exquisitely sensitive to human charm. This quality rendered him irritable in his dealings with his fellow-men, like an instrument of music, finely strung, and jangled on a slight occasion. In the third place we discover that, while accepting the mental influences and submitting to the personal attractions I have indicated, he strove, by indulging solitary tastes, to maintain his central energies intact for art—joining in no rebellious conspiracies against the powers that be, bending his neck in silence to the storm, avoiding pastimes and social diversions which might have called into activity the latent sensuousness of his nature. For the same reason, partly by predilection, and partly by a deliberate wish to curb his irritable tendencies, he lived as much alone as possible, and poorly. At the close of his career, when he condescended to unburden his mind in verse and friendly dialogue, it is clear that he had formed the habit of recurring to religion for tranquillity, and of combating dominant desire by dwelling on the thought of inevitable death. Platonic speculations upon the eternal value of beauty displayed in mortal creatures helped him always in his warfare with the flesh and roving inclination. Self-control seems to have been the main object of his conscious striving, not for its own sake, but as the condition necessary to his highest spiritual activity. Self-coherence, self-concentration, not for any mean or self-indulgent end, but for the best attainment of his intellectual ideal, was what he sought for by the seclusion and the renunciations of a lifetime.

The total result of this singular attitude toward human life, which cannot be rightly described as either ascetic or mystical, but seems rather to have been based upon some self-preservative instinct, bidding him sacrifice lower and keener impulses to what he regarded as the higher and finer purpose of his being, is a certain clash and conflict of emotions, a certain sense of failure to attain the end proposed, which excuses, though I do not think it justifies, the psychologists, when they classify him among morbid subjects. Had he yielded at any period of his career to the ordinary customs of his easy-going age, he would have presented no problem to the scientific mind. After consuming the fuel of the passions, he might have subsided into common calm, or have blunted the edge of inspiration, or have finished in some phase of madness or ascetical repentance. Such are the common categories of extinct volcanic temperaments. But the essential point about Michelangelo is that he never burned out, and never lost his manly independence, in spite of numerous nervous disadvantages. That makes him the unparalleled personality he is, as now revealed to us by the impartial study of the documents at our disposal.

IX.

It is the plain duty of criticism in this age to search and probe the characters of world-important individuals under as many aspects as possible, neglecting no analytical methods, shrinking from no tests, omitting no slight details or faint shadows that may help to round a picture. Yet, after all our labour, we are bound to confess that the man himself eludes our insight. "The abysmal deeps of personality" have never yet been sounded by mere human plummets. The most that microscope and scalpel can perform is to lay bare tissue and direct attention to peculiarities of structure. In the long-run we find that the current opinion formed by successive generations remains true in its grand outlines. That large collective portrait of the hero, slowly emerging from sympathies and censures, from judgments and panegyrics, seems dim indeed and visionary, when compared with some sharply indented description by a brilliant literary craftsman. It has the vagueness of a photograph produced by superimposing many negatives of the same face one upon the other. It lacks the pungent piquancy of an etching. Yet this is what we must abide by; for this is spiritually and generically veracious.

At the end, then, a sound critic returns to think of Michelangelo, not as Parlagreco and Lombroso

show him, nor even as the minute examination of
letters and of poems proves him to have been, but as
tradition and the total tenour of his life display him
to our admiration.   Incalculable, incomprehensible,
incommensurable : yes, all souls, the least and
greatest, attack them as we will, are that.   But
definite in solitary sublimity, like a supreme mountain seen from a vast distance, soaring over shadowy
hills and misty plains into the clear ether of
immortal fame.

Viewed thus, he lives for ever as the type and
symbol of a man, much-suffering, continually labour-
ing, gifted with keen but rarely indulged passions,
whose energies from boyhood to extreme old age
were dedicated with unswerving purpose to the
service of one master, plastic art.   On his death-bed
he may have felt, like Browning, in that sweetest
of his poems, " other heights in other lives, God
willing."   But, for this earthly pilgrimage, he was
contented to leave the ensample of a noble nature
made perfect and completed in itself by addiction to
one commanding impulse.   We cannot cite another
hero of the modern world who more fully and with
greater intensity realised the main end of human
life, which is self-effectuation, self-realisation, self-
manifestation in one of the many lines of labour
to which men may be called and chosen.   Had we
more of such individualities, the symphony of civili-
sation would be infinitely glorious ; for nothing is
more certain than that God and the world cannot be

better served than by each specific self pushing forward to its own perfection, sacrificing the superfluous or hindering elements in its structure, regardless of side issues and collateral considerations.

Michelangelo, then, as Carlyle might have put it, is the Hero as Artist. When we have admitted this, all dregs and sediments of the analytical alembic sink to the bottom, leaving a clear crystalline elixir of the spirit. About the quality of his genius opinions may, will, and ought to differ. It is so pronounced, so peculiar, so repulsive to one man, so attractive to another, that, like his own dread statue of Lorenzo de' Medici, "it fascinates and is intolerable." There are few, I take it, who can feel at home with him in all the length and breadth and dark depths of the regions that he traversed. The world of thoughts and forms in which he lived habitually is too arid, like an extinct planet, tenanted by mighty elemental beings with little human left to them but visionary Titan-shapes, too vast and void for common minds to dwell in pleasurably. The sweetness that emerges from his strength, the beauty which blooms rarely, strangely, in unhomely wise, upon the awful crowd of his conceptions, are only to be apprehended by some innate sympathy or by long incubation of the brooding intellect. It is probable, therefore, that the deathless artist through long centuries of glory will abide as solitary as the simple old man did in his poor house at Rome. But no one, not the dullest, not the weakest, not the laziest and lustfullest, not the most indifferent to ideas or the most tolerant of platitudes and paradoxes, can pass him by without being arrested, quickened, stung, purged, stirred to uneasy self-examination by so strange a personality expressed in prophecies of art so pungent.

Each supreme artist whom God hath sent into the world with inspiration and a particle of the imperishable fire, is a law to himself, an universe, a revelation of the divine life under one of its innumerable attributes. We cannot therefore classify Michelangelo with any of his peers throughout the long procession of the ages. Of each and all of them it must be said in Ariosto's words, "Nature made him, and then broke the mould." Yet if we seek Michelangelo's affinities, we find them in Lucretius and Beethoven, not in Sophocles and Mozart. He belongs to the genus of deep, violent, colossal, passionately striving natures; not, like Raffaello, to the smooth, serene, broad, exquisitely finished, calmly perfect tribe. To God be the praise, who bestows upon the human race artists thus differing in type and personal quality, each one of whom incarnates some specific portion of the spirit of past ages, perpetuating the traditions of man's soul, interpreting century to century by everlasting hieroglyphics, mute witnesses to history and splendid illustrations of her pages.

PEDIGREE OF THE BUONARROTI SIMONI FAMILY

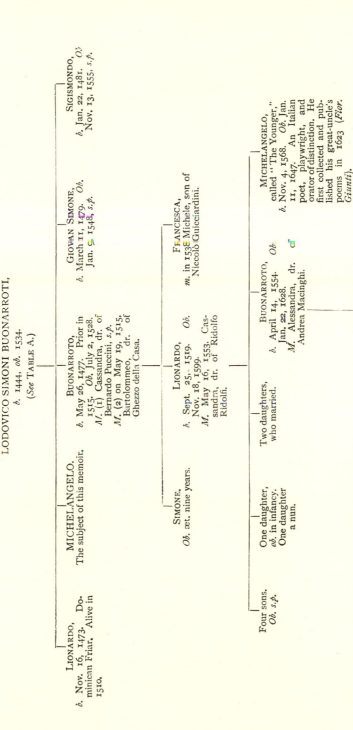

LODOVICO SIMONI BUONARROTI,
b. 1444, *ob.* 1534.
(*See* TABLE A.)

LIONARDO,
b. Nov. 16, 1473. Dominican Friar. Alive in 1510.

MICHELANGELO.
The subject of this memoir.

BUONARROTO,
b. May 26, 1477. Prior in 1515. *Ob.* July 2, 1528. *M.* (1) Cassandra, dr. of Bernardo Puccini, *s.p. M.* (2) on May 19, 1515, Bartolommeo, dr. of Ghezzo della Casa.

GIOVAN SIMONE,
b. March 11, 1479. *Ob.* Jan. 9, 1548, *s.p.*

SIGISMONDO,
b. Jan. 22, 1481. *Ob.* Nov. 13, 1555. *s.p.*

SIMONE,
Ob. æt. nine years.

LIONARDO,
b. Sept. 25, 1519. *Ob.* Nov. 18, 1599. *M.* May 16, 1553, Cassandra, dr. of Ridolfo Ridolfi.

FRANCESCA,
m. in 1538 Michele, son of Niccolò Guicciardini.

Four sons,
Ob. s.p.

One daughter, *ob.* in infancy. One daughter a nun.

Two daughters, who married.

BUONARROTO,
b. April 14, 1554. *Ob.* Jan. 22, 1628. *M.* Alessandra, dr. Andrea Macinghi.

MICHELANGELO,
called "The Younger," *b.* Nov. 4, 1568. *Ob.* Jan. 11, 1647. An Italian poet, playwright, and orator of distinction. He first collected and published his great-uncle's poems in 1623 (*Flor. Giunti*).

Elder line extinct in the person of Cosimo Buonarroti, who died Feb. 12, 1858, bequeathing the Casa Buonarroti to the town of Florence. The family is said still to exist in the male line of a younger branch.

APPENDIX.

No. I.

NOTE ON THE BUONARROTI PEDIGREE.

1. The family of Lodovico Buonarroti in the year 1480. Archivio di Stato, Firenze. Catasto, 1480 ; Leon Nero, ac. 265. Portata di Francesco e Lodovicho di Lionardo di Buonarotta Simoni.

Bocche [these were the persons maintained in the family] :—

Francesco di Lionardo sopra detto d'età d'anni . .	45.
Lodovicho di Lionardo sopra detto d'età d'anni . . .	34 [*sic*].
Mᵃ Lesandra nostra madre d'età d'anni	71.
Mᵃ Chasandra donna del sopra detto Francesco d'età d'anni	25.
Mᵃ Francesca donna di Lodovicho sopra detto d'età d'anni	25.
Lionardo figliuolo di Lodovicho sopra detto d'età d'anni	7.
Michelangniolo figliuolo di Lodovicho detto d'anni . .	5.
Buonarroto figliuolo di Lodovicho detto d'anni . . .	3.
Giovan Simone figliuolo di Lodovicho detto d'anni . .	1½.

2. In the Catasto 1469, Leon Rosso, ac. 808, Portata delle Rede di Miniato della Sera, Francesca (Lodovico's first wife) is said to be twelve years old. This does not agree with the age of twenty-five given her in the Catasto of 1480 above, and is possibly a mistake for fourteen. But her registration among the heirs of Miniato proves her to have been living in her father's home in 1469. Her eldest son, Lionardo, was born in 1473, if he had reached the age of seven in 1480. Her youngest son, Sigis-

375

mondo, was born in January 1481. When she died remains uncertain.

3. Lodovico's second marriage, to Lucrezia Ubaldini, took place in 1485. She died in 1497, and was buried at S. Croce on the 9th of July in that year. Libro de' Morti, 1457–1506. Anno 1497, Luglio: "La donna di Lodovicho Bonaroti fu riposta in Santa ✠ [Croce] a dì 9."

4. Proofs of the births of Giovan Simone and Sigismondo. Archivio di Stato di Firenze. Archivio delle Tratte, Libro ii. delle Età (Gonfalone Leon Nero), foglio 84 :—

> "Giovan Simone di Lodovicho di Lionardo di Buonarroto Simoni, 11 Marzo 1478." (79 common style).
>
> "Gismondo di Lodovicho di Lionardo di Buonarroto Simoni 22 Gennaio 1480" (81 common style).

These Registers of the age of Florentine citizens were kept because it was the custom to ballot for public offices, and when a man was elected, his age was duly inscribed. It is from the same source that we know Lodovico to have been born in 1444. This date does not agree with the age of thirty-four assigned to him in the Catasto of 1480 quoted above.

No. II.

TRANSLATION OF LETTERE, No. CCCLXXXIII., FROM MICHELANGELO BUONARROTI TO SER GIOVAN FRANCESCO FATTUCCI.

Rome, January 1524.

You write to ask me how my affairs with Pope Julius stand. I assure you that if I could claim an estimate of losses and gains, the balance would turn out rather to my credit than my debit. The matter stands thus: When the Pope sent for me from Florence, I think in the second year of his pontificate, I had begun to paint one half of the Hall of the Council, and was to be paid 3000 ducats; the Cartoon was finished, as is known to all Florence; and the money seemed to me already half earned.

Also, of the twelve Apostles ordered for S. Maria del Fiore, one was blocked out, as any one can see still; and I had brought down nearly all the marbles necessary for this work. When Pope Julius called me away, I made no profit by either of these undertakings. Afterwards, when I went to Rome with the said Pope Julius, he gave me a commission to make his tomb; the marble was to cost 1000 ducats; and he commissioned me to pay for it, and sent me to Carrara to have it quarried. There I stayed about eight months, directing the work of blocking out; after which I brought nearly the whole of it to S. Peter's, though a part remained at the Ripa. When I had finished paying for the transport of these marbles, and all the money was spent, I furnished the house I had upon the Piazza di S. Pietro with beds and utensils at my own expense, trusting to the commission of the tomb, and sent for workmen from Florence, some of whom are still alive, and paid them in advance out of my own purse. Meanwhile Pope Julius changed his mind about the tomb, and would not have it made. Not knowing this, I went to ask him for money, and was expelled from the chamber.[1] Enraged at such an insult, I left Rome on the moment. The things with which my house was stocked went to the dogs. The marbles I had brought to Rome lay till the date of Leo's creation on the Piazza of S. Peter's, and both lots were injured and pillaged. Among other details which I can prove, two blocks of four and a half cubits a piece were carried away from the Ripa by Agostino Chigi; these had cost me more than fifty golden ducats; and the money might be sued for, since there are witnesses to the fact. But to return to the marbles; more than a year elapsed from the time I went to quarry them and settled at Carrara to the day when I was expelled the Palace. For all this time I never received any pay, and spent some scores of ducats out of my own pocket.

Proceeding with my statement, when Pope Julius went to

---

[1] In the *abbozzo* (ccclxxxiv.): "Finding myself engaged in great expense, and seeing his Holiness indisposed to pay, I complained to him; this annoyed him so that he had me turned out of the ante-chamber. Upon which I became angry, and left Rome suddenly."

Bologna the first time, I was forced to go there with a rope round my neck to beg his pardon.[1] He ordered me to make his statue in bronze, sitting, about seven cubits in height. When he asked what it would cost, I answered that I thought I could cast it for 1000 ducats; but that it was not my trade, and that I did not wish to bind myself by contract. He answered: "Go to work; you shall cast it over and over again till it succeeds; and I will give you enough to satisfy you." To put it briefly, I cast the statue twice, and at the end of two years, at Bologna, I found that I had four and a half ducats left. I never received anything more for this job; and all the moneys I paid out during the said two years were the 1000 ducats with which I promised to cast it. These were disbursed to me in several instalments by Messer Antonio Maria da Legniame, a Bolognese.

When I had placed the statue before S. Petronio and returned to Rome, the Pope was still unwilling that I should complete the tomb, and ordered me to paint the vault of the Sistine. We agreed for 3000 ducats. The first design I made for this work had twelve Apostles in the lunettes, the remainder being a certain space filled in with ornamental details according to the usual manner.

After I had begun, it seemed to me that this would turn out a poor affair, and I told the Pope that the Apostles alone would make a poor effect, in my opinion. He asked me why; I answered, because they too were poor. Then he gave me a new commission to do what I liked best, and promised to satisfy my claims for the work, and told me to paint down to the pictured histories upon the lower row. Meanwhile, when the vault was nearly finished, the Pope went back to Bologna; whereupon I went twice to get the necessary funds, and obtained nothing, and lost all that time, till I returned to Rome. Then I began to make Cartoons, that is, for the extremities and sides around the said chapel, hoping to get money at last and to complete the

---

[1] In the *abbozzo*: "After some seven or eight months, during which I remained almost in hiding and in fear, on account of the Pope's anger, I was compelled, being unable to stay at Florence, to go and crave his mercy at Bologna."

work. I never could extract a farthing; and when I complained one day to Messer Bernardo da Bibbiena and to Atalante, representing that I could not stop longer at Rome, and that I should have to go away with God's grace, Messer Bernardo told Atalante that he must bear this in mind, for that he wished me to have money whatever happened. He had 2000 ducats of the Camera paid out to me; and this sum, together with the first 1000, is what they lay to my account for the tomb. I expected to get more for my lost time and the work I had done. Of this money, as Messer Bernardo and Atalante had raised me up, I gave the former 100, and the latter 50 ducats.

Afterwards, came the death of Pope Julius; and at the beginning of Leo's reign, Aginensis wished to enlarge his uncle's tomb, that is, to make something on a larger scale than my original plan. So we drew up a contract. I objected to the 3000 ducats which I had received being put to the account of the tomb, explaining that I ought to have a great deal more. Upon this Aginensis told me that I was a cheating rascal.

No. III.

DOCUMENT RELATING TO THE WOOL USED BY MICHELANGELO IN FORTIFYING FLORENCE.

Die xiiii ottobris 1531.

Essendosi nel tempo dello assedio qui della cipta, per ordine di quelli Magistrati che allora governavano, intrapreso e tolto di dogana e di più magazini dimolte balle di lana di diversi merca- *Montis* tanti e lanajuoli qui della cipta e d'altri; e quelle adoprate per *officialium auctoritas* fare ripari e altro, secondo che allora occorse, delle quali lane *danda* parte se ne sono salvate e hoggi si truovono ragunate nella Casa *super re-feriendis* di Horto San Michele e nel Fondaco del guado; e perchè le sono *lanis erep-tis e Doana* molto mescolate e male agevolmente si ricognoschono di chi le *tempore* siano, pur per renderle in verità a di chi elle fussino e trovarne *belli.* più il vero che sia possibile. Il Magnif^{co} Gonfaloniere di Giustitia e gli altri Spectabili Cittadini della presente Balia hanno nello infrascritto modo proveduto.

Che per virtù della presente Provisione alli Spectabili Ufficiali di Monte s'intenda essere e sia data auctorità e facoltà di potere fra X dì, dal dì della finale conclusione di questa, eleggere et havere electo quattro ciptadini e' quali parrà loro più idonei e approposito; et intendasi essere e sia per la presente data loro auctorità di potere tutti a quattro, o almeno tre di loro daccordo, rinvenire e ritrovare in quanto si possa e' padroni di decte lane e che quantità e qualità di lana invero a ciascheduno di loro fossi stata tolta; e di poi havere, infra dua mesi dal dì della loro electione, renduto, dato e consegnato e restituito decte lane, e partitale a chi giudicheranno che siano e' veri padroni di quelle; cioè rendendo a ciascheduno quella tanta rata e parte a lira e soldo che li toccassi. E tanto quanto così dichiareranno e consegneranno, tanto s'intenda essere e sia ben giudicata dato e consegnato, e a quello ciascheduno debba stare tacito e contento e non si possa per alcuno muovere, contradire o alterare im modo alcuno.

Non obstantibus, &c.

Copia estratta del Libro di Provvisioni della Balia a C. 49, che si conserva nel R. Archivio di Stato di Firenze.

No. IV.

LETTER FROM BATTISTA DELLA PALLA.[1]

Al Molto honorando Michelagnolo buonarotj simonj amico carissimo, Vinetia in casa Ec^{mo} panciatichi.

Doppo la de xxj tenuta a xxij per lo scarpellino a posta ui scrissj a xxiiij per la quale oltre allo hauerui rafermo tutto il dettoui per la dauanti ni promessi dopo esser parato per piu nostra satisfattione et sicureza uenire fino qui a leuarui et per

---

[1] Arch. Buon., vol. vii. No. 196.

tenerui compagnia fino drento di fiorenza ogni uolta che da uoi fussi chiamato et parendomi essere trascorsi tanti giorni che di gia qui douessi essere comparso alli xj di questo me ne uennj qua con tale ordine da toruj dello animo ogni sospettione del camino et cosi mi ci sono trattenuto infra pisa et qui fino a questa mattina. Ma non comparendo, ne sentendo alchuna nouella di uoj, ne auanzandomj piu tempo della licentia concessami da cot^i Sig^{ri} (cotesti Signori) me ne ritorno di presente alla uolta di casa che scriuendo questa sono stiualato et col pie alla staffa et perche io non mi posso persuadere che uoj non uegniate in ognj modo ui fo intendere per questa : se per sorte anchora non fussi partito che i beni di quelli che cascarono nella contumacia in compagnia uostra gia si uendono et che se non uenite nel termine del tempo cioe per tutto questo mese conccessoui per el saluo condotto si fara il simile di uostri senza uno remedio al mondo et uenendo come al fermo confido fate motto qui al mio Hr^{do} M. Filippo Calandrinj al quale ho lasciata M^{ria} (= memoria) del sopra detto modo di condurui sicuro senza un pensiero. Dio ci guardi di male et facciacj riuedere presto inella patria per sua bonta uittoriosa I. di Lucca a di xviiij° di nouembre 1529. Racomandatemj al bruciolo al quale scriuerò di fiorenza di nuovo del caso suo al mio partire lasciato in assai buon termine.

Nostro b. d. p.

BATTISTA DELLA PALLA.

No. V.

ON MICHELANGELO'S TEMPERAMENT AND ITS BEARING ON HIS POETRY.

I had written the sections of Chapter XII. which deal with Michelangelo's loves and friendships, and was in some uneasiness as to the propriety of publishing the results I had arrived at, when a series of new works came beneath my notice, rendering it totally impossible to avoid the problem in question. As far back as the year 1888, F. Parlagreco published a little essay at Naples, in which he strongly insisted upon Michelangelo's indifference to women and his partiality for male friends as the sign of radical psychical unsoundness. The views taken by this author are extreme and exaggerated. Still they approved themselves to the eminent Italian psychologist, Lombroso, who condensed and adopted them in a paper contributed to the *Archivio di Psichiatria*, vol. xi. Fasc. 3 and 4, 1890. Both Parlagreco and Lombroso treated the theories of Guasti, Milanesi, and Gotti with ridicule, and ran to the conclusion that Michelangelo was a victim of mental disorder bordering upon hysteria. Lombroso repeated these views regarding Michelangelo's congenital morbidity in his "Uomo di Genio," with some important modifications. They were echoed, with omissions and reticences intended for the English public, by Mr. Nisbet in "The Insanity of Genius." Personally, I do not accept the theory of Michelangelo's morbidity, or the hypothesis which makes all genius a diseased manifestation akin to vice and crime. Yet the diffusion of such opinions confirmed me in my own sense that the time had arrived for dealing frankly with the great artist's psychology by the light of his correspondence and ungarbled poems. I could not, moreover, neglect the fact that Anton Springer, in what is now the most authoritative book on Michelangelo in German, followed an erroneous line of explanation. He describes the Cavalieri episode in Buonarroti's life as "a paroxysm of friendship," an "illness," an "aberration of fancy," from which the sufferer emerged into healthier feelings and a purer air when he became attached to Vittoria Colonna.[1] Springer refused to recognise, what all the documents make manifest, that the Cavalieri episode was only a marked instance of Michelangelo's habitual emotion, whereas the friendship for Vittoria Colonna is unique in his biography, and belongs to the latest phase of his spiritual experience.

When I had advanced so far, and while the sheets of Chapter XII. were going through the press, I received an essay published in the present year. It is entitled "Michelangelo: Eine Rénaissance Studie," by Ludwig von Scheffler: Altenburg, Geibel, 1892.

---

[1] Springer, ii. 299–301.

This book of 227 pages is almost entirely devoted to the analysis of Michelangelo's psychology, as revealed by his letters and poems. Von Scheffler arrived independently at conclusions which are in all essential points coincident with those I had expressed upon the problem. I welcome his work, therefore, as a corroboration and justification of my own. He demonstrates with subtlety and vigour that Buonarroti's leading passion was a purely Hellenic enthusiasm for beauty exhibited in young men, regarded as the supreme manifestations of eternal loveliness, and admired more as works of art than as carnal personalities. This passion, when it found utterance in poetry, owed its literary colour and complexion directly to Platonic sources, especially to the *Phædrus* and *Symposium*. Von Scheffler is of opinion that in no case was Michelangelo's intenser feeling excited by the female sex, and argues with much plausibility that Vittoria, "il grande amico," exercised a peculiar influence over his nature in old age by supplying what he had always been seeking—a calm and spiritual communion of minds, a haven and refuge from stormy perturbations of the sense of beauty, an atonement of conflicting impulses through the vivid awakening of religious instincts—at a period of life when distinctly æsthetical enthusiasms and the powerful attractions of physical charm were beginning to lose their force. In support of these opinions, Von Scheffler traces, in the same way as I have done, the falsification of documents and traditions, beginning with Michelangelo himself, who substituted *donna* for the male *signore* of his poems, passing through Condivi's apologetic treatment of his erotic tendencies, touching on Aretino's malignant insinuations, exposing Michelangelo the younger's pious frauds, and finally condemning in no measured terms the Florentine group of scholars who used the knowledge acquired in their privileged inspection of the Buonarroti Archives to bolster up an obvious fiction. Von Scheffler maintains, with justice I believe, that Michelangelo's emotion was ideal, imaginative, chaste: such, in fact, as the philosophers of Athens in the best age conceived and formulated. Here he vindicates his hero, as I seek to do, against the injurious hypotheses of Parlagreco, Lombroso, Springer, and the no less injurious apologies of Guasti, Milanesi, Gotti, W. Lang. Not having had access to the Archivio Buonarroti, he makes some minor mistakes and lacks some substantial information. He does not know, for instance, that Febo di Poggio was a real man, and thinks the letter addressed to him by Michelangelo in December 1534 was meant for Cavalieri. He is also, of course, unacquainted with Pierantonio's correspondence. But I discovered nothing in the documents inaccessible to his inspection which invalidates the main line of his argument.

At this point I am bound to sum up my own final conclusions regarding the delicate topic which I have been obliged to handle.

It is clear, I think, that Michelangelo Buonarroti was one of those exceptional, but not uncommon men, who are born with sensibilities abnormally deflected from the ordinary channel. He showed no partiality for women, and a notable enthusiasm for the beauty of young men. There is nothing in his letters, in the correspondence addressed to him, in his poetry, or in any of the numerous contemporary notices of his daily life, to raise any suspicion regarding his moral conduct. On the contrary, the whole weight of argument adduced from documents and corroborative statements leaves the impression on our mind that he was a man of physically frigid temperament, extremely sensitive to beauty of the male type, who habitually philosophised his emotions, and contemplated the living objects of his admiration as amiable not only for their personal qualities, but also for their æsthetical attractiveness. In this connection, it is not insignificant to notice that Michelangelo was one of five brothers, four of whom (himself included) did not marry, and had no ascertained progeny, while the fifth, Buonarroto, left only one heir-male to carry on the family. The Buonarroti-Simoni breed, in his generation, appears to have been partially sterilised. He complained frequently and sadly to his nephew Lionardo that the race appeared to be dying out from want of heirs-male. Individuals of Michelangelo's peculiar temperament cannot be characterised as morbid, although the medical psychologists of modern Europe seem now agreed to do so. The history of ancient Hellas precludes this explanation of the phenomenon.

In Hellas they found a social environment favourable to their free development and action, but in Renaissance Italy the case was different. Society did not recognise the possibility of elevating and purifying these passions on the Socratic method. It is not impossible that the tragic accent discernible throughout Michelangelo's love-poetry may be due to his sense of the discrepancy between his own deepest emotions and the customs of Christian society. He was versed in the chivalrous poetry of Dante and Petrarch; he was also acquainted with the Platonic writings—how, or through what medium, we do not know : yet he had certainly appropriated the mysticism of the *Phœdrus* and *Symposium*, the doctrine of anamnêsis, the imagery of the soul's wings, and many other details which contributed to a philosophy based upon erotic principles. In this philosophy he seems to have sought, and perhaps to have found, a refuge from dominant emotions. When he wrote verses, he cast his Greek feeling for the beauty of young men in forms which recall the Dantesque tradition, using at the same time metaphors and symbols derived immediately from Plato. His poems, therefore, present a singular example of psychological and literary hybridism. The tap-root of feeling is Greek. The form given to it in the sonnet, the madrigal, the capitolo, is medieval. The imagery is Platonic. The personality of the beloved object, though passionately felt, remains abstract. So far as this is possible, the person is addressed as *tu ;* when further particularisation is needed, generally as *Signore ;* very rarely as *Donna*, and then, for the most part, in cases where the text has been deliberately altered. This vagueness regarding the sex and individuality of the beloved person may be ascribed in part to the poet's ideal feeling, which excluded concrete or sensual touches, partly to the obscuring medium of the double literary conventions he adopted in his method of self-expression.

No. VI.

LETTERS FROM BARTOLOMMEO ANGELINI TO MICHELANGELO.

Addi vij di settembre 1521.

Michelamgelo mio Car^mo al passato non uo schriptto che nŏn me hochorso nŏn gia che sempre nŏn u abbj nel quore come ui sono hoblighato d essere & che di molte uolte nŏn ragionj di uoj coɱ bastiano uiniziano & mastro giouannj darreggio del quale sera dua inchluse in questa quale ui pregha li facciate risposta & selle date costa a bonifazio fazzj aranno sempre bonifsimo richapito / & ui pregho che se di qua ho da fare per uoj cosa alchuna che mi sera somma grazia mi chomandiate & sia di qual si uoglia cofa / & uoy di comtinouo mi rachomando & il uostro mr giouannj il simile ch iddio in sanita ui chomseruj.

Vrŏ Bartholomeo Angielinj in Roma.

A tergo :

Al suo Car^mo Michelan
giolo Bonarrota schultore
iɱ fiorenza.

fate bem dare ch e d amicho.

———

ihesus addi xx^vij d giugnio 1523.

Cmŏ michelangelo e piu tempo nŏn uo schritto che no me ochorso noñ istamte che sempre u abbj nel quore e auero finch aro uita ma trouandomj pochj giornj fa chol Cardinale grimaño ueniɱo a ragionamento di uoj doue mi pregho ui schriuessj e ui preghassj che fussj chomtemto farlj quel quadretto per'uno studiolo chome di gia u adimando & dice li promettestj e rimette in uoj della materia della famtasia ho pittura ho getto & schultura quelo ch e piu chomodo a uoj quel facciate e che del prezzo la rimettera in uoj che quel tamto l adimanderete tamto ui dara & amchora fopra di piu restaruj hoblighatifsimo pero charo michelamgniolo perch io defidero faruj bene e chompiaceruj e alsi al luj quamdo e ui sia chomodo del paghamento lassatene a me la chura che ui faro paghare chosta li danarj e quam̃to adimanderete e certamente desidera tam̃to auer qual chofa di uostra mano quam̃to desidera la propia salute pero semdouj chomodo il rispondermj dell animo uostro me ne farete simghular piacere richordandouj che sempre soño uostro e nõn defidero altro che chompiaceruj e che mi chomandiate che iddio in fanita ui chonseruj / di nuoũo nõn so che dirmj siamo al prefente chom pocha ho niente di peste jddio grazia & uoj per l amore ui porto ui chomforto a lo stare a bona ghuardia che jddio in fanita ui chomseruj.

Vᵒ Bartholomeo Angielinj in Roma.

A tergo :

Allo suo carᵐᵒ Michelamgelo
Bonarrotj schultore in fiorenza.

---

ihesus addi xj di luglio 1523.

Michelamgniolo mio Carᵐᵒ jo o riceuto una uostra a me tamto grata quanto dir si possa e uegho che di quamto uo schritto del quadretto per il Carˡᵉ siate d animo di seruirlo e conseruarlj la promefsa chom tutto ch abbiate pocho tempo da lauorare pure jo o fatto intemdere a . s . s . l animo . uostro . e perche defidera gramdemente d auerlo pemfa lo seruirete a ongnj modo e per una suo lettera in questa uedrete quam̃to ui schriue e pregha e achaulsa ueggiate e d animo l abbiate a feruire m a ordinato ch a uostro piacere ui faccj paghare scudi 50 dor larghi per arra e parte di paghamento & tam̃to ho fatto chome per una nostra in questa uedrete che ordino a bonifazio fazzy & compangnj ch a uostro piacere ue li paghi in termini da questo di . a . 3 . mesj cioe che la chomefsione durj . 3 . mesj che sia in liberta uostra il pigliarlj & perche defidero chompiaceruj & desidererej schontare in parte del debito ho chon uoj che tutto questo ch o fatto & che . fo lo fo per faruj bene pero femdouj in piacere il seruire il Carˡᵉ al luj e a me ne farete finghular piacere & nel prezzo chome per altre u o detto sara rimessa in uoj che u

a in tamto grado & uenerazione che nõn ue lo potre ma dire & co
che l adimanderete tañto ui dara & di questo a me ne lassate la
brigha che fatto arete l opera ho prima chome uorrete mi direte
quañto u o da far paghare e tañto faro chostj a bonifazio fazzy
ſi che di questo nõn ue ne date brigha che stimo forse molto piu
l amicizia uostra & chonoscho l obligho ho choñ uoj nõn uj pem-
ſate & uolessj iddio un dj ue lo poteſsj dimostrare.

A bastiano a mr giouannj & a l altrj amicj uostrj a tuttj
ho fatto le rachomandazione & a uoj tutti si rachomandano
infinite uolte e jo inſieme chom loro che iddio in ſanita ui
chomſeruj.

VꝛŏBartholomeo angielinꞀ in Roma.

A tergo :

Vblj . d . Michelangnio lo Bonarrotia
schultꝝ amicho hrᵐᵒ jn propria.

---

ihesus addi xxviiij d aprile 1531.

Honrᵈᵒ michelangniolo jo ho sempre deſiderato far chosa che
ui ſia grata chom e mio hobligho di fare chon uoj e nõn potendo
farlo di chose gramde nõn manchero maj a quelle porro / · il
nostro bastiano non ſapeua doue ſ indirizare una suo lettera per
uoj a me la data e in questa ue la mando e uolendo fare risposta
al luj fate dare la lettera a loremzo mannuccj˙ bamderaro in
piazza il quale la mandera chon la ſua e jo la daro ſubito in mano
propria a bastiano e se altro posso per uoj richordateuj richordateuj (sic) che dou i sono ui auete un fratello che nõn deſidera
che ſeruiruj fedeliſsimamente e basti.

Ne altro per questa iddio jn ſanita ui chonferuj etc.

V° Bartolomeo angielinꞀ jn Roma.

A tergo :

Al ſuo Hnrᵈᵒ Michelangniolo
bonarrotj jn fiorenza.

Ihesus addi xviiij di giugnio 1531.

Honrᵈᵒ etc. sabato paxato ui schriſsj chom aueuo riceuto la
uostra . e dato la ſua a mastro ſebaſtiano il quale di poj questo

di m a portato l inchluxa per risposta alla uostra la qual aro charo arriuj a boñ faluamento & se altro ochorre fono al ufato tutto il uostro.

jddio in fanita ui chonseruj etc.

VRŌ Bartolomeo angiolini jn Roma.

A tergo :

A lo . fuo . Car^{smo}. e Honr^{do} michelangniolo otj jn propria.

---

ihesus addi xxij di luglio 1531.

Honr^{do} michelangniolo la prefente fara per far chouerta al uostro febastiano & jo prima nõn u o risposto alla uostra aspettando la fua & le uostre rachomandazione l o fatte al uostro mr paulo Gallo il quale ui fi rachomanda & u e tamto afezionato quamto dir si possa & nõn defidera che di riuederuj & di chompiaceruj in quel che per lui fi possa & che la chasa & co ch anno al mondo & tutto a uostro comando. jo nõn emterro piu chon uoj inn altre cirimonie paremdomj fuperflue bastauj che nõn o maggior piacer al mondo fe nõn quamdo pemso potere far qual chosa per uoj che ni sia grata & quamdo mi chomandafsj qua chosa pero fatelo fe defiderate farmj piacere restandouene fempre obligatifsimo.

Ne altro per questa jddio di mal ui guardj etc.

V° Bartolomeo angiolinj jn Roma.

A tergo :

Allo . fuo Honr^{do} michelangniolo otj jn fioremza.

Honr^{do} michelangniolo o riceuto la uostra chom l inchluxa al nostro febastiano la quale li dettj in propria mano e in questa ne fara la risposta a ochorendo altro che per me fi possa chomandatemj che altro non defidero che feruiruj & bene ualete in Roma die xviiij d aghosto 1531.

VRŌ Bart° angiolinj.

A tergo :

Allo fuo Honr^{do} Michelangelo re jn fiorenza.

Honr^{do} michelangniolo fra bastiano nostro m a detto che di giorno in giorno u attemde di qua che jddio sa quamto n o piacere & dice uoresti schaualchare in chasa uostra & fappiemdo che nõn u e altro che lle mura & jo trouafidomj certe po di masserizie lo fatte condurre in chasa uostra di modo ch auerete da dormire & da federe & qualch altra po di chomodita / da mangniare n auete in uicinanza da prouederuene a uostra uolonta pero uenite a uostra comodita che defidero di seruiruj inn altro che questo & pagare in parte del tamto debito che o chon uoj se jddio me ne presterra grazia pero uolendo ch i facca chosa alchuna per uoj comandatemj che jddio in fanita ui chonseruj jn Roma addi xvj d aghosto 1532.

Vrõ Bartholomeo angielinj.

A tergo :
    Doño Michelangniolo
    Bonarotj fuo Honr^{do} jn propria.

Honr^{do} michelangniolo jo ho parlato a quel delli danarj & lunedj ce li dara . rimandouj la lettra . & mi faro fare la forma delle quitamze . & ue le mandero . & a uoj m ofero & rachomando.

in roma addi xviiij di settembre 1532.

Tutto urõ Bart^o angiolinj.

A tergo :
    Le lectere de dugento ducatj.

---

ihesus addi xij di luglio 1533.

Honr^{do} & Car^{smo} michelangniolo di poj la partita uostra nõn ui o fchritto ne mancho ho noftre lettere . & tutti di qua defideriamo e amchora che tengniamo per certo ch ariuafsj a boñ falua mento pur ne faremo piu certj uedemdo uostre lettere / jo dettj quell anima a mr Thomao il quale molto ui fi rachomanda . & mi prego auemdo fuo lettere ne li mandassj & chosi li promifsj / fra bastiano amchor luj m a detto che . n . s . li a dimandato piu uolte fe a lettere da uoj . & sta bene . & ui fi rachomanda.

La chasa uostra . & di chomtinouo ongni notte guardata . & di giorno spefso da me uicitata le galline & mr gallo triomfano & le gatte molto fi lamentano della uostra afemzia amchor che nŏn manchy loro da mangniare.

La gita di . n. s . hongni giorno fi tieñ piu certa . & filippo strozzi dichono partira lunedj per chostj & che chomdurra la duchesfina a nizza & amchor uerra la duchessa di chamerino di modo che no resteremo qua foli ma aueremo pazziemza chome l altre uolte / nŏn ui diro altro ftate fano . & rachomandatemj a urbino & a tutti li altrj . & ochorremdouj di qua cosa alchuna chomandatemj . & uolemdo fchriuermj mandate le lettere a bonifazio fazzi ho amdrea ch e llj in por zamta maria all infemgnia dell amgiolo & tubbia che tutti le manderanno bene che jddio in sanita ui chonseruj etc.

TUTTO . URŎ . BARTHOLOMEO ANGIELINJ JN ROMA.

A tergo :

Al suo Honr^{do} & Car^{mo} Michelangniolo bonarrotj jn propria.

---

ihesus addi xviiij di luglio 1533.

Honr^{do} e Car^{smo} michelangniolo e l qual i amo fopra tutti l altrj ominj fabato pafsato jo ui schrifsj una lettera e di poj com piacere gramdifsimo n o auta una di urŏ chon una a fra bastiano la quale ebbe in mano propria e se ntefo chom ariuastj a buoñ faluamento e chome attemdete a spediruj chom piu presteza potete per ritornaruene in qua e che molto la defiderate che non e mancho il defiderio nostro ch abbiamo di riaueruj che fi sia il uostro d esercj che choll aiuto di dio di un e l altro (sic) succedera / Come ui difsj fabato le chose uostre ftanno bene & ne medefimj terminj che le lassastj faluo ch o leuato uia il uino & uemdutolo & alla tornata uostro ne richomperro dell altro meglio pero ftate fano & se sete manchato nŏn e marauiglia per lj gram chaldj che fono statj ma ne uerranno li fichj e tutti ci ristoreremo / di qua nŏn f attemde ad altro ch a metterfj a ordine per la gita di niza . & d e stato jntimato a tutta la chorte ch omgniomo allj vii . jd . agosto fia a ordine ma dichono andranno allj . xx . & aspettano

. 16 . galee framzese che li leueranno di modo resteremo folj
almancho per dua mefj fra bastiano m a detto che . n . s . a
studiato molto la uostra lettera & ch e molto desiderofo di
chompiaceruj ma le parole nŏn bastano non piu state fano e jo
foñ molto piu uostro che mio etc.

Tutto . urŏ . Bartholomeo angielinj jn Roma.

A tergo :

Al mio Car^{smo} & molto
Honr^{do} Michelangniolo
Bonarrotj jn propria.

---

ihesus addi xxvj di luglio 1533.

Honr^{do} & fopra tutti li altri da me amato michelangniolo
Car^{smo} i mi trouo la uostra coñ una a fra febastiano la quale li
fecj dare in mano propria & molto ui fi rachomanda / & fabato
pafsato ui mandaj una fua coñ una di mr Thomao uostro & per la
uostra intefo quanto fia l afezione li portate che jn uero che per
quanto in luy o uisto non ui ama mancho che ui amiate uoj luj
& perche in principio della uostra lettera auete fattj dua versj
bellj m auete amchor me fatto pemfare di dar principio di uoler
essere poeta amchora ch i nŏn pemfo auere adoperatj altro
alloro fe nŏn quamdo auefsj a chocere ho falsicca ho fegatellj
pero rideteuj di me piu onestamente potete & come per efso
ui dicho potete uiuere lieto perche l uostro defiderio & pari
tra uoi & Tho . & li o fatto la uostro inbascata . & com tutto il
chore ui fi rachomanda & quamto allo schriuere fi chomtenta di
quel ui chomtentate uoj tamt e l amore che ui porta . & jo
jnfieme com luj.

La chasa uostra com tutti l animalj & l orto ftanno bene al
folito & omgniomo ui defidera.

&l papa da lunedj in qua non a fatto che gridare delle podagre
pure adefso & migliorato & la' fua partita per nizza dichono nŏn
fara prima ch a fettembre perch auamtj fi parta uol auer noua
che fi sia comfumato il matrimonio della duchessina & po fubito
amdra.

jn questa fara una di fra baftiano jnfieme choñ li dua camtj delli uostri madrichali & altro non o che diruj faluo che fon fempre il uostro che jddio jn fanita ui chonferuj etc.

TUTTO URŎ BART° ANGIELINJ JN ROMA.

A tergo :

    Allo . fuo . Car^{smo} . & molto . Honr^{do} Miche
    Bonarrotj in fiorenza.

———

ihesus addi ij d aghosto 1533.

Michelangniolo mio Honr^{smo} alli xxvj del paxato ui schrifsj l ultima mia e dl poi mi trouo la uostra di xxviij ohoñ una inchluxa al uostro mr Thomao la quale dettj fubito in mano propria e molto ui fi rachomanda e per quamto ritrafsi del fuo parlare mostra nŏn auer altro desiderio al mondo che la tornata uostra perche dice quamd e chon uoj li par efer felice perch a tutto quel defidera in questo mondo di modo che mi pare che fe uo ui chonfumate di tornare luj abruca di defiderio che uo torniate fi che state comtemto e attemdete a fpediruj per tornare e dar quiete a uoj e ad altrj . ho uisto l anima uostra sta bene . & fotto bona chustodia & l corpo attemdecj uoj.

La chasa uostra fta al folito bene e l moschadello e prefso a maturo e chome fara bem fatto ne mandero la fuo parte a mr tomao e a fra bastiano fe lle ghazere nŏn fe lo mangiano tutto chom auien chomincato che fi portauañ difonestamente ma o foprito (?) con ispauemtachj fe basteranno jo u o fempre nel chore . & nŏn pemfo inn altro che di chompiaceruj e quamdo comfidero quamtj fieno l obrighi gramdifsimj o chon uoj giudicho che fe uiuefsj mill anno nod fare may per rimeritaruene la minima parte pero pregho iddio che ue ne rimeritj per me di modo ch e l chomtrario di quel par a uoj pero attemdiamo a uiuere & quamdo mi uolete fare gramdifsimo piacere comandatemj jo o auto questa mattina le uostre lettere . & manday fubito la fua a fra febastiano & ueramente che ui porta tamto amore per quel dimostra quamto portar fi posfa a un altro omo & fiate certo che nŏn mancha di teneruj richordato a . n . s . perche ui dia quel u a dato jntemzione che chome luj jo pemfo ch abbj da uenire a ogni modo.

Questa mattina il mastro di chafa del papa a fatto intimare

alla chancelleria che la ſi trouj a nizza allj 3 ho a . 4 . di settembre e ongniomo uada per che uia uole e luj amdera per terra fin all ſpezie di modo che paſsera di chosta m anchora nõn ſi sa apunto la ſtrada che . s^a^ . s^ta^ fara.

jo ſono ſtato a ſpettare ſino a notte per uedere ſe fra bastiano mi mandaua uostre lettere & nõn l a fatto mandouj una auta da mr tomao & s aro quella del frate ue la mandero.

Alli gallj uostri & mia patronj o fatto la uostra inbascata & ui ſi rachomandano.

TUTTO URÕ BART^O^ ANGIOLINJ IN ROMA.

A tergo:

Allo . mio . Car^smo^ . & molto . Honr^do^
chelamgiolo bonarrotj in fiorenza.

---

ihesus addi xvj d aghosto 1533.

Honr^do^ & Car^smo^ michelangniolo jo ui schriſsj l utima mia allj ij del presente e di poj mi trouo la uostra di . vj . choñ una a fra sebastiano la quale dettj in propria mano & di poj o auta un altra uostra al luj la quale li manday ſubito ma perche & ſtato un pocho indisposto pemſo nõn u ara riſposto chosj presto . ma jddio grazia & guarito & sta beniſsimo & molto ui ſi rachomanda.

jo ho auto piacere del uostro ſchriuermj perche mi dite aue tanto piacere del mio ſonetto che nõn lo fecj per altro comside ramdo che mandamdo una choſa gofiſsima a un omo &cellemte come ſiate uoj tamto ſe li da piu materia di ridere . & di chomſiderare la diferemza ch e dan noj a uoj ma ſapete ui ſchriſsj ui rideſsj di me oneſtamente & amchora comsiderato l amore & afezione che ſempre m auete portato mi fanno pigliar animo al mostraruj integramente il quore mio quale &gli e uerſo di uoj che altro non deſidera che di chompiaceruj & di ſeruiruj / a mr Thomao o fatto le uostre rachomandazione & jn molto piu numero indrieto ue le rimando & altro nõn deſidera chel la tornata uostra come noi altrj / Li fichj del uostro cortile ſoñ molto bonj quellj dell orto & l moschadello amchor ṅoñ som fatti . & jo comtinouo ci uo a uicitarlj . l altrj animalettj tutti ſtanno bene & l orto a comincato a beuere che c e un po piouto / Vo direte beñ ch i ui

schriua certe lettere famza fustanza alchuna perdonatemj che mj
pare che choll amicj char^smi fia lecito parlar liberamente e chom i
defidero facciate uoj chome / la partita di . n . s . fara alla fine
del prefente mefe o pocho prima ho poj fechomdo che piouera ma
l amdata & piu che certifsima ne altro a uoj mi rachomando
ftate fano.

TUTTO URŌ BART° ANGIOLINJ JN ROMA.

A tergo :

Allo · mio Car^smo & molto Honr^do
gielo bonarrotj jn propria.

---

ihesus addi xxiij d aghosto 1533.

Honr^do & Car^smo michelangniolo alli xvj del prefente fu l utima
mia e di poj questo di mi ritono dua uostre una per mano delli
uostri bastagi & l altra per il bamcho cofi una a fra bastiano la
qual fubito li manday a palazzo & a detto uolere parlare a . n . s .
& faruj rifposta & mandarmela che se l lo fara fara in questa / jo
ui dissj per l utima chome s era femtito di mala uoglia pur e
guarito & fta benifsimo & pero nōn ui a fchritto.

L altra lettera a mr Thomao l o data . & amchor luj a promefso
fare rifposta & molto defidera la tornata uostra & molto ui fi
rachomanda &d e tutto il uostro / ami detto dappoj che questo
dì nōn uj fara altra rifposta ma e tutto uostro.   (These words
were added, after the letter had been finished, in another ink.)

Dell amdata di . n . s . per amchor nōn f intemde quamdo
abbj da efsere questa partita perche dichono nōn f amdra piu a
niza rispetto che l ducha di sauoia nōn uol dare la fortezza . & per
questo . n . s . mando lunedj pafsato mr jaco° girolamj in poste al
re di framca per rifoluerfj doue f a d amdare dichono / moltj
dichono f amdra a marfilia altrj a pregni altrj a grassa & molti
che nōn f amdra i nefsuñ logo ma l papa dice f amdra a ongni
modo & nōn fi mancha di chomtinouo delle preparazione di modo
che tutta questa terra sta ambighua jn tutte le chofe jddio lafsj
feguire il meglio.

La chafa chon tutte l altre uostre cose fta al folito e jo uo a
uicitare spefso que uostri fichj che foñ moltj bonj e l moschadello

ne fecj parte all amicj uostri . ne altro m ochorre faluo fom fempre
a li feruizi uostri che jddio jn fanita ui chonferuj.

TUTTO URŏ BARTº ANGIOLINJ JN ROMA.

A tergo :

Allo mio Car^{smo} & Honr^{do} michelangniolo
Bonarrotj jn fioremza.

———

ihesus addi xxx d aghofto 1533.

Honr^{do} e Car^{smo} michelangniolo fabato pafsato fu l utima mia
choñ una del uostro fra baftiano & di poj noñ a fchritto altri-
mentj ma in quello ch auefsj manchato foperira (?) a bocha perche
. n . s . dichono ch al fermo partira uenerdj proximo e stara a
uiterbo e alla madonna dell auergna tutto lunedj & di poj per la
uolta di niza per la uia d'e paesi uostrj e fra bastiano m a detto
che . n . s . uole che parta dua dj auamtj perche uemgha chosta
a trouaruj di modo che farete raguagliato del tutto a bocha e aret
un po di brigha a raccettarlo per quel mi pemfo nŏn che m abbj
detto chofa nefsuna di questo / altro non o che diruj noj di qua
refteremo tutti foli e areñ tempo amdarcj a follazzo.

mr Thomao sta bene e ui fi rachomanda & jo infieme choñ n efso
che jddio in fanita ui chomferuj etc.

TUTTO URŏ BARTOLOMEO ANGIOLINJ JN ROMA.

A tergo :

Allo . fuo . Honr^{do} & Car^{smo}
michelangniolo bonarrotj
in propria.

———

ihesus addi vj di settembre 1533.

Honr^{do} & Car^{smo} michelangniolo jo o riceuto la uostra a me
Car^{sma} infieme chol uostro gemtile e bel fonetto del quale rifer-
batomene chopia o dato al uostro mr Thomao qual a uto molto
charo conofcemdo auer tamta grazia da dio d auer aquistato una
tamta amicizia choñ un omo dotato da tamte uirtu qual fiate uoj
& tamto piu l e stato grato quamto l o detto che la uostra tornata
fara presta il che defidera fopra ongni altra chofa.

Car^smo michelangniolo jo no mi pemti maj di piacer alchuno ch
i abbj ma fatto a neſſuno amzi mi dogo di que ch i non o poſsutj
fare & nŏn tamto alli stranj quamt all amicj . & uoj che ui
temgho primo . s^re . & padrone nŏn uo che pemsiate che m
inchrescha ſ i o fatto choſa che ui ſia stata grata perche ſa dio ch
i nŏn deſidero che di ſeruiruj & di chompiaceruj & questo nŏn m
inchreſce may n imchreſcera fim ch aro uita e ſ i ui manday
quel ſonetto abozzato cho pichonj ne fu chaulsa l amore ui porto
& la sichurta mi par auer chon uoj e per l amore che uoj ſempre
m auete dimostro pero amdiamo auamtj ſichuramente & ongnuñ
parlj chome l e chomodo e tutto ſi reputj a bom fine.

j o ſchritto questo di a m̃ loremzo del cone uett^le [= uetturale]
che ſta chostj fermamente &d e omo da bene e a dua fratellj che
di chomtinouo uemghono a roma fidatiſsimj il qual ui uerra a
parlare che li o detto uolete mandare certe uostre robe che ui
dicha quamdo e pemſa che un di que ſuo fratellj uemgha in qua
che per trouarſj loro qui per amdare alla ſpezie chol papa nŏn
ſo quamdo ſaranno tornatj chostj ma luj ue lo ſaperra dire e
tornañdouj chomodo ui potrete ſeruir di loro liberamente per eſer
fidatj fidatiſsimj.

E si dice per certo che l papa partira martedj ma moltj nŏn
lo chredono per non eſer piouto il che deſiderauano faceſsj auamtj
partiſsino pure pocho a piu ſaranno per ſoprastare jac^o ſaluiatj
questa mattina fu seppellito in ſam pietro e madonna luchrezia ſta
molto male . e l ſimile il uostro oratore di modo questa morte
non la perdona a neſsuno.

fra bastiano m a detto questa ſera che partiranno martedj e luj
per tutta quest altra ſettimana ſara chostj & a uoj ſi rachomanda
& jo inſieme con eſſo.

Ne altro per questa jddio di mal ui guardi etc.

TUTTO UR̃O BART^o ANGIELINJ JN ROMA.

A tergo :

Allo mio Car^smo &t Honr^do
Michelangniolo bonarrotj jn fiorenza.

ihesus addi xviij d ottobre 1533.

Honr^{do} and Car^{smo} michelangniolo jo mi trouo la uostra de di xj d ottobre infieme cholla di mr Thomao e li bellifsimj fonettj delli qualj n o feruato chopia e di poj datolj a chi amdauano per faper quamta afezione & porti a tutte le chofe uostre . & m a promefso faruj rifposta la quale fara in questa & per quamto o uifto comta l ore nõn che li giornj che uo dite d efer di qua pure a charo ongnj uostra comodita . & molto ui fi rachomanda la fettimana pafsata jo fecj la uemdemia delle melagrane uostre & ne mandaj una canestra a mr Thomao . & un altra al putto & fra bastiano & una parte ne ferbo a uoj che quest anno fono state bellifsime & la chafa chon tutta la uostra brigata ftanno bene & l mio fonetto fatto cholla zappa ui pare da chorregger ch i fo che nõn ui resteria niente ma mi basta che fanno chon uoj quell efetto che fa il fucile cholla pietra amchor che dimostrate che ce ne fia un altro che fa molto piu focho che l mio amchor che nõn fia di ferro / quamdo faremo di qua jnfieme ne riparleremo fpediteuj & uenite . & ochorremdo chofa alchuna auisate . & la stamza di roma & bona & fichura per quanto fi uede & jntemde.

Ne altro foñ fempre il uoftro jddio di mal ui guardi etc.

V^o BARTOLOMEO ANGIOLINJ JN ROMA.

A tergo :

Al mio Car^{smo} & Honr^{do} Mi
chelangniolo bonarrotj jn propria

Honr^{do} & Car^{smo} michelangniolo jo ho la uostra & intemdo la chaulfa che per amchora ui trouate chostj che tutto fia in bonora ch e forza a chi fi troua in quefto mondo fpefso far della uoglia fua quella d altri pure quamdo fi fa chon isperanza di qualche bene & mancho male.

jo ho fatto le uostre rachomandazione & schusa del nõn li fchriuere al uoftro mr Thomao le rachomandazione acetta ma l altra . no . ma dice bene nõn ui fchriuerra piu per non ui infastidire ma che uoj nõn l imfastidirestj maj ma piu ara chara

la prefemza uostra che le lettere . & che s a uoj par mill annj
di uenire qua al luj ne pare x mila che uoj arriuiate.

Quamto all efsere bon efsere in questa terra per quamto fi puo
giudichare per quel che fi uede . & bonifsimo chom bona iustizia
& dal pane in fora d ongni chofa a boñ merchato ma l grano ci
uale ▽ —◝ £ iñ . 8 . il rubbio & amchor che fi sia detto mille
nouelle di fospezione di nouj foladtj per uenire a questa uolta s e
chiarito che fono ftate bugie . & parmi che non f abbj d auer
paura fe nŏn de seruitorj chi a nome d auer danarj perche da
pochy giornj in qua & stato morto dua & rubatj da feruidorj
ma d altrj nŏn f intemde uñ minimo manchamento per quanto f
intemda.

La lettera di fra baftiano l o dato bonifsimo richapito jo ho auto
il uostro galamte e bel fonetto . & amchor che no me ne diciate
chofa alchuna uifto per chi e fatto gnien o dato il quali e ftato
molto acetto chome tutte l altre chose uostre / & perche pare che
per efso fonetto mostriate che l amore di chomtinouo ui tien
trauagliato . & a me pare il chomtrario ui mando in questa un
mio fonetacco che non e fe nŏn e il nome di fonetto e puofsj dire
pesce pastinacha ma nonn e boñ da magniare e chome l orfo
taluolta piace per la fua ghofeza chofj fi potre dir di questo
quamdo ui piacefsj pero pigliatene la mia bona afezione.

jo aspettauo pur che uo uenifsj a far la uemdemia delle
melagrane & delle perfiche del uostro orto ma uisto che ftate
tamto a chomparire & le fi chomincano a marcire ne faro come
del moschadello & ue ne faluero la uostra parte che foñ quest
anno bellifsime al folito tutto il resto della chafa fta benifsimo

Ne altro m ochorre ftate fano jddio di mal ui guardj.

VRŏ BARTHOLOMEO ANGIOLINJ JN ROMA.

A tergo :

Allo . mio . Honr^{do} & Car^{smo} michelangniolo
tj in firenze

No. VII.

LETTERS FROM TOMMASO CAVALIERI, FEBO DI POGGIO, LUIGI DEL RICCIO, AND ASCANIO CONDIVI, TO MICHELANGELO.

Ho receuuta una uostra littera quanto piu non sperata da me tanto piu grata non sperata dico reputadomi io indegno che un uostro pari si degnasse scriuermi : circa di quello che pierantonio in mia laude ui a detto e quelle opere mie che cō uostri occhi hauete uiste perl le quali mōstrate di mostrarmi non poca affectione ui rispondo che nō erano bastanti fare che u huomo eccellentissimo come uoi e senza secōdo non che senza pari in terra, desiderasse scriuere a un giouane appene nato al mondo e p questo quanto si puo essere ingnorante. Ne uoglio anchora dire che uoi siate bugiardo. Penso bene anzi son certo che de la affettione che mi portate la causa sia questa che essendo uoi uirtuosissimo o p dir meglio essa uirtu : sete forzato amar coloro che di essa son seguaci, e che lamano, tra li quali son io et ĩ questo secōdo le mie forze nō cedo a molti. Vi prometto bene che da mene receuete uguale e forse magior cambio che mai portai amore ad huomo piu che ad uoi ne mai desiderai amicitia piu che la uostra e se nō ĩ altro almāco in questo o bonissimo iuditio e ne uedreste le effettetto se non che la fortuna in questo solo a me cōtraria uuole che hora che mi potrei godere di uoi stia poco sano spero bene se ella nō mi uuole di nuouo cominciare a tormentare tra pochi giorni esser guarito et uenire a fare il mio debito in uisitarui se a quella piacera : Jn questo mezo mi pigliaro al manco doi hore del giorno piacere in cōtemplare doi uostri desegni che pierãtonio me a portati quali quanto piu li miro tãto piu mi piacciono et appagero ĩ gran parte il mio male pensando alla speranza chel detto pierãtonio mi a data difarmi uedere altre cose delle uostre. Per non esser fastidioso nō scriuero piu a lungo : solo ui ricordo accascãdo ui seruiate di me : et ad uoi di continuo mi racomãdo.

Di V. S affettionatissimo

seruo THOMAO CAUALIERE.

Unico signor mio ho riceuuta una de le uostre a me gratissima
per la quale ho inteso V. S. esserse non poco attristato di quel
dimenticare io gli scrissi : io ui rispondo che io non lo scrissi ne
per che V. S. non mi hauessi mandato niente ne per accrescerui
magior fiamma ma folo il scrissi per mottegiar con esso uoi che
credo certo posserlo fare pero non ui attristate per che io son
certo che non mi possete dimenticare. Jn quanto V. S. mi scriue
di quel giouane de nerli lui e molto mio e hauendosi da partire di
Roma mi uenne a dire sio uoleuo nulla da firenze io gli dissi che
no e lui mi prego che io lo lasciassi andare da parte mia a raco-
mandarmi a V. S. solamente per desiderio di parlarui : Altro no
so che scriuermi se no che V. S. torni presto perche tornando libe-
rarete me di prigione per che io fuggio le male pratiche e uolendo
fugire le (male pratiche) non posso praticare con altri che con uoi
non altro. A V. S. infinite uolte mi ricomando in Roma a di 2
de agosto 1533.

Vostro piu che fuo

THOMAO CAUALIERE.

A leccellentifzimo e fuo da
   magior honorãdo Mr miche
   langnolo buonarruoti
    Jn fiorenza.

Unico fignor mio alli giorni passati ebbi una delle uŕe a me
gratissima fi come per intendere il uostro star bene e fi ancora
per esser certo che la uostra tornata fia brieue : e afsai me increbbe
el non posserli responder : pure mi conforto che intefa la cogione
mi harrete per iscuso che il giorno ch io l ebbi mi era uenuto un
uomito fi fatto accompagnato con una febre che io hebbi a morire
e certo se non era quella che alquanto mi risuscito io moriuo poi
dio gratia son stato sempre bene : hora hauendomi misser Bartolomeo portato un fonetto da parte uostra, mi e parso fare il debito
mio circa il fcriuere : forse tre giorni fa io ebbi il mio fetonte
assai ben fatto e allo uisto il papa il cardinal de medici e ugnuno
io non so gia per qual causa sia desiderato di uedere : Il cardinal
de medici a uoluto ueder tutti li uostri disegni e sonnogli tanto

piaciuti che uoleua far fare quel titio el ganimede in cristallo e
nono saputo far si bel uerso che non habbia fatto far quel titio e
ora il fa maestro giouanni assai o fatto a saluare il ganimede
laltro giorno feci la uostra imbasciata a fra sebastiano e ue si
ricomanda per mille uolte non altro se non pregarui che tornate
di roma a di 6 đ settĕb.

di V. S. affettionato

Thomao caualiere.

A leccellentiſſimo e ſuo da
   magior honorãdo Mr mic
   helagnolo buõarruoti
   Jn fiorĕza.

Molto mag^{co} S^{or} miǫ.

Jo da certi giorni in qua mi sono adueduto che uoi haueui
con me non so pero che cosa ma pur ieri me ne certificai,
quando uenni a casa uostra, ne possendomi imaginarne la
causa, ho uoluto scriuerui questa, accio che piacendoui possiate
chiarirmene, et sono piu che certo non hauerui mai offeso, ma
uoi credete facilmente a chi forse meno deuereste et forse alcuno
ui a detto qualche bugia p dubbio che io pur un giorno non scopra
molte ribalderie che ſi fanno sotto il nome uostro che ui portono
poco onore et se le uorrete sapere le saprete, pure io non posso
ne manco possendo uorrei sforzarui, ma ben ui dico che se uoi
non mi uolete p amico, potete farlo ma non farrete già ch' io non
sia amico a uoi et sempre cercaro di farui seruitio, et pur ieri ueniuo
per mostrarui una lettera scritta dal Duca di Firenze et per leuarui
noie come sempre o fatto insin qui et sappiate certo che uoi non
hauete il migliore amico di me ne mi uogglio stendere sopra di
cio, ma se a uoi adesso pare altramente, spero che in poco tempo,
se uolete, ue ne chiarirete, et so che sapete ch' io ui sono stato
sempre amico senza interesse alcuno, ora io non uogglio dire altro
p che pareria ch' io mi uolesse scolpare di qualche cosa il che
non e . ne mi so imaginare p nessum uerso cħ cosa habiate meco,
et ui prego et scongiuro p quanto amore portate a Dio cħ me lo

uogliate dire, accio ch' io ui possa sgannare, et non mi occorrendo
altro me ui ricomando di casa il di 15 đ nouembre 1561.

Di V. S. S^{or}

THOMAO D CAUALIERI.

Al molto mag^{co} mr
    Michelangelo bonarroti
        padrone osser^{mo}.

FROM FEBO DI POGGIO (Arch. Buon., Cod. 8. 303).

N.B.—*The orthography, which is very bad in the original, has been modernised.*

Magnifico Messer Michelangelo da padre honorando.

Hieri tornai da Pisa che io era andato fin la per veder mio
padre, e subito fui giunto da quello vostro amico che sta insul
banco mi fu dato una vostra la quale ho vista con grandissimo
piacer, per aver inteso di vostro bene stare.   Il simile per lo Dio
gratia alpresente è di me.   Appresso ho inteso quanto dite circa
dello essermi io corucciato (chorucato) io con esso voi, che sapete
bene io non potrei corucciarmi (churucarmi) con esso voi per
tenervi io in luogo di padre, e poi i portamenti vostri non sono
stati di talsorte verso di me che io avessi a far talcosa.   E pensate
che quella sera voi partiste, la mattina io non mi potei mai
spiccare da M. Vincenzo che avevo grandissimo desiderio di
parlarvi.   Alla mattina venni a casa, e voi eri di gia partito che
ebbi dispiacere grande vi partissi senza che vi vedessi.

Io mi trovo qui in Firenze, e quando vi partesti mi diceste che
s' io avrò bisogno di niente, lo domandassi a quel vostro amico, e
perchè M. Vincenzo non si trova qua mi trovo bisognoso di
danari si per vestirmi e si per andar fino al Monte a veder combatter
coloro che la si trova M. Vincenzo.   Per tanto io andai a trovare
quel del banco, e mi disse non aveva da voi commissione alcuna,
ma che era uno che partira stasera e che arebbe risposta fra
cinque di cosi se voi li davi commessione che non mancherà.   Si
che vi prego vogliate essere contento di provvedermi e aiutarmi di
quel tanto che pare a voi e non mancate di rispondere.

Non vi dirò altro se non che quanto so e posso a voi mi raccomando Iddio pregando di mal vi guardi.

Da Firenze il giorno 14 di Gennajo 1534, vostro da figliuolo

FEBO DI POGGIO.

FROM LUIGI DEL RICCIO.

Mag^{co} et hon mr micħo.

Chi non ha da se et libisognia ritrouarsi con ch ha, uolendo aparire se non come loro almanco il meglio che puo, ci è forza seruirsi in qualche modo di quel d altri, il che usa con risico di rimanerne se ciascuno si uenisse per il suo, nudo et uituperato, pero coloro che lo fanno uoluntarii sono non poco da biasimare . et per ch io mi trouo nel medesimo grado con lo incluso madrigale, il quale ancora che fie in maggiore parte acchatato da uoi, che siete maestro perfetto, si è egli pur si brutto et mal composto che non ha simiglianza alcuna con le cose uostre . come interuiene che chi non sa da se mai intende interam^{te} ne sa ben usare le cose d altri : ho uoluto agiugnere q uersi in mia scusa et dirui che non uoluntario ma sforzato da uoi mi son messo a usar per necessita le cose u<del>r</del>e, che mi auete non solo detto che se non ui mando qualcosa del mio io non haro mai piu nulla del u<del>r</del>o ma hauete fatto di piu che di gia mi hauete tolto di quello che io haueuo, pero piu per ubidire che per altro quale egli è uelo mando con protestatione che sia primo et utimo che per sempre harete da me . perche non essendo la mia professione, è, un farsi scorgiere, anchora che, ogni cosa da uoi m' è dolcie onore ; conosco di non ui hauere ubidito perche mi hauete doman dato del mio et io ui mando del uostro . pero scusimi quanto di sopra et il non potere dare quel ch' io non ho : ho ben piacere pensando con questa occasione del domandarui, hauere da uoi la gratia chesta et che a possibile desidero come da quello che sapete, possete et uorrete, consolarmi di che ui haro perpetua obrigatione et diro che e mia uersi ui sieno piaciuti hauendo fatto frutto et se non ui parra fatica il far loro risposta sarete causa di farli conosciere et che qualcuno fara loro carezse per amore u<del>r</del>o come fanno a urbino uͬo sʳᵉ (servitore) che altra diferenza non è da loro a uͬi che da urbino a voi et mi ui racomando State sano et amatemi che iddio ui mantengha molti anni.

Di banchi alli 16 di Dic. 1543.

A com^di d. v. s.

LUIGI DL RICCIO.

1. Raro fattor' ch' el tuo bel' arno honori
   Piu ch' e' Romani il tebro e' Greci il Xanto
   Et a Natura il uanto
   Toi, nel far l'opre tue eterne et belle
   che a' celesti chori
   si assemblan tutte et apena di quelle
   fra mille una ne piacie, et quella il tempo
   Guasta et inuola in breue; alle tuo' dona,
   gratia et fauor; et uiuon seco apparo.
   Ond' io c' omai mi attempo
   per la nostra amicitia uera et buona
   ti prego fammi un dono onesto et raro
   che fia signor mio caro
   far l'alma donna nostra, bella et pia
   contento eterno della uita mia

   Mag^co mr micħlo
   chi non ha da se et è forzato a dare, bisognia
   Si acomodi di quel d altri et pero io
   ui mando del uͬo medexi°
   di la.

   Delle belle opre tua ch' l' tempo eterne
   conserua, e l secol nostro onoran tanto
   a che fuggir, le lodi, il pregio, el uanto
   ch' assai uie piu da ciascun merti hauerne.
   Potess' io pur mie giuste uoglie interne
   co' l opre dimostrar' al mondo, quanto
   t' honoro; enchino al uirtuoso e santo
   uiuer tuo dato alle gratie superne.

e ingrato se ben
Ma l' guasto et cieco che non sente o uede
opra se non fa sol quanto il mal uso seco apporta
parendoli il fiel dolcie el mele amaro
fuggiendo quel che mostra harabbe a tenere caro hauer piu caro
fara' come chi tardi si rauede
del danno suo e ua chiuder la porta
dicendo ancora, a lui mai nacque paro.

Mag^{co} et hon mr michlo
Voi mi hauete tanto mostro, nel leggere le
cose uostre, che forse qualcosa mi se^{ne} sara
apichata; pero qual' ella è uien da uoi et e uostra
Ch' io per me son quasi un terreno asciutto
colto da uoi, il pregio è uostro in tutto.

From Ascanio Condivi.

Vnico sig^{re} et padron mio oss^{mo}.

Ho gia scritte due lettere . dubito non glie sieno uenute alle mani non hauendo saputo altra noua di uoi . con questa dirò solo che ui ricordiate di cōmandarmi et seruirsi non solamente di me ma di tutta la casa Perche ui siamo tutti serui . Di gratia messere mio oss^{mo} et hon dignatiue ualerui et fare di me come d'un minimo seruo far si suole ; e l'hauete afare perche ho piu obbligo a uoi che a'mio Padre : et ue corrisponderò con gli effetti . farō fine per non annoiarui . Raccomandandomeni humilmente dignandoui darmi consolatione che stiate bene che la maggior di questa non potrei hauere . Stiate sano . di Ciuita noua li xxiiij di maggio del 1555 (?).

D. V. S. M.

Seruo perpetuo

Ascanio Condiuj.

A tergo :
A Michelagnolo Buonarroti, Pittore
Scultore et architetto Vnico.
A Roma uicino la piazza di s^{to} apostolo
canto la chiesa di loreto e casa Zanbeccari.

VIII.

ACCOUNT OF THE CODEX VATICANUS OF MICHELANGELO'S RIME.

The Vatican MS. of Michelangelo's poems (No. 3211) consists mainly of a copybook which must have belonged to Buonarroti, and which he began to use for the preservation of madrigals and sonnets. The first fourteen pages are filled with thirty five poems, four sonnets, the quatrain on La Notte, together with Strozzi's verses, and the rest madrigals. All these are entered in one handwriting—perhaps Luigi del Riccio's. They finish with the word ΤΕΛΟΣ. That the book was kept for Michelangelo's use appears probable from the fact that we find at least eleven alterations in his own handwriting. One of these is *caro* for *grato* in the quatrain on La Notte. On the back of page 14 a madrigal is written by the same scribe, together with part of a sonnet (*Dal Ciel Discese*). Page 15 opens with the second part of this sonnet in a different and more clerkly hand. Three madrigals follow by the second scribe. Pages 16 to 22 return to the first handwriting, with four madrigals and three sonnets. From the back of page 22 to the end of the Codex, the whole is written in Michelangelo's autograph. It should here be said that there are 103 pages in the book, mostly written upon both sides. There are about 120 poems or fragments of madrigals and sonnets, among which must be reckoned very frequent repetitions of the same pieces with various readings. In addition, we find five letters and three closely written pages of medical prescriptions relating to ways of treating the eyes in disease and health, all in Michelangelo's autograph. The prescriptions may belong to the time when he suffered in the eyes from painting the Sistine vault. It is clear from many indications that the poems entered by Michelangelo himself belong to the later portion of his life. I doubt whether a single one is antecedent to the year 1544. Several of those entered by the scribes are referable to an earlier date. The original copybook is a small quarto. It has been broken up, and each leaf neatly inserted into a large sheet of paper. When this book comes to an end, the Codex has been made up of scattered manuscripts, and the whole is bound handsomely in red calf.

<hr>

IX.

REPLIES TO CRITICISM.

On Michelangelo's Unfinished Statues.

Reviewing what I have written about Michelangelo's work in sculpture, some of my critics think I am wrong in maintaining that he invariably aimed at finish, and never left a statue imperfect unless he was forced to do so by external circumstances. It is ingenious to plead that the two male figures in the Sacristy of S. Lorenzo, which are called Day and Twilight, owe their effect to the vagueness of their blocked-out forms. But this is sentimental, not scientific criticism. The polish given to the Night and Dawning, and to the statue of Giuliano de Medici, proves that Michelangelo, if he had not been interrupted in his labours at Florence, intended to work the whole series of monumental figures up to the highest pitch of completeness. Examining the long list of his statuary, we shall find that at no period of his life did he deliberately and voluntarily leave a piece unfinished. The Bacchus, Cupid, and Madonna della Febbre of his early Roman residence; the David of his early Florentine period; the bronze statue of Julius II.; the Bruges Madonna; three, at least, of the figures in the Sacristy; the Risen Christ of his full manhood; the Moses of his declining years; and, later on, the Madonna and two female Allegories on the tomb of Pope Julius in S. Pietro in Vincoli—all of them confirm my view. On the other hand, we know for certain what changes of residence, of work, of ground-plan in the monuments projected, caused him to lay down his chisel before large portions of the sculpture for the mausoleum of Julius, the allegories of the Medicean Sacristy, and the Façade of S. Lorenzo, were completed. Both finished and unfinished statues support my argument. Those which are brought in parts to a high state of finish, and which yet remain imperfect—such as the Captive of the Louvre, and the great Pietà in the Duomo at Florence—establish it beyond all power of refutation.

On the Influence of Della Quercia.

One of my critics says that I ought to have alluded to the influence of Jacopo della Quercia on Michelangelo. Herein he is right. It was not through ignorance, but through inadvertance, that I failed to do so. I have always felt, and still feel, that in the bas-reliefs upon the portal of S. Petronio at Bologna we find the germ of those frescoes on the vault of the Sistine which portray the creation and the fall of man. In the continuous development of these particular motives, from the Pisani at Orvieto and the school of Giotto, through Ghiberti and his contemporaries, down to the period of Michelangelo and Raffaello, it was Jacopo della Quercia who formed the vital link between Buonarroti and his earliest predecessors.

On Michelangelo's Ideal of the Female Form.

I have been taken to task for misconceptions and confusions of ideas regarding Michelangelo's female type. I never denied, however, that he was as great a master of female as of male form. It seems to me self-evident that, so far as the nude goes, his Eve, Night, Dawn, Leda, are unmistakably women and not men, and also that they are equal in vigour of conception and profound anatomical science to his idealised men. What I did say was that he nowhere makes it clear that the secret of feminine charm—the youthful, the virginal, the graceful—was felt by him as keenly as he felt the charm of masculine adolescence. The matron is the woman he portrays. A powerful ephebus is the man he prefers. And on this point it will not do to tell me that the exigencies of plastic art on a huge scale—Sistine vault, Sacristy of S. Lorenzo—forced him to create that colossal type of adult brawny womanhood. Whoever carved the pediments of the Parthenon, did not feel obliged to violate the truest truth of femininity because he was working on a large scale; and yet the pediments of the Parthenon are far removed above the head of the spectator, whereas the allegories of the Sacristy are on the level of our eye. Here, if anywhere, was the opportunity for a sculptor, who truly felt the charm of woman, to have represented her with her own sexual grace as adequately rendered as are the sexual graces of the male adolescents on the Sixtine vault.

On Michelangelo's Ideal of Form in General.

It has been objected that, in what I say about Michelangelo's gradual departure from the model and formation of a schematic ideal of the human figure, I do not lay sufficient stress upon the conditions of extensive monumental work. It is of course true that when a master is called to paint a whole chapel or to carve a mass of marble into plastic shapes, he cannot follow nature as displayed in the model so closely as when he is designing an easel-picture or a single statue. Not only would time fail him, if he sought to study each and every attitude in hundreds of figures from the life; but it is also desirable in vast decorative schemes that a certain unity of type should govern all the parts. This is so self-evident as not even to require stating. But it does not weaken my contention that Michelangelo, having originally followed the model very closely, in course of time adopted an ideal system of proportions, which he applied to his whole treatment of the human form. The ideal type appears in the Adam of the Sistine, and runs thenceforward through all of Michelangelo's great works. With respect to the female figure, it cannot, I think, be proved that Michelangelo at any time studied the model very closely. The designs which he actually made from living women are extremely few; so few as almost to excuse the paradox of

Parlagreco, who asserts that he only knew the female nude by dissection.[1] However that may be, it is certain that his principal attention was devoted to the male figure, and that he allowed masculine attributes to dominate his ideal of the female. This tendency reveals itself in the Madonna della Febbre, that is to say, in the first of his masterpieces which idealizes woman. It never disappears in any later work of sculpture, painting, or design. By this, I do not mean that figures like the Eve of the Sistine, the Night and Dawn of S. Lorenzo, are not distinguished by a profound knowledge and a keen perception of what is characteristic in female anatomy. Nay, Michelangelo was careful to suggest the greater fulness of adipose tissue, the lesser development of muscles, the suaver curves and the more rounded surfaces, which differentiate women from men. Still, the ideal he formed of female beauty continued to the last to be what I have described. All this amounts in fact to nothing more than that Michelangelo, like every other artist of the first rank, developed his own specific language of plastic form, a style peculiar to himself, a mode of expression through plastic shapes consistent with his severe and sublime imagination.

On the Frescoes of the Sistine and their Meaning.

It has been objected that, in my account of the Sistine Chapel, I refuse to explain what I think about Michelangelo's intentions —the inner spirit and meaning of his scheme of frescoes. This was due in part to a growing conviction that such eloquent passages of interpretation as Michelet, for example, poured forth upon the relation between Michelangelo's thought and its plastic expression in painting, are too subjective to be valuable ; that in fact we ought to consider art-work more from its purely artistic, less from its literary side, than has been usual in æsthetic criti-

---

[1] We possess at least one fine chalk drawing which refutes this paradox. It is the woman curled up in a seated attitude (dated Rome, 1560, March 27, now in the Uffizi). But his rare drawings of women are nearly always draped. His studies of the male nude, on the other hand, are innumerable.

cism. But I also felt that the vault of the Sistine and the Last Judgment do not require elucidation. The choice of subjects, to begin with, was not Michelangelo's, nor the Pope's. Patron and artist concurred in following medieval tradition. Had the Fall of Lucifer been painted on the eastern wall, then the digest of Christian history contained in the "Speculum Humanae Salvationis" would have received fairly full expression through the works of all the artists who concurred in the decoration of the Chapel. I alluded in my text to the absence of any representation of the crucifixion, as singular; but I did not think it necessary to publish a suggestion which has often occurred to my own mind —namely, that the crowning act in the drama of man's redemption, the sacrifice of Christ, was continually repeated in the consecration of the Host upon the altar. With regard to those wonderful adolescents on the vault, the "certi ignudi" of Condivi's narrative, whom I call Genii, it seems to me more profitable to contemplate their sensuous beauty and to feel their mental music, than to search for any definite intellectual ideas which they express. I am here in full agreement with the views of my friend Von Scheffler, who connects these most attractive products of Michelangelo's genius with his Platonic mysticism, and his sensibility to the loveliness of male adolescence. Like the boys in the National Gallery Madonna, the naked youths in the Doni Madonna, the Captives on the tomb of Julius, these nude ephebi are, to use Von Scheffler's phraseology, Michelangelo's canon of perfection in the human form. Inspired by the erotic "mania" of the *Phædrus*, they breathe what Bruno called "heroic fury," the intense and rapturous enthusiasm for what is purely beautiful in form. Like strophes in some sublime hymn to intellectual beauty, like phrases in some vast symphony, they possess a meaning irreducible to words, but clearer and more penetrative than words are. To call them the majestic sculptor's *chant d'amour* would not be wrong; but to tie their interpretation down to any scheme of thought more definite than this, would be to miss their music and to violate their rhythm.

On Berni's Capitolo to Sebastiano del Piombo.

I am reminded by the foregoing paragraph that when I spoke about Michelangelo's Platonism in Chapter xii., I inadvertently omitted a confirmatory passage which, coming from a contemporary poet, carries great weight. Berni, in one of his Capitoli addressed to Sebastiano del Piombo, composed a splendid panegyric upon Michelangelo as sculptor and architect. He also alludes to his poetry—

> Ho visto qualche sua composizione;
> Sono ignorante, e pur direi d'havelle
> Lette tutte nel mezzo di Platone.

" I have seen some of his compositions in verse; I am an ignorant fellow, and yet I could have sworn that I had read them all in Plato's writings." The answer to Berni's Capitolo, " written in the name of Sebastiano del Piombo," has been ascribed to Michelangelo himself. The external evidence for this attribution is a copy of the poem in the Buonarroti archives, which distinctly states that it was composed by the sculptor. Internally, the style does not differ in any important respects from that of Michelangelo's familiar verses.

On Michelangelo's style in Architecture.

The impression produced by works so original as the Laurentian Library and Sacristy must of necessity vary according to the taste and sensibility of the spectator. To certain of my critics it seems that I have been unduly fault-finding with regard to these buildings, and also that I have fallen into an error which I blame in others, that, namely, of judging them by standards which are not really applicable. I am not insensible to the audacity of conception displayed in the vestibule to the Library. It breathes the " terribleness " of its Titanic creator, and no one but Buonarroti could have imagined it. Nor do I deny the subtlety and beauty of the mouldings, the grace in detail of the orders, and the novelty displayed in all the ornamental parts, which may be so well studied in Rossi's book upon the edifice. But I still feel justified in condemning the principles upon which doors, windows, columns of Roman buildings have here been applied to the flat decoration of the inside of a vestibule. And I repeat that, in my own opinion, their only excuse must be found in Michelangelo's obvious intention to fill them up with statuary and bronze reliefs. The staircase may be beautiful, although I do not think so. But, at any rate, as we learn from Vasari's correspondence with Buonarroti (see chap. xiv. section 2 of this book), Michelangelo was not responsible for its design or its construction. About the dignity and harmony of the Library itself there can be no doubt; and all its fittings in desks, panellings, pavement, which may, in part at least, be ascribed to Michelangelo, are executed with refined Tuscan taste. With regard to the Laurentian Sacristy, I need hardly repeat what I have frequently stated—that its marble panels, friezes, orders, mouldings, are carried out with exquisite sense of their subordination to the sculpture in the chapel. The statues in their turn are exactly suited to the illumination. Had the stucco and fresco ornaments upon which Giovanni da Udine was at work (when the disasters of Rome and Florence put an end to the building) been completed according to Michelangelo's intention, and had the numerous figures in marble and bronze which were to have filled the niches (see chap. x. section 7) been executed under his superintendence, there is little doubt but that this sacristy would have displayed the sublimest, richest, and most picturesque collection of associated art-works to be found in any single chapel of Italy.

INDEX.

and pardons Michelangelo, 186 ; commissions him to cast his statue in bronze, 187 ; and to paint the vault of the Sistine, 198 ; refuses to listen to any arguments against the proposal, 200 ; visits the artist on the scaffold while at work, 209 ; his death, 300 ; on Michelangelo's violence of temper, 347 ; in debt to him at the time of his death, ii. 137

Julius III., Pope, a friend and admirer of Michelangelo, ii. 226

KUGLER, i. xvi.

LABACCO, Antonio, makes Sangallo's wooden model for S. Peter's, ii. 217 *note*

Landino, Cristoforo, his theory regarding the number of days spent by Dante in his journey through Hell and Purgatory, i. 337

Lang, W., cited for Michelangelo's letter to Febo di Poggio, ii. 156

Languet, his letters to Sidney illustrative of personal emotion at the end of the sixteenth century, ii. 154, 159

Laocoon, discovery of the, i. 154

Lapo, Lapo d'Antonio di, sculptor, an assistant of Michelangelo, i. 189

Lasca, Il. *See* Grazzini

Last Judgment, the, in the Sistine Chapel, Michelangelo begins the work, ii. 42 ; Aretino's criticism on the fresco, 50 *sq. ;* contemporary opinions on its nudity, 56 ; exposed to view, 58 ; criticism of the work, 59 ; its immediate fame, 67

Laurentian Library, the, Pope Clement's ideas regarding, ii. 2 ; the vestibule, 15 ; difficulty about the staircase, 253

Leda and the Swan, Michelangelo's picture of, i. 441 ; disapproved of by the Duke of Ferrara's agent,

442 ; taken to France by Antonio Mini, *ib. ;* copy by Benedetto Bene, *ib. ;* sold to the King of France, 443 ; ordered to be destroyed because of its indecency, *ib. ;* restored and taken to England, *ib.*

Legniame, Antonio Maria da, ii. 378

Lenoir, M., purchases Michelangelo's Bound Captives for the French nation, ii. 86

Leo X., Pope, grants an augmentation of the family arms to Buonarroto Buonarroti, i. 2 ; rejoicings in Italy on his election, 300 ; his character, 301 ; employs Michelangelo, 311 ; his triumphal entry into Florence, *ib. ;* meets Francis I. at Bologna, 312 ; re-enters Florence, 313 ; conceives the idea of finishing the Church of S. Lorenzo, 314, ii. 2 ; orders Michelangelo to construct a road at Santa Pietra, i. 330 ; changes his mind about S. Lorenzo, 350 ; offers Sebastiano del Piombo a hall to paint, 355 ; his vacillation, 356 ; purchases the library of S. Marco, ii. 3 ; commissions Raffaello to continue Bramante's design for S. Peter's, 215 ; appoints Antonio da Sangallo to assist him, *ib. ;* death, i. 365 ; estimate of his character, 366

Leoni, Diomede, corresponds with Lionardo Buonarroti regarding Michelangelo's bust, ii. 269, 271 ; apprises Lionardo of the grave condition of his uncle, 318 ; and of his death, 320

Leoni, Leone, his tomb at Milan for Gian Giacomo de' Medici, ii. 79 *note ;* his medal of Michelangelo, 258 ; his wax model and medallions of the artist, 274

Le Pileur, A., i. ix.

Leyden, Lucas van, his copper-plate

SPECIAL INDEX

TO SOME OF

MICHELANGELO'S WORKS

WHICH ARE PARTICULARLY MENTIONED IN THIS BOOK.

ARCHITECTURE.

Capitol, Rome, ii. 245 *sq.*
Lorenzo, S., Library, ii. 2–4, 15, 253
Lorenzo, S., Sacristy, i. 375 *sqq.*, ii. 19 *sqq.*

Maria, S., degli Angeli, ii. 255
Peter's, S., cupola of, ii. 218, 231, 238 *sqq.*, 241, 244
Porta Pia and other gates, Rome, ii. 254

DRAWINGS, SKETCHES, &c.

Anatomy, study of (Oxford), i. 44
Arcieri, or Bersaglio (Windsor), i. 296
Cartoon of the Battle of Pisa, i. 119, 161–170
Cartoons for the frescoes of the Sistine, i. 240 *sqq.*
Crucifix carved in wood, i. 43
Crucifixion, ii. 98, 197
David, the second (Louvre, Paris), i. 107
Designs for a Naked Man (Louvre, Paris), i. 109
Ganymede (Windsor), ii. 142, and *note*
Madonna (Louvre), i. 294
Male Nude (Albertina, Vienna), i. 294
Middleton's Reconstruction of the

Tomb of Julius II. (Cambridge), i. 138
Monument of Julius II. (Uffizi, Florence), i. 133–135, 137
Phaëthon, ii. 141
Pietà, ii. 98
Revel of Children (Windsor), ii. 125, 141, 142
Saint, Bearded (British Museum), i. 89 *note*
Salt-cellar, ii. 43
Samson slaying a Philistine, i. 439
Satyr (Settignano), i. 19
Sword-hilt, i. 191
Tityos (Windsor), ii. 141, 142
Various drawings, i. 295

PAINTINGS.

Entombment (? National Gallery, London), i. 67, 68 *note*, 114 *note*, ii. 199
Francis, S., receiving the Stigmata (S. Pietro a Montorio, Rome), i. 57
Frescoes on the vault of the Sistine Chapel, i. 208 *sqq.*, 237 *sqq.*
Leda and the Swan, i. 259, 440–443

Madonna and Child (National Gallery, London), i. 65
Madonna and Child—the Doni Holy Family (Uffizi, Florence), i. 114, and *note*
The Last Judgment, ii. 42 *sqq.*
The Pauline Chapel, ii. 181 *sqq.*

448